Performance Coaching For Dummies®

C000214939

Setting SMART Goals

One aspect of successful Performance Coaching is ensuring that the goals set by the individual are clear, behavioural, and realistic. Make goals:

- ✔ **Specific.** Ensure that the goal is stated in specific terms (for example, 'To make a presentation to the board at the next quarterly meeting regarding the advantages of a global strategic response').
- ✔ **Measurable.** Ensure that the goal can be measured (either the individual will make the presentation concerned or not).
- ✔ **Achievable.** Check to see that the goal can be achieved in the time available and whether the goal is within the individual's ability (there are two months before the next board meeting so there is enough time to prepare the information required and your colleague has given presentations before and has the skill to deliver).
- ✔ **Relevant.** The goal should be relevant to success in a specific area. Ensuring the goal is important encourages commitment (that is, this presentation will open the way to position the department and your colleague more favourably).
- ✔ **Time Bound.** Check the timeframe that the goal needs to be achieved in (the date of the next quarterly board meeting).

Coaching Questions for Different Stages

Stage	Sample questions	Purpose
Stage 1: Agreeing Aims	What are you trying to achieve?	Clear objectives
	When are you going to do it?	Agreed dates
	How will you know you have succeeded?	Measurement
Stage 2: Awareness	What is happening now?	Clear picture of current actions
	What have you done so far?	Review of relevant achievements, however slight
	What are the consequences?	Effect of current actions
	What do you want to be different?	Where your colleague is and where he wants to be
Stage 3: Analysis	What can you change?	Identify possibilities
	What are the options?	Broaden vision
	How can you change it?	Seek solutions
	What are the risks?	Evaluate choices
	What are the barriers?	Obstacles to overcome
Stage 4: Action	What are you going to do?	Clear action steps
	Who is going to do what?	Define responsibilities
	When are you going to do it?	Agree milestones
	What do you need to help you?	Determine support
Stage 5: Assessment	What actually happened?	Clarify outcomes
	Was this what you wanted?	Evaluate degree of success
	What have you gained from this experience?	Discoveries made
	How can you improve?	Establish further potential

For Dummies: Bestselling Book Series for Beginners

Performance Coaching For Dummies®

Cheat Sheet

Asking the Right Questions

As a Performance Coach, you have a number of different styles of questions at your disposal:

- **Closed questions: 'Do you like her?'** Closed questions are good for helping people to focus but don't encourage people to open up because only a 'yes' or 'no' is likely to be the answer.

- **Hypothetical questions: 'What do you think he would say if you told him?'** This type of question can be useful because you're asking the person to use his or her imagination. Doing so encourages someone to think beyond his or her current situation and into the realm of possibility.

- **Open questions: 'What steps have you already taken to change your situation?'** Open questions help people to consider options and are the most useful form of questioning. Turn to Chapter 5 for more on questioning.

You may find the following questions useful when coaching for change:

- How do you know that the information you have is accurate?
- What's happening at work for you at the moment?
- What other factors are relevant?
- What is the other person's perception of the situation?
- What have you tried so far?
- How do you feel about the feedback you've received?
- What can you do to change the situation?
- What alternatives to that approach do you have?

- Would you like some suggestions from me?
- What are the benefits and pitfalls of these options?
- Would you like to choose an option to act on?
- What possibilities for action do you see?
- What are the next steps?
- When will you take the next step?
- What may get in the way?
- What support do you need?
- How and when will you enlist the support you've identified?
- How can we overcome the obstacle you've identified?

Achieving Excellence

Here are the 10 commandments for coaching excellence (also head to Chapter 16):

- Know who you are
- Communicate well
- Work co-operatively
- Be credible
- Give others credit

- Aim for results
- Give up the easy stuff and tackle the difficult things
- Consult with others
- Develop influence
- Get things done

For Dummies: Bestselling Book Series for Beginners

Performance Coaching
FOR DUMMIES®

Performance Coaching
FOR
DUMMIES®

by Gladeana McMahon and Averil Leimon

John Wiley & Sons, Ltd

Performance Coaching For Dummies®

Published by
John Wiley & Sons, Ltd
The Atrium
Southern Gate
Chichester
West Sussex
PO19 8SQ
England

E-mail (for orders and customer service enquires): cs-books@wiley.co.uk

Visit our Home Page on www.wiley.com

Copyright © 2008 John Wiley & Sons, Ltd, Chichester, West Sussex, England

Published by John Wiley & Sons, Ltd, Chichester, West Sussex

For general information on our other products and services, please contact our Customer Care Department within the U.S. at 800-762-2974, outside the U.S. at 317-572-3993, or fax 317-572-4002.

For technical support, please visit www.wiley.com/techsupport.

Wiley also publishes its books in a variety of electronic formats. Some content that appears in print may not be available in electronic books.

British Library Cataloguing in Publication Data: A catalogue record for this book is available from the British Library

ISBN: 978-0-470-51748-2

Printed and bound in Great Britain by Bell and Bain Ltd, Glasgow.

WILEY

About the Authors

Gladeana McMahon is considered one of the leading personal development and transformational coaches in the UK. She was instrumental in founding the Association for Coaching for which she now holds the positions of Fellow and Vice President. She is also a Fellow of the British Association for Counselling and Psychotherapy, The Institute of Management Studies, and The Royal Society of Arts. Gladeana is widely published with some 16 popular and academic books on coaching and counselling. An innovator, Gladeana is one of the UK founders of Cognitive Behavioural Coaching and currently works as the Head of Executive Coaching for Fairplace plc and is Co-director of the Centre for Coaching. She is passionate about her work in coaching business and public sector leaders to master the psychological complexities of 21st-century corporate life. Gladeana was named as one of the UK's top ten coaches by the *Independent on Sunday* and *Sunday Observer*.

Averil Leimon made a name for herself in coaching before anyone knew that was what it was called. As a clinical psychologist, she pioneered the transfer of techniques, knowledge, and academic discipline from the reserve of the damaged to the domain of the eminently normal (well, relatively speaking), becoming a Coaching Psychologist as a result. Averil is co-editor of an ever-increasing coaching series. A founder member of the Association for Coaching (AC), Averil was one of the first people accredited by the AC and now works as an accreditor herself in order to ensure high standards in coaching.

Also hailed as one of the top ten coaches in the UK, Averil and Gladeana make a formidable team of heavy hitters in the coaching world.

Averil's company, White Water Strategies, combines the best of psychology and business knowledge to coach and develop rounded leaders who get things done successfully, time after time.

Authors' Acknowledgements

From Gladeana: To all the very many coaching clients who have allowed me to help them and have taught me as much about how to be a good performance coach as I have taught them. To Averil who has been a joy to work with on this project. To Mike who helped me achieve my dream of being a writer, and to my partner Will who makes me laugh and provides me with much needed coffee to make sure I meet my deadlines!

From Averil: I can only thank my family for having such faith in my ability to write this book while running a business, a home, and a family, they completely ignored the fact that I was doing it! Just wait – my daughters are writing the next book with me so that will be fun. My husband Julian Bird's own writings in communication in medicine have been very helpful. My daughters, Natasha and Jessica, have a capacity for both writing and hard work that is inspirational. Working with Gladeana was, as always, great fun. Thanks also to all the many and varied coaching clients over the years. I am grateful to be just as fascinated by the coaching process now as I was right at the start. And finally thanks to Rachael Chilvers at Wiley for keeping us right so charmingly.

Publisher's Acknowledgements

We're proud of this book; please send us your comments through our Dummies online registration form located at www.dummies.com/register/.

Some of the people who helped bring this book to market include the following:

Acquisitions, Editorial, and Media Development

Development Editor: Rachael Chilvers

Commissioning Editor: Samantha Spickernell

Content Editor: Nicole Burnett

Copy Editor: Kim Vernon

Proofreader: David Price

Publisher: Jason Dunne

Executive Project Editor: Daniel Mersey

Cover Photos: © GettyImages/George Doyle

Cartoons: Ed McLachlan

Composition Services

Project Coordinator: Erin Smith

Layout and Graphics: Alissa D. Ellet, Joyce Haughey, Melissa K. Jester, Christine Williams

Indexer: Ty Koontz

Brand Reviewer: Jan Sims

Publishing and Editorial for Consumer Dummies

    Diane Graves Steele, Vice President and Publisher, Consumer Dummies

    Joyce Pepple, Acquisitions Director, Consumer Dummies

    Kristin A. Cocks, Product Development Director, Consumer Dummies

    Michael Spring, Vice President and Publisher, Travel

    Kelly Regan, Editorial Director, Travel

Publishing for Technology Dummies

    Andy Cummings, Vice President and Publisher, Dummies Technology/General User

Composition Services

    Gerry Fahey, Vice President of Production Services

    Debbie Stailey, Director of Composition Services

Contents at a Glance

Introduction 1

Part I: Getting to Grips: Introducing
Performance Coaching 5
Chapter 1: Coaching for Performance 7
Chapter 2: Getting the Process Right 21
Chapter 3: Deciding What You Want to Achieve and Setting the Structure 39

Part II: Does Your Face Fit?: The Personal
Attributes of a Performance Coach 53
Chapter 4: Starting the Relationship with Trust and Respect 55
Chapter 5: Getting Your Hands Dirty: The Practical Skills
of Performance Coaching 67
Chapter 6: Advancing Your Skills: The Magic of Motivation 91
Chapter 7: Equipping Your Coaching Toolkit 107

Part III: Applying Performance Coaching 117
Chapter 8: Getting the Best: Talent Management 119
Chapter 9: Managing Change 127
Chapter 10: Following the Organisational Life Cycle 139
Chapter 11: Managing Careers 157
Chapter 12: Getting the Best Out of Your Teams 171

Part IV: Troubleshooting in Performance Coaching 189
Chapter 13: Coping with Difficult Situations 191
Chapter 14: Overcoming Negativity 203
Chapter 15: Managing Organisational Problems 213

Part V: The Part of Tens 229
Chapter 16: Ten Steps to Performance Excellence 231
Chapter 17: Ten Steps to Coaching Yourself 239
Chapter 18: Ten Useful Resources 249

Appendix: Forms 253

Index 265

Table of Contents

Introduction *1*

About This Book..1
Conventions Used in This Book 1
Foolish Assumptions 2
How This Book is Organised...2
    Part I: Getting to Grips: Introducing Performance Coaching..........2
    Part II: Does Your Face Fit?: The Personal Attributes
      of a Performance Coach...3
    Part III: Applying Performance Coaching 3
    Part IV: Troubleshooting in Performance Coaching 3
    Part V: The Part of Tens...4
Icons Used in This Book..4
Where to Go from Here..4

*Part 1: Getting to Grips: Introducing
Performance Coaching* *5*

Chapter 1: Coaching for Performance 7

Defining Performance Coaching..7
What Performance Coaching Is Not...9
    The remedial class 9
    The psychiatrist's chair..9
    The 'I didn't get where I am today by . . .' spot 10
Looking at an Overview of the Coaching Process 10
Checking Your Potential as a Performance Coach....................11
Balancing In-House and External Coaching 13
Overcoming Resistance to Coaching..14
Structuring the Process...15
    Agreeing aims: Are we on the same page? 16
    Awareness: Where am I right now? 16
    Analysis: What are my options? 17
    Action: So, what can I change? 17
    Assessment: How did I do? 17
    Activity: Here's the script!..18

Chapter 2: Getting the Process Right 21

Considering What You're Trying to Achieve by Coaching.......21
Introducing Two Types of Performance...................................23
Managing the Performance Coaching Process 24
    Painting the picture...24
    Not a flash in the pan 25

Using the ACE coaching structure 25
So, how did it go? 27
Climbing the Ladder to Success 28
Measuring outcomes 31
Considering other people's feedback 33
Introducing Performance Coaching to Your Workplace 34
You mean I don't tell them? 34
Who are these people I work with anyway? 35
What's this got to do with work? 35
Keeping everybody happy 36

**Chapter 3: Deciding What You Want to Achieve
and Setting the Structure** **39**
Seeing from the Coach's Perspective 39
Performance Recovery Coaching 40
Coaching for Excellence 40
Ensuring that Your Colleague Is Ready to Change 41
Scribble here: Drawing up a Behavioural Contract 42
Differentiating between the hares and tortoises 43
Seeing from Your Colleague's Perspective 43
Holding a chemistry meeting 44
Continually developing 44
The Six-Session Model 45
First formal meeting 46
Ongoing sessions 46
Session 6: Final meeting 47
Reviews 48
Evaluation 49
Avoiding Performance Coaching Road Blocks 51
When coaching is not the answer 51
When the person is unable to change 52

**Part II: Does Your Face Fit?: The Personal
Attributes of a Performance Coach** **53**

Chapter 4: Starting the Relationship with Trust and Respect **55**
Building the Foundations of the Relationship 55
Getting to know you 56
Trust me – I'm your coach! 57
Fancy meeting you here 57
Showing Respect 58
Being respectful while coaching 58
Avoiding judging people 58
Developing respect 59
Even Attila the Hun had good points – finding the best
in people 60

Establishing the Ground Rules 61
    Confidentiality 62
    Writing the rules of engagement 63
Working in Partnership 66

Chapter 5: Getting Your Hands Dirty: The Practical Skills of Performance Coaching **67**

Letting Your Body Do the Talking 67
    Responding to non-verbal cues 68
    Unlocking the secrets of the voice................................69
Hear, Hear! Using Listening Skills 70
    Attending 70
    Listening to the end of the sentence...........................71
    Using silence 71
Asking Different Types of Questions 72
    Using open questions 72
    Asking motivational questions 74
Probing to Get to the Point 75
Sounding It Out: Paraphrasing 77
Reflecting Feelings 79
Challenging with Care..80
    Ensuring that you have the right to challenge 80
    Understanding the key skills of challenging 82
    Getting the timing right 82
    Challenging effectively...84
Through a Glass Clearly: The Five Domains of Emotional Intelligence...85
    Improving your EQ 86
    Recognising your own feelings 86
    Recognising others' feelings 87
    Reading emotions 87

Chapter 6: Advancing Your Skills: The Magic of Motivation **91**

Getting People Excited 92
    Remembering they're not all like you.............................92
    What gets you out of bed in the morning? 92
    Considering career drivers 93
    Looking at deeper motivators 95
    Playing to people's strengths...96
    Being your best..97
Aiming for Change...98
Discussing Feedback...99
    Giving positive feedback 99
    Conferring constructive criticism 100
    Motivating people with feedback 101
Are We There Yet? 104
    I spy changes 104
    Delaying gratification..104

Chapter 7: Equipping Your Coaching Toolkit 107
    Introducing the Seven-Stage Problem-Solving Model.................107
    Testing, Testing.................109
        Using the Myers-Briggs Type Indicator (MBTI).................109
        What shape are you?.................113
    Seeing the Value of 360-Degree Feedback.................115

Part III: Applying Performance Coaching 117

Chapter 8: Getting the Best: Talent Management 119
    Fighting for Talent.................120
    Encouraging Talent.................121
        Determining your strategy.................122
        Coaching the leaders of tomorrow.................123
    Measuring the Impact of Company Culture on Talent.................124

Chapter 9: Managing Change 127
    Coping with Changing Times.................127
        Can't live with change; can't live without it.................127
        Change and survive.................128
    Cutting Costs and Speeding Up the Process with Coaching.................129
    Coaching through Change.................130
        Understanding the impact of change.................131
        Taking control of negative thoughts.................132
    Helping Colleagues Make Use of Their Support Systems.................135
    Understanding Stress.................135

Chapter 10: Following the Organisational Life Cycle 139
    Understanding the Organisational Life Cycle.................139
        Growing up is hard to do.................141
        Creating the best blend.................142
        What goes around, comes around.................143
    Being Prepared for a Recession.................144
        Adopting the brace position.................145
        Finding that old wartime spirit.................145
    Riding the Wave of Expansion.................148
    Getting Back to Normal: Performance Recovery.................150
        Assessing what went wrong (without blaming).................150
        Remembering that when one door closes another one opens.....151
        Becoming resilient and having a plan.................152

Chapter 11: Managing Careers 157
    Stepping Out on the Career Path.................157
        Looking where you're going.................157
        Understanding personal strengths and limitations.................159
        Developing a career plan.................160

What Really Matters to Me?..161
Excelling During the First 100 Days 162
    Ta-da! – Making the right impact 163
    Hitting the ground running 163
Balancing Life and Work..166
    Look at me – the plates are all spinning.........................166
    Getting out of the comfort zone 168

Chapter 12: Getting the Best Out of Your Teams **171**
Delving Deeper into Teamwork 171
    The team works! 172
    Coaching individual team members 173
    Starting to team coach...174
Identifying Strengths and Weaknesses in Team Roles..........177
    Using Belbin Team Roles 178
    So, what are you good at? 180
    What can't you do?..181
Minimising Team Weaknesses 182
Ensuring Effective Communication...185
    Being clever isn't good enough! 185
    Seeing the blind spots in communication 186
Coaching Teams: A Case Study 186
Avoiding the Pitfalls 188

Part IV: Troubleshooting in Performance Coaching 189

Chapter 13: Coping with Difficult Situations **191**
Dealing with Negative Reactions...191
    And, breathe: Keeping calm in a crisis 192
    Fanning the flames or putting out fires?..........................192
Coping with Anger...194
    What lights your fuse? 194
    Dealing with anger..196
Handling Distress 197
Managing Personality Clashes...199
Avoiding 'Scapegoating' 199
    It wasn't me: Avoiding the blame 200
    Dealing head-on with organisational issues....................200

Chapter 14: Overcoming Negativity **203**
Overcoming Negative Emotions with Motivation 203
Reaching for the Stars: Raising Aspirations 204
Challenging Overconfidence and Lack of Insight....................205
Seeing Yourself as Others See You: The Johari Window 206
Careless Whispers: Overcoming Anxiety About Confidentiality..........207

Overcoming Setbacks 208
     Strategies for dealing with setbacks 209
     Getting back on the horse 210

Chapter 15: Managing Organisational Problems 213

Improving Communication 213
     Auditing communication 214
     Coaching for communication 216
Coaching an Uncertain Organisation 217
     Dealing with uncertainty 218
     It's good to talk 219
Preventing the Loss of Good People..220
Avoiding Litigation 222
     Beating bullying 223
     Counting the cost of stress 225

Part V: The Part of Tens 229

Chapter 16: Ten Steps to Performance Excellence 231

Strive to Achieve Interdependence..231
Ensure Good Communication Channels...232
Work Co-operatively 233
Improve Your Credibility...234
Notice Other People's Achievements 234
Focus on Outcome 235
Delegate to Stretch Yourself 235
Let Others Have a Say...236
Develop Your Influence 237
Get Things Done..237

Chapter 17: Ten Steps to Coaching Yourself 239

Improve Your Confidence 239
Create a Positive Lifestyle..240
Manage Your Money 241
Get Creative 242
Float into Relaxation 243
Deal with Criticism Assertively...244
Give Criticism Assertively..245
Increase Your Chances of Success 245
Successfully Manage Your Time 246
Keep Stress Under Control...248

Chapter 18: Ten Useful Resources 249

Finding Wise Words in Books 249
Entangling Yourself in Web Sites 250
Getting Advice from Professional Bodies..250

Appendix: Forms *253*

    Performance Coaching Checklist 253
    Coach Them! 254
    Setting Goals 254
    Delegating Tasks 254
    Performance Coaching Evaluation 256
    Sample Coaching Contract 258
    Talking Feelings 259
    Your Positive Introduction 259
    The Seven-Stage Problem Solving Model 260
    Using Psychogeometrics 260
    FENO-menal Feedback 262
    Four Windows on Reality 263
    Team Performance Checklist 263
    The Responsibility Pie 263

Index *265*

Introduction

*P*ut simply, Performance Coaching means getting the best out of people at work, and we are passionate about it. If coaching conjures up an image of men in bad shorts with megaphones yelling at would-be sports people, think again. That's not what we do. This is a practical, helpful, and hopefully fun book for you out there who just need to get a good job done well.

About This Book

We care passionately about facilitating change, and *Performance Coaching For Dummies* is the written result of that passion.

We like to roll the sleeves up and start making a difference rather than sitting around defining things. In this book, we encourage you to do the same. Good coaching is highly effective. We really can't stand wimpy, ineffectual coaching. Let's make a difference out there!

We won't pull the wool over your eyes by brandishing jargon at you and creating a mystique around the coaching process. We're straight talkers. We know that you can get great results with your colleagues and staff and make a difference to your business, whatever it is, with insight into our techniques. We hope you enjoy.

Conventions Used in This Book

To help you navigate through this book, we set up a few conventions:

- *Italics* are used for emphasis and to highlight new words, or define terms.
- **Boldfaced** text indicates the key concept in a list.
- `Monofont` is used for Web and e-mail addresses.

Sometimes we (the authors, Averil and Gladeana) use the pronoun 'we' to signify both of us or 'I' followed by '(Averil)' or '(Gladeana)', depending on who the author writing that particular paragraph is.

Also, when speaking generally we use the female pronoun 'she' in even-numbered chapters and the male 'he' in odd-numbered chapters, just to be fair to both genders!

Foolish Assumptions

We assume, and correct us if we're wrong, that you:

- Are quite a sensible, pragmatic person.
- Are a manager who wants to get the best out of your team.
- Have a good reason for using Performance Coaching but don't have time to read a wordy tome or a whole panoply of books.
- Know that quite a lot of psychology is behind Performance Coaching but don't really want to get too scientific.
- Need some quick hits and the tools to achieve them.

How This Book is Organised

For Dummies books give you answers – fast. You may need to know something specific right now; and other situations that crop up along the way will drive you back to read different sections.

You don't need to read this book from cover to cover – unless you'd like to (and we secretly hope you do!). Look up the bit you want. Check out the table of contents and the index to find what you need.

The next sections tell you what you can look forward to.

Part 1: Getting to Grips: Introducing Performance Coaching

This part is all about painting the big picture. Find out here what Performance Coaching is all about and how to use it. This is where you can begin to work out what you really mean by 'performance'. Successful Performance Coaching needs an underlying structure and philosophy in order to succeed. This part helps you understand and set up the structure and decide on the goals to shape your coaching.

Part II: Does Your Face Fit?: The Personal Attributes of a Performance Coach

Part II is all about the characteristics you need to hone to be a Performance Coach and how to begin Performance Coaching at work. Really good, successful coaches share a range of attributes that are core to their coaching. Read this part to find out what qualities you need to develop for successful Performance Coaching. Find out how to build the coaching relationship and establish the ground rules. Consider the impact of body language, motivation, and listening skills. Start to build up a repertoire of more advanced skills that can transform your Performance Coaching.

Here's where you get to grips with the basics of setting up Performance Coaching to engage people in the most effective way. In this part you consider the stages of Performance Coaching from agreeing a contract, to giving positive feedback and constructive criticism, through to charting progress and managing emotions confidently as you go along. We share some very simple ways of doing things that make all the difference.

Part III: Applying Performance Coaching

In this section, we put Performance Coaching to the test. If you're gearing up to face some big organisational challenges, this is the part for you. You find out how you can use Performance Coaching as a weapon in the war for talent, as a tool to facilitate change, and as a safety device during organisational turmoil. In this part you contemplate how effective coaching can be in career planning at all stages and in building team effectiveness.

Part IV: Troubleshooting in Performance Coaching

In Part IV we deal with a range of tricky things that can crop up in Performance Coaching. Let's face it – even if you've done all the groundwork, prepared well, and developed the appropriate skills you can still experience obstacles. Personalities clash sometimes. Life in organisations is complicated, with ups and downs, change and uncertainty. In this part you find out how to overcome negativity and deal with strong emotions, difficult relationships, and organisational challenges.

Part V: The Part of Tens

In this part you find a bunch of punchy chapters to contribute to your Performance Coaching excellence and self-development. Even when not Performance Coaching, this section may transform your life!

We also include ten resources to professionalise your Performance Coaching

Icons Used in This Book

A number of icons help you find the juiciest bits of the book.

Throughout the book we use anecdotes to illustrate Performance Coaching in action, and we use this icon to highlight them.

This icon draws your attention to an important point to bear in mind.

Keep your sights on the target for particularly useful shortcuts or hints.

Sometimes you really have to roll up your sleeves and try something. This icon draws your attention to more practical exercises – we hope you have fun with them!

Performance Coaching is pretty exciting stuff and it's easy to get carried away. This icon asks you to hang on for a minute and think about the consequences of what you're doing.

Where to Go from Here

Jump right into any part of the book that interests you the most. Have fun. Flick through and dip in wherever takes your fancy – you're bound to find something useful. For example, if you want to know more about giving useful feedback, turn to Chapter 6. If you're having problems with an angry colleague, we offer advice in Chapter 13. Above all, enjoy this book, and your Performance Coaching journey!

Part I
Getting to Grips: Introducing Performance Coaching

'They're getting instructions from
the Ultimate Performance Coach!'

In this part . . .

In these chapters you begin to get the big picture. This is where you really find out what Performance Coaching is, and can sample some theories and applications. You start thinking more clearly about what you want to achieve and how you can go about it. You also see how to set up and structure your Performance Coaching.

Chapter 1

Coaching for Performance

. . . .

In This Chapter

▶ Finding out what Performance Coaching is – and isn't

▶ Ensuring that you're cut out for the job

▶ Understanding the Performance Coaching process

▶ Applying Performance Coaching in the real world

▶ Putting a structure in place

. . . .

*W*hat is Performance Coaching, and are you the right person to be delivering it? This chapter gives you the answers. We explain the Performance Coaching process and how to apply it in day-to-day corporate life.

Defining Performance Coaching

How many flavours of coaching have you heard of? We have life coaching, business coaching, executive coaching, career coaching, personal coaching, corporate coaching, sports coaching, and coaching psychology, to name just a few. They all have the positive purpose of skilfully enabling someone to change and achieve valued goals but it seems almost everyone who coaches invents a new title for himself. So what are the distinguishing characteristics of Performance Coaching?

Sir John Whitmore, in his book *Performance Coaching*, states that: 'Coaching is unlocking a person's potential to maximise their own performance. It is helping them to learn rather than teaching them.' Performance Coaching means:

✔ Accessing potential

✔ Facilitating the individual to make the changes required

✔ Maximising performance

✔ Helping people acquire skills and develop

✔ Using specific communication techniques

The Performance Coach works with people, often colleagues, using coaching methods to enhance their existing behaviours and develop new ones central to personal and professional success and, in business situations, the success of the organisation.

Performance relates to effectiveness in terms of leadership, decision-making, relationships, creativity, stress, time management, meetings, and dealing with day-to-day tasks and aims to significantly increase your colleague's effectiveness.

Performance coaching uses many models and theories from business and psychology as well as from general management approaches. Put simply, Performance Coaching is all about making an individual more effective and efficient.

Coaching can be useful in the following situations:

- Something going right – a success is a good opportunity to build confidence and guarantee repeated success
- Something going wrong – mistakes and failures create opportunities for development
- Planned delegation
- A new job, or a new role within an existing job
- Talent management
- Special projects
- Attending meetings

Information about all these scenarios is included in this book.

Seeing how it all started

Sports coaching usually gets the credit for having started the whole coaching business. If you suffered through school PE lessons, however, you may wonder if sports coaching ever made it further than the elite sportsmen and women of Olympian levels. Tim Galwey, writer of the *Inner Game* book series, applied cognitive psychology techniques to the sports field, working on the thought processes of players in order to increase their skill at the sport of their choice. Athletes who trained this way took their skills out into a variety of other applications where they thought coaching may transform performance, and Performance Coaching was born.

What Performance Coaching Is Not

Sadly, people can make mistakes when trying to Performance Coach. In this section we warn you against inappropriate or ineffective approaches and beliefs about Performance Coaching.

Coaching is still largely unregulated rather than an established profession.

The remedial class

Coaching often used to be perceived as remedial; sorting out problems and putting things right. All coaching has an element of removing blocks to success – the ideas or behaviours that stand in the way of your colleague's best efforts. However, in Performance Coaching, the basic assumption is that your colleague has the capacity to perform even better, rather than that he must rectify issues. Performance Coaching is not about:

- ✔ Highlighting flaws or weaknesses
- ✔ Correcting failures
- ✔ Managing poor performance

Performance Coaching is about helping individuals be the best they are able to be. Sometimes this means helping someone improve his performance to the required standard. Coaching can also mean working with a talented individual to develop his skills even further. The idea that Performance Coaching is always about catching up is only part of the story. Many colleagues who go through the coaching process do so to ensure they are able to continue to develop their considerable skills.

The psychiatrist's chair

Performance Coaching isn't your opportunity to grab a pipe, install a couch, and draw out deep-seated issues in an Eastern European accent. Everyone has problems. Delving into the origins of issues as a precursor to working them out and fixing them may be interesting. However, Performance Coaching takes the premise that your colleague 'ain't broke' and that he has the reserves he needs to move forward through coaching. Performance Coaching is about the future rather than the past.

The 'I didn't get where I am today by . . .' spot

One of the Videoarts teaching videos, featuring the comedy actor John Cleese, used to start this way: 'Let me give you a piece of advice from my experience. Never give anyone a piece of advice from your experience.'

Old-fashioned mentoring used to use this technique of benefiting from another's experience. Performance Coaching is not about exhorting people to listen to your wisdom, mistakes, and experience. Instead, Performance Coaching means helping people to improve their existing skills and develop new ones.

Looking at an Overview of the Coaching Process

Traditional styles of management may be effective some of the time but are limited in their ability to effectively access people's potential. The 'command and tell' style tends to work best when the boss remains on the premises. When the boss is absent, people are less likely to be self-activated, preferring to wait and be told what to do because they know that's what's going to happen in the long run. Old-fashioned management that treats people like children results in childish behaviour such as 'the cat's away, the mice will play'. Performance Coaching as a management tool gives back to the individual the responsibility for his own development and career.

A myriad of opportunities for coaching present themselves on a daily basis. *Water cooler coaching* involves coaching on the hoof; in the train, at the photocopier, wherever necessary, as the situation unfolds. On other occasions, setting aside designated time to coach a colleague about his development and future is a mark of true respect and good management.

For example, your colleague may be struggling with a new piece of work. In the old-school style of management you'd tell him what to do and how to do it. However, as a manager who using Performance Coaching skills, you may decide to sit down with the individual and encourage him to consider ways in which he can deal with the task in hand. This type of approach encourages your colleague to think through situations rather than simply do what he's been told.

Checking Your Potential as a Performance Coach

Everyone has potential. However, no one can do everything, otherwise we'd all be geniuses, as well as exhausted!

However experienced or knowledgeable you are, at times and for a variety of reasons you won't be able to meet all the demands that are made of you as a Performance Coach.

- ✔ **Too much to do and too little time!** On occasions, you won't have the time to meet the needs of your colleague. In such situations, help the person concerned access a range of additional sources of help, from external coaching to internal training programmes. In this type of situation, limit your time, energy, and input to simply guiding the process.

- ✔ **Not got a clue!** If someone presents with difficulties that are outside your competence level, helping the person concerned is impossible. In such cases, refer your colleague to the appropriate source of help. Don't be ashamed to admit a lack of experience or knowledge.

- ✔ **Oh no – not you!** At times you may find your colleague difficult to communicate with. You may have to manage the person concerned, but managing someone is quite different to providing any kind of in-depth Performance Coaching support.

  Additionally, your colleague may simply not warm to you for whatever reason. In such cases, save yourself a great deal of emotional conflict and provide your colleague with the best chance of success by referring him on to someone more compatible with him.

- ✔ **You're fired!** In cases where formal disciplinary action is taking place or is likely to take place, it's unlikely that you can develop the appropriate coaching climate. At best your colleague is likely to feel stressed and at worst antagonistic towards you. He may see you as responsible for his current situation or acting as an agent for the organisation.

  In addition, it is confusing for you, as the Performance Coach, if you have to deliver bad news from a managerial perspective one minute and be supportive as the Performance Coach the next. Instead, you need to find the right person or combination of services to best meet the needs of the individual.

Reality check: You're not superhuman

Here are a few examples of situations where the Performance Coach needs to consider finding someone else to coach a colleague, however briefly:

- ✔ **Amal** had been promoted into a new role that required him to present to large audiences. Previously competent enough with small groups, he wasn't highly inspirational in the way he needed to be to get commitment to big changes. Having worked on the fundamentals of public speaking, confidence, and body language with his coach, Amal had polished his speaking style quite a bit – but not quite enough. After discussion, Amal agreed to bring in the big guns – a voice coach who, by working with the way Amal stood, breathed, and projected his voice, transformed the sense of gravitas he emitted on stage.

- ✔ **Jonathan** was entering his early 40s. His weight had been gradually increasing and he had little time for regular systematic exercise. His diet and drinking were excessive because of all the business entertaining he did. Constant travel and crossing time zones meant Jonathan's sleep patterns were seriously disturbed. His coach was conscious of the strain Jonathan was under. In a throw-away remark, Jonathan mentioned that his own father had died aged 41 of a heart condition. Recognising that health was a crucial issue for Jonathan, the coach encouraged him to work with a sports science coach to devise an exercise and diet programme that fitted in with his demanding lifestyle.

- ✔ **Susan** began to talk more often about the strain in her marriage because of the demands of her job. Her coach had tried to help her juggle her goals to achieve a balance but it became obvious that the strain between Susan and her husband was not letting up. Through coaching, Susan realised that she needed counselling and her coach helped her assess who'd be best to approach for help.

Remember, looking for the best specialist help for your colleague isn't weakness on your part.

You cannot be all things to all people. Make sure that you play to your own strengths fully so that you can develop others to their fullest.

You can usually gain a lot of assistance by working in conjunction with your Human Resource, Learning and Development, or Occupational Health colleagues, who already have a lot of the contacts you seek.

Balancing In-House and External Coaching

Performance Coaching can take place *in-house*, where you're an employee of the organisation as well as a Performance Coach, or you're directly appointed as Performance Coach without any other organisational responsibility. External coaching is where coaches are commissioned and brought into the organisation to undertake specific coaching assignments. Each has benefits and drawbacks:

- **Internal Performance Coaches.** In-house coaches already have knowledge of the culture, history, and politics of the organisation. They are available, less expensive, and more easily managed by the organisation. Individuals can also benefit from developing long-term relationships with their coaches. An internal coach can help develop a coaching culture within an organisation in a way that an external coach cannot.

- **External coaches.** External coaches benefit from their independence, objectivity, and wider range of experience. They're often able to provide sensitive feedback to senior staff, which an internal coach would find harder to do. External coaches are perceived as being more confidential. Colleagues may also find that an external coach is able to give a new perspective because he's able to view the bigger picture. External coaches are perceived as being unbiased because they're not involved in or part of the day-to-day culture and benefits of the organisation.

'People are our most valued asset' – yeah, right!

You hear companies say that people are their most valued asset all the time, but when does it actually mean anything? Companies are haemorrhaging money on a daily basis through inadequate use of their people's talents – round people in square holes, competent workers demotivated by micro-managing bosses, people overworked and bored at the same time, the over-promoted finding themselves out of their depth. This kind of management does not make sound business sense.

A survey by Towers Perrin in 2006 of 86,000 employees in 16 countries came up with these shocking statistics on employee engagement levels:

- 24 per cent of people were disengaged
- 62 per cent were moderately engaged
- 14 per cent were highly engaged

Engaging people in the workplace is the easiest way to improve the performance of both individuals and the organisation. You can use Performance Coaching as the obvious tool to encourage engagement.

This book helps you focus on your Performance Coaching skills as a manager rather than as an external Performance Coach.

Overcoming Resistance to Coaching

If coaching is so terrific and has such great results, then why doesn't it happen? Sadly, many other activities are really good – such as eating healthily and taking exercise – but people somehow just don't get around to doing them. Good habits don't always automatically make their way into our behavioural repertoire.

You may encounter resistance to Performance Coaching from your manager, colleagues, or the company.

Here are just some of the arguments that may be going through your employer's mind:

- **There just isn't time.** Taking time for coaching can save time in the long run. One of our coaches was working with Andrew, a senior manager, known as a bit of an Attila the Hun. Andrew said: 'I can see that this soft stuff may be effective but I just don't have time in the real world.' The coach rather cleverly asked him to role-play how he would normally deal with a situation and then again how he would deal with it using the Performance Coaching approach. Both were videotaped. Andrew normally spoke sternly to the individual, which led to an argument that wasted time and left both of them frustrated. In the re-run, Andrew listened to what his colleague was saying and used open questions to elicit answers. He spoke in a quieter tone. The issue was sorted far more quickly and amicably, leading Andrew to recognise the benefits of changing his style of communicating. Idea sold!

- **I'm not sure that this coaching really works.** Why would your company believe in Performance Coaching if they're not convinced of the benefits? Your company may not see sufficient evidence of the return on investment (ROI) for coaching and because considerable time and money is spent on coaching, your company may want to be reassured that the outcomes are valuable. Many companies using both internal and external coaching fail to set up objective systems of measurement, and certainly measuring the impact of investments in people is notoriously difficult.

    Across all the data available is general agreement that Performance Coaching pays for itself six times over. Here are a few examples:

    - In 2001, Metrix Global was employed to undertake a Return on Investment Study at Nortel and computed a return of 530 per cent based on 43 interviews, or 790 per cent taking into account the impact on staff retention.

- *CA Magazine*, in a March 2004 article, reported that Price Waterhouse Coopers has been using coaching worldwide since 1998 and estimates its return at six to one.

- In 2004 Manchester Consulting (US) reviewed 100 coached clients and also showed a six times return. The review (published in the *Manchester Review*) notes that significant business results were:

- Improved productivity (53 per cent)

- Better quality work product (48 per cent)

- Greater organisational strength (48 per cent)

- Better relationships with direct reports (77 per cent)

- Better relationships with supervisors (71 per cent)

- Improved teamwork (67 per cent)

- Better relationships with peers (63 per cent)

- Greater job satisfaction (61 per cent)

Six to one is an enormous ROI. If you get even a fraction of that success through coaching, you're probably going to be extremely satisfied. The techniques have been tested for many years.

✔ **Will your behaviour at work change?** If adopting a coaching style seems out of character for you, your colleagues may justifiably be wary of the changes and be unsure about how you can sustain your new style. Be absolutely honest about why you're using coaching and the contexts in which you plan to coach people. You can even give permission for people to point out any occasions when you may lapse from Performance Coaching style. Coaching is a legitimate, work-related activity.

✔ **How confidential is this discussion?** People are more likely to open up and give personal opinions and information when a Performance Coaching approach is used. You need to reassure people about how you use such data. Is it to end up on their Human Resources record and affect their chances of advancement or next bonus? If so, they are likely to remain pretty tight-lipped. All parties agree the boundaries in which confidentiality will operate. We consider confidentiality in more detail in Chapter 4.

Structuring the Process

Unlike most social interactions, professional communication is planned communication. When you're coaching, keep a clear idea of where you're going, what you're trying to achieve, and how much time you have available. In this section we give a coaching structure and associated tools to help you shape your Performance Coaching. Chapter 3 gives you a more in-depth structure to work from.

Taking stock

You probably do more coaching than you realise. Reflect for a few moments and consider the following:

- ✔ Over the last month, when have you used coaching techniques?
- ✔ Who was involved?
- ✔ What was your purpose?
- ✔ What went well?
- ✔ What could have been better?

- ✔ What was the outcome?
- ✔ What outcome did you want?
- ✔ Where do you see giving coaching as being of most use to you?
- ✔ What specific people do you have in mind to coach?
- ✔ What do you feel your best coaching skills are?
- ✔ What do you need to take away from this experience?

Agreeing aims: Are we on the same page?

The first stage of the Performance Coaching process is to agree the aims of the coaching activity with your colleague. This discussion need not be a lengthy process but make sure that you're both on the same page and that the agreed aims are achievable. Ask for your colleague's understanding of the purpose and possible outcome of the Performance Coaching. How realistic is it? Careful exploration at this stage avoids a false start and disappointment on both sides when goals are not achieved.

The primary aim of Performance Coaching is to improve performance. For the coaching to be successful, you need to agree detailed specific aims for the various elements that make up the area identified for development. You must also ensure that these aims are measurable and have agreed completion dates. (For more on setting goals, see Chapter 3).

Awareness: Where am I right now?

In Performance Coaching, you must ensure real awareness of what's currently happening for yourself and your colleague before embarking on a process of change. As Performance Coach, you can guide colleagues to a clearer understanding of their situation. Don't make assumptions. Talk with the people being coached about what you see happening and try to get them to understand and agree.

Clarity about what is happening at the moment is perhaps the most important aspect of coaching. You don't always have to know why something is happening – what's important is discovering how you can coach your colleague to do things differently in order to improve. Knowing what is happening now is the starting point in recognising the gap between where you are and where you want to be.

Analysis: What are my options?

The next step is to analyse what you've observed and what your colleague has experienced. From this analysis, you can discuss and evaluate the options to determine what can be done differently. Your aim is for your colleague to recognise things that he can do for himself.

During the analysis stage the aim is for you and your colleague to get ideas from the experience, not to find fault or focus on errors.

Action: So, what can I change?

In Performance Coaching, the action stage is an opportunity to discuss options rather than a test or challenge that you put your colleague through. To make the action stage effective, you can prompt your colleague to work out what he can do with your support.

You may find that your role is to encourage your colleague to test out new horizons, or to rein in his impulsive desire to try everything. Being able to calibrate actions to the exact abilities and stage of the individual is more likely to ensure success at each stage.

Although action is the bit of the process that gets things done and is highly visible, make sure that you fully explore the other stages so that you can be sure that the actions are the right ones at the right time.

Assessment: How did I do?

After coaching, the final element of the process is assessing the performance to enable further progress. The first opinion that matters here is that of your colleague. How does he feel he did? How realistic is he in his assessment? If you're dealing with a perfectionist, he may believe nothing has been achieved and he may regard the whole exercise as a failure. Your job is to be the voice of reason, challenging assumptions and demanding more balance in his assessment. Honest feedback and positive reinforcement are vital at this stage.

Use the assessment as a review mechanism to evaluate the degree of success achieved and the insights gained, and to identify further opportunities for improvement. The assessment also gives you the chance to reflect on your own development and performance.

Perhaps your colleague has an over-inflated sense of achievement. In such cases you need to help your colleague evaluate the outcomes he's achieved and, if possible, to seek external feedback from others.

When Performance Coaching, recognise that the people you coach may often have greater skill and ability in their specific field than you do, but that without your impartial eye and experience they may find it difficult to improve. For example, Wimbledon finalists are usually far better players than their coaches, but the coaching makes all the difference.

Activity: Here's the script!

Of course, you wouldn't dream of slavishly sticking to a script during actual coaching. However, sometimes a clear structure and examples can be useful – and a good discipline. Try working through the questions in Table 1-1 with your colleague and see just how far you can get. Adapt the questions to your own style of language where necessary. Record your answers and check whether they achieved your purpose. The Appendix has a blank form that you can photocopy and fill in.

Table 1-1	Coaching Questions for Different Stages	
Stage	*Sample Questions*	*Purpose*
Stage 1: Agreeing Aims	What are you trying to achieve?	Clear objectives
	When are you going to do it?	Agreed dates
	How will you know you've succeeded?	Measurement
Stage 2: Awareness	What is happening now?	Clear picture of current actions
	What have you done so far?	Review of relevant achievements however slight
	What are the consequences?	Effect of current actions
	What do you want to be different?	Where your colleague is and where he wants to be

Stage	Sample Questions	Purpose
Stage 3: Analysis	What can you change?	Identify possibilities
	What are the options?	Broaden vision
	How can you change it?	Seek solutions
	What are the risks?	Evaluate choices
	What are the barriers?	Obstacles to overcome
Stage 4: Action	What are you going to do?	Clear action steps
	Who is going to do what?	Define responsibilities
	When are you going to do it?	Agree milestones
	What do you need to help you?	Determine support
Stage 5: Assessment	What actually happened?	Clarify outcomes
	Was this what you wanted?	Evaluate degree of success
	What have you gained from this experience?	Discoveries made
	How can you improve?	Establish further potential

EXAMPLE

Different strokes for different folks

Here are a few illustrations of how Performance Coaching can help many different people:

✔ **James.** You know that James just carried out an excellent piece of work for your key client. Why would you want to carry out Performance Coaching? 'If it ain't broke don't fix it' would be a common cry. On the contrary, this success is an excellent opportunity for coaching. Ask James questions such as, 'What went right with this client?', 'What was the most critical activity?', 'What would you do differently?', and 'Which of your particular behaviours led to the success?'. In this way, you lock in the components of success and build James's confidence so that he performs even better next time.

✔ **Helen.** Helen shows great promise, has met all her targets, and is beginning to grow out of her current job. Now is the time to start coaching her to take over some of the activities you, as her manager, normally carry out. Perhaps you want her to take your place at a key meeting. Prior to the meeting, coach her using questions such as, 'What do you expect the key issues to be?', 'How would you need to prepare in order to feel confident about taking part in the discussion?', and 'What would you need to do to feel that you'd performed at your best?'

✔ **Louise.** Although she has excellent qualifications and has done good work, you're sure that Louise is capable of a great deal more. You suspect that low confidence is holding her back. You want to help her develop, so you need to focus on ensuring that she's aware of her successes and can build on these by expanding her repertoire. Start by asking her, 'How do you feel you're getting on?', 'What has been a real success?', 'What would develop your confidence?', and 'What help do you need to reach your potential?'

✔ **Sanjeev.** Sanjeev is full of energy, has no idea how to say 'no', and usually pulls things off even though he sometimes has to stay up all night. In order to keep his performance more consistent and help him to go the distance, you need to challenge him about prioritising. Ask, 'What is the key issue here?' and 'How can you select the critical things to focus on?'

Chapter 2

Getting the Process Right

. . . .

In This Chapter

▶ Exploring performance

▶ Making the process work

▶ Acquiring Performance Coaching skills

. . . .

*P*erformance means the effectiveness with which someone does her job: that is, the manner in which she operates and behaves at work to achieve defined results against specific agreed targets. Performance Coaching works well in a culture of continual development, improvement, and advancement. Nowadays, a person's performance can rarely afford to stand still in either the workplace or in her personal life, where she may want to improve and expand her talents, hobbies, and sports.

In this chapter, we look at the practical applications of Performance Coaching in the work setting, what it entails, and what you're hoping to achieve by coaching.

Considering What You're Trying to Achieve by Coaching

Before embarking on Performance Coaching with a colleague, think carefully about your agenda. Here are some questions to consider:

- ✔ As the Performance Coach, what are you hoping to achieve?

- ✔ How realistic are your hopes and intentions?

- ✔ What do you know of your colleague's past performance, attitudes, hopes, and aspirations?

- ✔ Are you looking for radical change in a short period of time or very gradual fine-tuning?

✔ Are you prepared to play the long game, investing time now in the belief that you'll reap the benefits later?

✔ How much of your coaching needs to be about technical issues (such as business strategy or presentation skills) and how much about issues concerning people (such as building confidence)?

How you answer these questions helps you structure your Performance Coaching process.

How much change can you achieve with people? How you answer this may have serious consequences for your coaching. All coaches need to possess a sound belief in the capacity of others to learn and change. Ask veteran coaches like us and we admit to boundless optimism. We've seen, first-hand, the type of change in people that takes your breath away. But we're doing this professionally, have years of experience, and all sorts of tricks up our sleeves. You may suspect that achieving change may not be so easy for you. You'll be surprised by how successful you can be by adopting some of the tips we give you throughout the book. Here are some of the key factors you need to consider in order to achieve really successful coaching:

✔ **The nature of the coaching relationship.** Your ability to engage with the person you're coaching in such a way that she wants to change is the fundamental issue. After she makes the decision to change, you can, in sense, sit back and watch her do all the work.

✔ **The fact that change is uncomfortable.** Transition from entrenched habits to new, different behaviour can be unpleasant at times. When coaching, your job is to help your colleague see the benefits and maintain the motivation to get through the less rewarding times.

✔ **How you agree goals is critical to success.** People have a tendency to set themselves goals that are doomed to failure. Just look at New Year's resolutions. By aiming for a big and impressive goal, people sometimes make getting started impossible because they know deep down that they can never make it. (See the section 'Climbing the Ladder to Success' later in this chapter, which has more about setting goals.)

Making the journey

'If you don't know where you're going, you'll end up somewhere else', is the old cliché. The analogy of a journey is simple but appropriate in coaching. Think of Performance Coaching as embarking on a journey with another person. You want to succeed in reaching your destination in the most effective or scenic manner, arriving when you want, and avoiding misunderstandings about direction. Plan well so you can really enjoy the journey.

Introducing Two Types of Performance

In Performance Coaching, you're usually working on one of the following:

- ✓ **Development of high performance in a person's current job at the present time.** Performance coaching at this stage focuses on achieving improvement in a range of activities within the scope of your colleague's current role.

- ✓ **Development of heightened performance to reach full potential in a person's future roles**. Performance coaching here focuses on raising your colleague's sights in line with her next promotion.

These two aims may lead to different styles of coaching:

- ✓ **Getting better.** You examine your colleague's current performance carefully to see in which areas she can improve. She's no doubt already doing well in her job so your focus is on where targets can stretch her and lead her to a better use of her potential. You can also focus on her developing additional strengths to improve her overall performance.

Anne has been in her post for a while now. She has the hang of the job and her recent appraisal was excellent. When coaching her, the focus is on discovering what she feels could help her to do her job even better. During coaching, Anne reveals that she's had little experience of public speaking and is unsure of how good she is at it, but recognises that the next step is to take part in more meetings in order to get her views across. Coaching focuses on how she can prepare and practise for such events, how she can build her confidence, and which meetings she needs to target.

- ✓ **Getting ahead.** Your colleague's current job may have little scope for improvement. However, as a part of her talent and career management, you need to line her up for a new role which, at some time in the future, will require a different range of abilities. This may be part of an organisation-wide talent management procedure, succession planning, or a one-off situation concerning a very able colleague. Whatever the circumstances, you need to plan ahead. This is the time to begin the coaching process to ensure that your colleague is ready when the opportunity presents itself.

Vikram is ambitious. He's been in his current role for eighteen months now and is beginning to think about his next move. In other circumstances, he might start looking outside for a new job. You really want to keep him because he's done very well and you believe that he can go far. Performance Coaching for Vikram entails considering what moves are possible and agreeing his personal development goals in light of his future role. He may have come this far purely on technical ability. For the next stage of his career, his interpersonal skills will be essential in helping him to become a more effective manager. Coaching focuses on reviewing and expanding his communication style.

Managing the Performance Coaching Process

In this section we get you thinking about the overall Performance Coaching process. You need to decide whether you're aiming for an organisation-wide intervention, where everyone receives comparable focus and coaching linked to strategic organisational changes, or you may want to help one person with her career or her current challenges through coaching. Whatever your purpose, successful outcomes are more achievable when you manage the process professionally from start to finish.

Painting the picture

When you first introduce Performance Coaching, you have the opportunity to win hearts and minds and create enthusiasm and demand for the process . . . or you can really put people's backs up. You need to make a positive impact from the start or an initiative can fail. Announced in a negative way, Performance Coaching can easily sound remedial and critical. People may react with defensiveness and resistance and make your coaching job hard to do.

People who have suffered from bad or ineffectual management in the past are understandably wary about new initiatives, especially when they're aimed at themselves. Gaining your colleagues' commitment at this stage involves focusing their attention on the benefits and outcomes of coaching. Although coaching has obvious benefits for your company (refer to Chapter 1 for a run-down of these benefits), you need to emphasise what the process will do for your colleagues. Table 2-1 shows just some of the 'what's in it for you' (WIIFY) and 'what's in it for them' (WIIFT) factors.

Table 2-1	Benefits of Performance Coaching
What's in It for You	*What's in It for Them*
Better use of colleagues' potential	Recognition and use of strengths
More skilled colleagues	Expanding repertoire of skills
More versatile colleagues	Giving new opportunities
Close monitoring of performance	Providing one-to-one support
Harnessing emerging talent	Opportunities for advancement
Participative relationship with colleagues	Participation in their own development and advancement

Be absolutely clear about your purpose in initiating Performance Coaching as a general process and later as a specific intervention for the individual.

Not a flash in the pan

Organisations can throw initiatives at employees until they become punch drunk, immune, or just cynical. Because people are often overloaded and overextended at work, many good initiatives and strategies slip through the cracks or happen too infrequently to be effective or valued.

Some people who were once open and positive to new ideas and activities may now want to wait and see before committing themselves. You'll be tested on everything you do. So, when you embark on Performance Coaching, take the long view into consideration when you decide:

- ✔ Your overall purpose in Performance Coaching
- ✔ Your immediate and eventual goals
- ✔ Your commitment to the process
- ✔ The frequency with which you coach
- ✔ The number and selection of people you coach
- ✔ The length of time required to achieve the change
- ✔ The time commitment you need to make to coaching

If you're aiming to achieve continual development in your colleagues, you must cost carefully the commitment it may require and the overall timescale. Not everyone develops overnight after coaching, and the needs of the organisation will continue to change all the time. Your sustained attention is vital. If you coach well, people typically want more, whereas they may become demotivated if they find you're under too much pressure to give them the attention and consistency they require.

Using the ACE coaching structure

You need to create the best Performance Coaching structure for your situation. Spending time getting the process appropriate to your goals can save time long-term and produce better results. Considering the structure of each session you have allows you, rather paradoxically, to relax and be flexible when you need to be. By having a structure, you know where the coaching is going, what you have to achieve with your colleagues, and, if it deviates, you can return and hit your marks accurately if you need to.

You can find almost as many different coaching models as coaches. When coaching, you need to develop a framework that makes sense and helps shape proceedings to a productive outcome.

Use our simple ACE model in Figure 2-1 and Table 2-2 as a basis for your own Performance Coaching structure. The ACE model emphasises all phases of coaching, from the face-to-face coaching to the ongoing process that contributes to a successful outcome. Refer to Chapter 1 for more detail about Awareness, Analysis, and Action.

Analyse

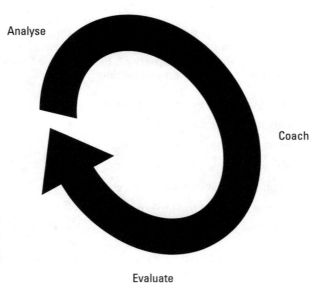

Coach

Evaluate

Figure 2-1:
The ACE
model

Table 2-2	The ACE Model for Performance Coaches
Analyse	Who do I coach?
	What are my aims?
	What does my colleague want?
	What do I know of my colleague already?

Coach	Awareness: taking stock of the situation
	Analysis: working out the options
	Action: deciding where to make the change
Evaluate	How did I do?
	What support will they need?
	What do I need to do next time?

The ACE tools that shape the Performance Process are useful, but don't be too wedded to the script. Every coaching experience is different but it helps to have some underlying structure in your approach.

So, how did it go?

When you first design the Performance Coaching process, think about how you're going to evaluate the outcome. All too often, all the planning and forethought goes into designing the coaching initiative, and assessing the impact and the worth of the exercise is neglected. Here's why considering outcomes from the start is worthwhile:

- ✔ You get the reward of measuring results against effort.
- ✔ You have data against which you can plan the next phase of the coaching.
- ✔ You can build a case for return on investment (refer to Chapter 1 for more on ROI).

You need to decide what data you want to collect in order to do a *cost-benefit analysis* of the process. In reality, what that piece of jargon means is measuring the outcome so that you can decide whether the results really justify the effort – the cost-effectiveness. If you're putting time and energy into Performance Coaching, is it worth it? How formally you do a cost-benefit analysis differs between organisation and individuals and depends hugely on your purpose in embarking on coaching. You and your organisation may be quite happy with simply saying you can see the difference in people who've been coached. Other organisations prefer a more quantitative approach. Using a technique such as the scorecard shown in the later section, 'Walking the line: 'Before' and 'after' self-report' you can state the result. For example, Vikram's performance improved by an overall 30 per cent on the three items measured.

Climbing the Ladder to Success

Setting huge goals beyond initial reach can set people up for failure. In coaching, you need to help your colleagues break down their goals into all the small steps that lead to success. Try the following 'Ladder of Success' exercise, mapping out each step. Then reconsider the ultimate goal and check whether it really is the one your colleague needs to aim for.

Think of a goal of your own from your personal or professional life. Perhaps you want to lose weight, learn French, or get promoted within the year. Write your ultimate goal at the top of Figure 2-1 and then start at the bottom, breaking down all the steps to achieving your goal. Your ladder may end up with a hundred steps. What matters is that you're now in a position to take the first one, making the very last one more of a possibility. You may realise that you need to renegotiate the goal for something more realistic and achievable.

Figure 2-2 shows how you can break down the goal of becoming a concert pianist into several steps on the ladder to success. Check that you're approaching the goals in the right order. In the example in Figure 2-3, the aspiring concert pianist may need to buy a piano earlier in order to practise frequently and pass the exam.

In this instance, maybe being a concert pianist is a goal too far but having started towards the goal you may love the fact that you're now equipped to play in church or have a singsong in the pub.

Serving up some tennis coaching

I, Averil, am learning to play tennis. Ray, my calm, patient, amateur coach has gradually, through many small steps, built up my technique so that I have a relatively predictable forehand and an improving backhand. However, now that I have some competence, when he asks me to change something – my grip, stance, footwork – there's a really good chance that everything will go to pieces and the experience will be less than satisfying. To be honest, I find myself getting irritable and a bit miserable at losing the advances I thought I'd just made. However, because I trust Ray's judgement, I go for it, knowing that, after a while, the new learning will lock in and my shot will be improved.

Everyone going through coaching tends to feel this way at some point – a bit cack-handed and vulnerable to criticism. When this happens, you need to inspire confidence, provide emotional support, and reward any steps in the right direction to ensure that your colleague progresses through this stage. Chapter 5 has more about providing support through your coaching relationship and skills.

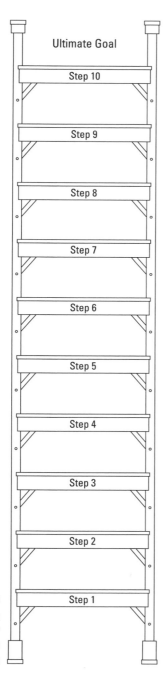

Ultimate Goal

Step 10

Step 9

Step 8

Step 7

Step 6

Step 5

Step 4

Step 3

Step 2

Step 1

Figure 2-2:
The ladder
to success

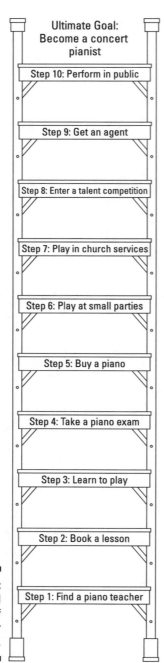

Ultimate Goal: Become a concert pianist

Step 10: Perform in public

Step 9: Get an agent

Step 8: Enter a talent competition

Step 7: Play in church services

Step 6: Play at small parties

Step 5: Buy a piano

Step 4: Take a piano exam

Step 3: Learn to play

Step 2: Book a lesson

Step 1: Find a piano teacher

Figure 2-3:
A worked example of the ladder to success.

Measuring outcomes

Why bother measuring the outcome of Performance Coaching? Well, looking back and seeing how far both you and your colleague have come is really rewarding. You may know that you're doing good work, but if you want to make a case for the use of your time or if you simply want to chart your effectiveness, consider the various ways in which you can measure outcome. Your colleague may adjust quite quickly to changes in her performance, and begin to take her new abilities for granted. She may begin to feel despondent at her apparent lack of progress. By measuring outcomes you can reassure her by giving proof of how far she's come. This is especially useful when she feels that her progress is stuck for some reason or feels as if she's getting nowhere. You can point out where she started and what she's achieved, and this encouragement can help her overcome the obstacle.

If, when you measure the outcome, you find that your colleague hasn't really made any progress, you may have to go back to the start. Check whether:

- ✔ You were working on the right goals
- ✔ Her motivation is high enough
- ✔ There are blocks to success

Perhaps your colleague's situation is that she has a really difficult goal and she can't expect to see results for a long time; in which case you're both going to have to work hard at keeping the motivation going. Try Chapter 6 for tips on motivation and Chapter 7 to review your goal setting.

Measurements don't have to be of a complex statistical nature. The following sections show some of the simplest.

Walking the line: 'Before' and 'after' self-report

Ask your colleague to rate herself on the aspect of her performance she wants to change at the start of coaching and again at the end. You can do this using a questionnaire or ask her to score herself out of 10 or 100 on a range of targets she chooses. This scoring type of measurement is especially useful when you're assessing concepts such as your colleague's confidence in a particular area.

Anne wants to increase her professionalism by becoming a better and more confident public speaker. Ask her to define the key areas that she wants to work on and then to rate those aspects of her performance at both the beginning and end of coaching by putting a mark at the corresponding point on the scale. The closer to 100 the mark, the happier Anne is with that aspect.

Anne's scorecard before and after coaching
Before

Confidence	0_____X_____100	
Clarity of the message	0_____X_____100	
Impact on the audience	0_____X_____100	
Pleasure taken in presenting	0__X_____100	

After

Confidence	0_____X_____100	
Clarity of the message	0_____X__100	
Impact on the audience	0_____X_____100	
Pleasure taken in presenting	0_____X_____100	

Although Anne may not score 100 on every one of the aspects, she can see that real change has taken place. The scorecard also makes clear that any further coaching needs to focus on making sure Anne has the maximum impact on her audience and that her confidence and enjoyment also increase.

For Vikram, who wants to prepare for the next big job, the goals are wider. He may establish the following goals on which to assess his progress:

Vikram's scorecard

Knowledge of market	0_____X_____100	
Range of experiences	0_____X_____100	
Number of contacts	0_____X_____100	

By establishing a baseline perception of his experience and knowledge, Vikram can pinpoint exactly where he needs to improve.

Ensuring clear goals
Establishing clear, measurable goals means that you can regularly monitor and celebrate achievement as and when it happens. Be vigilant for the sloppily stated goal. Be careful not to jump to conclusions and assume that you know exactly what the other person means when she states her goal. If someone says she wants to 'improve my public speaking', what exactly does she

mean? Goals need to be clearly tied to a person's behaviour. What does your colleague need to do to improve her public speaking? You need to clarify whether the goal concerns the research that goes into the speech, the way it's delivered, or how your colleague controls anxiety at the time – or all three. You can state these different goals as:

- ✔ I want to prepare consistently for speeches by reviewing the research and choosing my key points carefully.

- ✔ I want to achieve a lively style of presentation by working on improving my voice – expression, emphasis, and tone.

- ✔ I want to be calm and confident when I get up to speak by using positive self-talk and relaxation exercises.

This is the information you need in order to complete your goal ladder correctly. Each of these three examples would generate a different ladder of steps, yet they all come under the heading of 'improving public speaking':

- ✔ The first ladder would focus on how she organised her advance reading, selected the best points, and structured the talk.

- ✔ The second ladder would have steps involving practising delivery.

- ✔ The third ladder would have steps concerning monitoring what she's saying to herself, how she's managing anxiety, and building her confidence.

This is where individual Performance Coaching can hit the mark – by being geared exactly to the individual needs rather than offering a blanket solution.

Considering other people's feedback

Feedback from other people about your colleague is an excellent way of assessing changes. Bear in mind, however, that people don't always update their preconceptions about other people, despite evidence to the contrary. Ask other colleagues at the start of the coaching process to be vigilant and feedback achievements about their coached colleague as you go along. Avoid asking *closed* questions (questions that can only result in a 'yes' or a 'no'). Asking 'Have you seen any change in Anne?', is likely to result in a vague 'no'. Asking, 'What differences have you noticed in Anne's style of presenting over the last three months?' produces more useful feedback.

If your company has very specific professional targets linked to pay or bonuses, employees receive feedback at yearly or half-yearly intervals. This feedback may be quite remote from the event itself and may not say much about how the target was achieved. Nonetheless, it still points to real, measurable, and widely respected achievement.

Introducing Performance Coaching to Your Workplace

Many people who manage others learn their management skills while on the job rather than through formal qualifications. A work environment where action and results are highly prized leaves little time for reflection and consideration of the process by which results are achieved. As a result, managers may not have had time to chart why some people have flourished on the job, while others have not fulfilled their earlier promise.

People are your most valued asset, so you need to develop the techniques that will ensure that you access their potential successfully. Many good communicators automatically and naturally shift into more of a coaching style when opportunities permit. Sadly, under any time or personal pressure these skills may disappear very fast. Other people, for a variety of reasons, may fail to question or modify their communication and behaviours. This section covers some of the basic requirements for developing your coaching skills.

You mean I don't tell them?

Simply telling people what to do seems so easy but is often ineffective. It works while you remain on site with your colleagues, but the effect erodes quickly when you're absent. Managers may say, 'I don't know how many times I've told her how to do it and she still does it wrong.' Hmmm – what does that tell you about the way people function? Telling people what to do, without their active participation in the process, is the least effective way of communicating. Old management styles of the command and control variety have been proved to be less effective and are even less acceptable to younger generations who haven't been raised to just do as they're told. You might not feel you order people about but consider for a moment how you engage with people. How much direction do you give them? How much scope is there for them to use their initiative? How much do you give instructions rather than ask questions? Coaching is always about engaging the other person and encouraging her to commit to action through taking responsibility and making choices. You can find out more about effective communication in Chapter 5 and specific skills of Performance Coaching in Chapter 6.

Who are these people I work with anyway?

If you're coaching colleagues – direct reports perhaps – you probably know a great deal about them already. You need to take that into account when considering how you coach for performance. Some very self-starting, self-directed people need little more than a nudge in the right direction to set them driving towards their goals. Others need to be prised out from their position of safety to take some initial risks to change their performance through coaching. You already have information about where colleagues have performed best in the past and what circumstances tend to motivate them most. If not, start reviewing all the data available to you from observations and company records. The more you know about your colleagues, the more exactly you can target their development. Some questions to consider are:

- ✔ What are your colleagues' real strengths?
- ✔ In what circumstances have they done their best work?
- ✔ What has motivated them best in the past?
- ✔ How do they like to make changes in their lives?

What's this got to do with work?

You have 'real' work to do and you're working all hours already, so where will you find the time to coach? Many managers feel too busy carrying out tasks to have the time to develop their staff. When you're firefighting just to keep up, you may find it hard to believe that investment now in Performance Coaching will pay off in terms of better performance and maximum use of potential later. Coaching requires a considerable investment of time and energy in the short term to reap long-term gains.

Whatever business you're in, any products can be copied and improved on – your main competitive advantage has to be your people. You need to use every opportunity to bring them on.

Where do you find the time? An excellent coaching opportunity arises when you can *delegate* a task or project that someone else would regard as a career development.

Imagine, if you will, that you're unexpectedly abducted by aliens. Nothing unpleasant will happen but you'll be absent from work for the next three months.

On a piece of paper, list everything your job entails. For each task decide:

- ✔ Who could do it now, if necessary? Highlight in green.
- ✔ Who could do it if they received some coaching? Highlight in yellow.
- ✔ What jobs are left that only you can do. Highlight in pink.

What do you notice about how much of your job could be done by someone else? What you regard as routine work could be a fantastic development opportunity for someone more junior. Notice how you feel about relinquishing some of the tasks – relief or loss?

You may not be in a position where you can delegate any of the more routine tasks. In order to find time to do some Performance Coaching you may need to double-check your prioritising. Somehow things that are put in the diary usually happen. Be realistic about the amount of time you can afford, then set it in stone. One hour a month spent Performance Coaching for definite is worth much more than, 'I'll do it when I get some free time', because free time just isn't going to happen.

Another time-waster is procrastination. Are you possibly putting off doing any coaching? Check whether this is actually about your confidence or skill levels rather than time itself.

Finally, consider how you'd like to develop your job after all these other tasks are taken care of. What would this exercise free you up to achieve? Coaching can make this a reality.

Keeping everybody happy

Ideally, coaching takes place as part of a wider talent-management process so people are always aware of its positive and developmental nature. Only when there's uncertainty or a lack of transparency do people become uncomfortable or suspicious.

Think about who else is involved in the process of Performance Coaching. What impact will your coaching of one or more individuals have on the functioning of others, the team, or the organisation itself? Coaching can have a destabilising effect in a number of ways:

- ✔ **The coached individual.** When someone is coached effectively, her confidence grows. She becomes more aware of her skills and more eager for challenges. If no challenges are forthcoming, then disaffection can set in. In coaching, you need to cover how to deal with the frustration of delay in advancement in the real organisation.

✔ **The great un-coached.** Other people may feel threatened by seeing one of their number moving ahead as a result of coaching, and react by suppressing that person in some way. They may scorn some of the new ideas put forward by their coached counterpart. Clarity of communication about who's being coached, and why, will bring out some of these reactions early in the process and avoid this happening. If other people clearly understand their place in the scheme of things, you can often avoid this type of resistance.

With Performance Coaching, always consider the process of re-entry. You can't take someone out of context, cause dramatic change, and then toss her back into an unchanged environment. Throughout the coaching process, you need to examine the impact the individual's changed behaviour and style has on other colleagues and team members. By dealing with it throughout the coaching process, she won't experience the shock of re-entry that people often feel when returning from an intense course or programme.

✔ **The organisation.** How do you keep the business happy? If people's goals are clearly aligned to the business direction, you can clearly link results in coaching to business success. That would please most organisations and is rewarding for the individual who can recognise her contribution to the overall success. So, you need to align the goals of the individual and the organisation. People may be quite happy to work on development in all sorts of areas of their lives but your job as a Performance Coach is to help people test whether the goals they want to pursue are appropriate for the organisation at this moment in time.

The organisation may not be delighted if everyone you coach leaves for a new and better job with the competition. However, if someone's unhappy in her job or with the company, you need to work on that within coaching. If you can't overcome these issues, you need to effect the resolution of a potentially damaging situation. Rather than shoring someone up in a job she increasingly hates, you may need to negotiate with the organisation a new goal of achieving a move.

If no opportunities exist within the organisation, helping people to leave may seem disloyal. Supportive organisations often consider that helping someone to find the next good job is worthwhile, even if that job is external. If someone needs more experience, she gains it on someone else's time and may return to you mature and better qualified if she parts on constructive terms. However, you might need to clear this with your organisation first. As you can imagine, an external coach finds it easier to deal impartially with this type of issue.

Chapter 11 gives insights about the different stages of careers, and Chapter 8 looks at how you keep talent in the organisation.

Chapter 3

Deciding What You Want to Achieve and Setting the Structure

· ·

In This Chapter
▶ Coaching for recovery
▶ Coaching for excellence
▶ Introducing the six-session coaching model
▶ Overcoming obstacles

· ·

*I*n this chapter we outline the basic concepts of the Performance Coaching process to enable you (as the Performance Coach) and your colleague (as the recipient of your coaching) to maximise the benefits of Performance Coaching.

Before you can effectively begin your Performance Coaching work, you need to be clear about what Performance Coaching actually means and what you're trying to achieve. (Refer to Chapter 2 for more on this subject.)

Each coaching situation is different. For example, your colleague may have taken on new responsibilities and be finding it difficult to reach the required standard or manage his workload. Alternatively, an individual may have a personal crisis that is impacting on his ability to work effectively. Sometimes an individual may be really good at what he does but wants to get even better.

Seeing from the Coach's Perspective

As a Performance Coach, having an idea about the type of Performance Coaching that is appropriate for your colleague is helpful.

Performance Recovery Coaching

Performance recovery is the term normally associated with rectifying performance because it usually refers to someone who, for whatever reason, isn't achieving the quality of performance you or he expects. The aim of Performance Recovery Coaching is to help your colleague get back to his former level of output or achieve an acceptable baseline in relation to consistent effective work performance.

The reasons you may engage in Performance Recovery Coaching include:

- An individual receives a poor appraisal interview that outlines areas of disappointing performance.
- The individual approaches you with concerns about poor performance.
- You, as the manager of the individual, may identify areas of weakness.
- Human Resources (HR) have become involved in a disciplinary matter where the individual's poor performance is a key issue.
- An individual is promoted but is unsupported in the new role and requires help in rising to the challenges.

Coaching for Excellence

Many people seek coaching for performance enhancement rather than for performance recovery purposes. *Coaching for Excellence* is a type of Performance Coaching for individuals who are already good at what they do but who want to be even better. Coaching for Excellence is sometimes called Performance Enhancement.

Coaching for Excellence is similar to coaching world-class athletes – you're working with people who are already achieving great results. Just as the world-class athlete wants to continue to get better and refine his performance to go on to win more medals by getting faster or jumping higher, so the competitive person who engages in Coaching for Excellence wants to be the best that he can be at work.

Coaching for Excellence is *staying sane and ahead of the game.*

Staying sane

Coaches of top athletes have to ensure that their clients don't over-train because otherwise injuries can occur to put them out of the game. You, as manager, need to ensure that your colleagues aren't on the path to burnout – after all, what's the point of being a bright star in an organisation only to find that a few years down the line that star has faded? High achievers are often competitive (if not with others then certainly with themselves), hate boredom, have a high capacity for work, and push themselves physically, emotionally, and psychologically. These personalities are more likely to end up burning out and/or causing themselves physical harm in the longer term than less competitive types. These people want to achieve at all costs.

Coaching for Excellence means ensuring that your colleague develops a style that ensures sustained performance. You need to coach the personal management strategies required to sustain long-term success and this book can help you.

Ahead of the game

The world of work, marketplaces, and the global economy are changing at such a rapid rate that successful individuals need to ensure that they're up to date on the best ways of making the most of their abilities. People who are creative and adaptable, keep up-to-date on developments, and are able to add value to organisations are well equipped to stay ahead of the game.

To ensure that an individual stays motivated, he needs a game plan relating to future aspirations. Where does he want to be in two or five years' time? What's next on the agenda in relation to career progression and skill enhancement?

In today's competitive environment, your colleague needs to keep physically and psychologically healthy, ensuring that his skills and knowledge are up to date and that he has the ability to think ahead. He needs these attributes to achieve success for the future, and to stick around to enjoy that success.

Ensuring that Your Colleague Is Ready to Change

When working with your colleague to improve performance, you need to be clear about what you both want to achieve, and your colleague needs to be clear about the developments and changes required.

You and your colleague face the challenge of taking into account the needs of the organisation you work for as well as any personal goals your colleague may have.

Scribble here: Drawing up a Behavioural Contract

Your first task, as the Performance Coach, is to identify what changes need to take place. To start this task, you can complete what's called a *Behavioural Contract*, which aims to outline the changes the individual needs to make.

A Behavioural Contract brings together the changes required by the organisation with the changes the individual decides he wants to make. If you're the individual's manager, you already know what changes you want your colleague to make and you simply need to discuss these with the person concerned and elicit his requirements from the coaching process. However, if your colleague works for another manager, you need to discuss the type of outcomes required with the manager concerned.

Whether you're speaking to the individual or to the individual and his manager, you need to clarify the changes needed by answering the following questions (we provide example answers).

- ✔ **What change is needed?** Here you, as the Performance Coach, set an overall objective with your colleague (or with your colleague's manager and your colleague) against which you can eventually measure the outcome.

- ✔ **What are the Coaching Objectives?** A *Coaching Objective* is a very general goal elicited by asking questions.

  - **Individual's Manager:** I would like to see John become a better communicator.

  - **Colleague:** I would like to be more assertive.

- ✔ **What is the reason for change?**

  - **Individual's Manager:** John has taken on a role with a much higher profile in the organisation which requires him to communicate with a wider group of individuals across all levels, both internally as well as with external clients.

  - **Colleague:** I'm now finding myself having to make difficult decisions and to delegate and negotiate more. I am not delegating enough because I find it hard to ask people to do things for me.

- ✔ **What negative outcomes are likely to happen if the changes aren't made?**

  - **Individual's Manager:** If John is unable to fulfil the requirements of this role effectively, then we may need to consider a change of position.

  - **Colleague:** My stress levels will continue to rise and I won't be able to cope or fulfil my role effectively.

 ✔ **What positive outcomes would result if the change is successful?**

- **Individual's Manager:** If this current situation can be addressed, I'd like to consider John for future promotion.

- **Colleague:** If I can become more effective in my communications with others and find out how to be more assertive, I'll decrease my stress levels, become more effective, and position myself well for future promotion.

Differentiating between the hares and tortoises

Everyone adapts to change at different rates, so as a Performance Coach you need to develop strategies at a pace that suits the individual.

Going too slowly for someone able to go faster leads to frustration, and you also don't get results as quickly as possible. On the other hand, coaching too fast may mean that your colleague doesn't really understand what's required. People want to show themselves in a good light, especially if you're their manager. Some people engage in 'nodding dog' syndrome. You know – the nodding dogs in the back of cars. People often look as if they're agreeing when, in fact, they don't understand you or feel pressurised to agree to avoid appearing stupid.

As the Performance Coach, your job is to ensure that you're pitching and pacing your interventions in the most appropriate way to ensure that your colleague gets the best from the process.

To ensure that you get your pacing right with an individual, check your colleague's understanding from time to time. Use questions such as, 'I wonder what you're thinking about what we've discussed?' Transmit to your colleague that you're not judging him but that you want to ensure that he gets the best out of the Performance Coaching process by *pacing* your discussions in the way that's most helpful to that person. Pacing means ensuring your colleague has time to consider and process your discussions.

Seeing from Your Colleague's Perspective

After you've given some thought to your role as the Performance Coach, think about what your colleague may need from you.

For example, you need to consider whether you're the best person to work with your colleague, and whether your colleague is clear about whether he's engaging in performance recovery or Coaching for Excellence.

Holding a chemistry meeting

Sometimes you may coach direct reports who you know well; at other times you may know little about the person you're going to work with. An initial *chemistry meeting* is a good way of seeing whether the Performance Coach and the individual can work together. Your colleague can ensure that you're the right person to work with and you can see whether the coaching you offer is right for the individual. Most Performance Coaches begin to show their coaching potential in these meetings as a way of giving colleagues a feel of what coaching would be like if they decided to proceed.

In a chemistry meeting, you can begin to firm up on the assessment of needs process (covered in the previous section 'Ensuring that your colleague is ready to change'), identifying objectives and possible outcomes.

When setting the scene with your colleague at a chemistry meeting, you need to provide a clear explanation of what Performance Coaching is and whether the work you're about to embark upon is performance recovery or Coaching for Excellence. Be clear in your mind about what you can offer.

John is the Marketing Manager for a major high-street retailer. He's risen swiftly through the ranks and is well regarded. However, having been recently promoted, he now finds himself struggling to meet targets, a new and some- what uncomfortable experience for him. He knows his performance has slipped and, following a discussion with the Director of Marketing, they ami- cably and mutually agreed that Performance Recovery Coaching may prove helpful in assisting John adjust to the additional demands of his new role.

Continually developing

Individual performance in anything has an element of continual development, because no job stays exactly the same. The Performance Coaching programme builds on success while identifying areas of work required.

Successful Performance Coaching breaks down what needs to be achieved into small, manageable stages, each building on the other. All of these, over time, come together to achieve the desired result.

Your colleague needs to consider where he is now, where he needs to be, and how many stages he needs to achieve each goal.

The Six-Session Model

When starting the Performance Coaching process, you need to have a structure to help you and your colleague gain the best from the work you do together. Most Performance Coaching programmes are designed to run over a predetermined number of sessions.

The number of sessions and duration of sessions may vary depending on the original assessment, the needs of the individual, and any coaching policy that your organisation already has in place. However, most Performance Coaching is offered in blocks of six 90-minute sessions over anything from a three- to six-month period with a mid-point agreed review and an evaluation at the end. You can then agree on additional further sessions.

Table 3-1 shows a breakdown of the six-session model.

Table 3-1	The 90-Minute, Six-Session Performance Coaching Model
Session 1	Session 1 is the chemistry meeting and Behavioural Contracting, assessing your colleague's needs and behavioural changes. In this session, you and your colleague firm up on the objectives and associated outcomes required from the coaching.
Session 2	In the second session, you refine information about your colleague's situation. Together, you set goals for the coaching process to empower your colleague to behave more effectively in real-life work situations. You develop and agree strategies for reaching goals.
Sessions 3–5	During the middle sessions, you review the coaching that's taken place, discuss progress towards goals, and find out if anything's blocking progress. You provide additional techniques for making further progress. You may use role-play to deepen the acquisition of techniques. You encourage your colleague to work out solutions for himself so that his own abilities are revealed and developed and he gains confidence.
Session 6	In your last session, review what your colleague has discovered and used. Review objectives to ensure that they've all been met. Agree plans for your colleague to ensure ongoing progress.

First formal meeting

Coaching is a formal activity and the first formal meeting is important because it sets the tone for the work you and your colleague will be doing together. Your colleague may have asked for coaching or may have been advised by his manager that coaching may help him.

Here's a rundown of what you need to cover in your first formal meeting:

1. Confirm coaching arrangements and your colleague's understanding of Performance Coaching to ensure that you're both clear about all the parameters.

2. Ask what your colleague wants to achieve from the coaching process and give him the opportunity to 'tell his story'.

3. Come up with a *Coaching Agenda* – a list of topics to explore. The Coaching Agenda relates to all the changes your colleague and his manager would like to see take place. This part of the process relates to the Assessment of Needs part of the Performance Coaching process. For example, your coaching agenda may include mention of areas of professional development such as needing to devise ways of communicating more regularly with colleagues, increasing individual profile within the organisation, or developing better time management skills.

4. Begin work in the session on ways of moving forward – ideas and strategies for reaching the goals.

5. Set a *Coaching Assignment* – what your colleague can do between now and the next time you meet to move towards a successful outcome. For example, your colleague may want to speak to key individuals to ascertain their thoughts on how he's performing; undertake research on internal training programmes to assist development; or simply take time to reflect on his achievements to date. Performance Coaching is a proactive form of help.

6. Ask for feedback from your colleague about the session – did he find your discussions useful, what went well, and what might have been done differently that would have made your time together more fruitful? End each session by asking for feedback on how the coaching session has been.

Ongoing sessions

All ongoing sessions include a review of your colleague's mood as well as focusing on agenda items for that session.

1. Review your colleague's mood and current situation – this reflection helps to break the ice for the session and gives you both the opportunity to catch up on what's been happening that may be of relevance. It also

gives you the chance to check in on the emotional mood of your colleague to help you gauge the way in which you can work with him.

2. As you listen make a list of Agenda items for the current session.

   At times during the Performance Coaching process you may want to take notes, so explain this to your colleague. Tell him that these notes are to help you and aren't for inclusion on your colleague's work record.

3. Check on assignment progress since the last session (what went well, what could have been done differently, what got in the way or assisted?).

4. Work on the chosen Agenda item from the list you both devised at the beginning of the programme. Each session builds on the last in relation to picking up on themes and topics and building on progress and experience. Sometimes you may want to act out a situation that your colleague is facing. For example, your colleague may need to have an important conversation with his manager. You take on the role of the manager while your colleague practises what he can say and how to say it.

5. Help your colleague to set the next Assignment. Your colleague needs to devise his own action points for follow-up between sessions because it encourages him to take responsibility for the changes required. Doing so also ensures that your colleague begins to take the actions required to ensure the goals that he has set are achieved.

6. Ask for feedback on the coaching session. Performance Coaching is a collaborative process.

Session 6: Final meeting

Now that you and your colleague are coming to the end of the coaching process, you both want to review what's happened and what you've achieved.

1. Review your colleague's views on how the coaching has been for him. Ask how it's helped, what he's gained from it, and what he'll take away with him.

2. Check how your colleague intends to maintain progress. Maintaining progress is particularly important if he had issues around areas such as stress and work-life balance. You want to ensure that your colleague doesn't fall back into bad habits. Discuss the idea of maintaining progress, to reinforce the need to keep up newly gained healthy practices. For example, if your coaching programme included the need for your colleague to develop a better work-life balance, then you can discuss the ways in which those new behaviours will be maintained. This may be as simple as a reminder that if he returns to his old ways the same issues will recur.

3. Discuss options for follow-up sessions, if any. Some people find it helpful to agree a follow-up meeting for 8–12 weeks in the future as a kind of 'check-in' or 'top-up' session.

4. Use evaluation sheets if appropriate – external coaches always use evaluation sheets to check how successful the coaching has been in relation to achieving the original set of objectives. Although you're most likely working with your colleague and are not an external coach, some type of evaluation is still of use. (See the later section 'Evaluation'.)

5. Steps 3 and 4 lead to a natural ending where you can reflect on your work together. You'll probably wish your colleague well and end with a handshake.

Reviews

Each coaching session has time for a mini-review of work at the end, and setting specific dates for more formalised reviews can also be helpful. If, for example, you and your colleague have decided on a 12-week programme, you may want to set a formal review of your progress at around Session 6.

The review is a two-way process. It's a chance for your colleague to reflect on the coaching process, what's been achieved, the challenges and successes, and what still needs to be done. The review is also an opportunity for you to provide your colleague with any feedback that you feel may be appropriate and useful. Each session has a mini-review when you, as the Performance Coach, ask your colleague how he's found the session. However, as you've set dates for more formal reviews (say, at the halfway point of the agreed number of sessions) you may want to structure your questions to ascertain more detailed information.

The more formal review comprises three simple questions:

✔ **How did you feel when you first started the Performance Coaching process?** This encourages your colleague to reflect back on how things were at the beginning.

✔ **Where do you think you are now in terms of the goals you set for yourself?** This encourages your colleague to evaluate how far he's come.

✔ **What is left for you to achieve?** This enables your colleague to consider how much more work needs to be done to reach the goals that have been set.

Evaluation

After taking a colleague through Performance Coaching, you may think that a review suffices as an evaluation tool. However, you may want to put into place something more structured such as an evaluation form with a series of questions. The evaluation can be a paper or online questionnaire. Use your last meeting with your colleague to introduce the idea and ask whether he'd like to complete the evaluation form. Explain what it will be used for and who will probably see it. The following section shows an example of an evaluation form:

Answer the following questions (with 1 meaning that you don't agree and 5 meaning that you very much agree).

Coaching Fundamentals

Did your Performance Coach:

- Keep agreed appointments?

- Allow you to set the agenda for your sessions?

- Keep a check on the points agreed during your sessions and feed these back to you including reviewing points from previous sessions?

- Share experiences and ideas as options for you to consider?

Coaching Process

Did your Performance Coach:

- Establish rapport with you – listening to what you said and displaying empathy with your thoughts and ideas, giving clear responses and summaries, and communicating openly with you?

- Explain clearly any necessary concepts, information, and techniques, giving concise and constructive feedback?

- Ensure that you retained responsibility to solve your own problems and change your own behaviour, committing to a Coaching Agenda.

- Assert him/herself without being aggressive or passive?

- Show that he/she was knowledgeable, skilful, and willing to liaise with other appropriate experts?

- Demonstrate good time-management practices?

- Communicate a genuine belief in the potential for people to improve their performance?

- Manage any relevant emotional issues that occurred during the coaching (if appropriate)?

- Act as a good role model?

What do you need to measure?

Measuring the effectiveness of coaching can be tricky. You can see measurable outcomes as follows:

✔ If your colleague used to avoid giving presentations but now successfully does so on a regular basis.

✔ If your colleague is reaching his sales targets which he previously struggled with.

✔ On a larger scale, if an organisation used to suffer from loss of staff because of lack of support and effective career enhancement and now effectively retains staff.

As the Performance Coach, you need to consider measurement at both

✔ **The micro level:** That of each individual being coached

✔ **The macro level:** That of organisational benefits

Coaching Outcomes

Answer the following questions as best you can:

- Are you now able to assess your current levels of competence effectively (if appropriate)?
- Has your work performance improved?
- Are you able to maximise opportunities to progress?
- Are you able to set yourself development targets and prioritise your development needs?
- Are you able to set yourself new goals?
- Do you feel positive about your development?
- Did Performance Coaching raise your morale?

Organisational Benefits

Rate the following statements between 1 and 5 (with 1 meaning 'I don't agree' and 5 meaning 'I very much agree').

- Providing Performance Coaching demonstrates to me that this company cares about my development.
- My motivation has increased as a result of coaching.
- I'm more likely to stay with the company as a result of receiving coaching.
- I'm able to demonstrate how coaching has improved my personal performance at work.

- My coaching has *directly* resulted in business benefits.
- My coaching has *indirectly* resulted in business benefits.

Coaching Objectives

Write down your original objectives and rate each one 1 to 5, with 1 being 'I haven't met this objective' and 5 being 'I have definitely met this objective'.

Avoiding Performance Coaching Road Blocks

People sometimes come into coaching with issues and emotional reactions that are beyond the scope of Performance Coaching. For example, your colleague may be going through a difficult divorce or have suffered a recent bereavement and is finding coping difficult. No amount of coaching can help in such situations. Instead, you need to refer the individual on to a more appropriate source of help, such as a counsellor.

Dealing with people experiencing psychological or emotional problems can be taxing so you may need someone to share your challenges with. Bearing in mind issues of confidentiality, who in your organisation can function as a supervisor? Would entering into a formal supervision arrangement be appropriate?

Keep a list of possible referral sources and know who within your organisation takes responsibility for helping individuals if they face difficulties.

When coaching is not the answer

At times you and your colleague may identify a barrier that's outside of the remit of coaching. For example, your colleague may require training in addition to coaching. In such cases, although Performance Coaching has been proven to embed knowledge gleaned from training more effectively than training alone, it cannot be a substitute for training itself. If you and your colleague identify a need for another form of assistance, ensure that he gains access to it.

When the person is unable to change

No amount of coaching can help if what is being asked of your colleague is outside his ability range. Locating the resources to begin the process of gaining such skills is one step. However, sometimes Performance Coaching highlights to the individual that he doesn't have the aptitude for or desire to make the changes required. In this case, Performance Coaching can be a way of helping the individual clarify his thinking and set about putting actions in place to benefit the organisation as well as the individual. For example, an individual may decide that a particular job isn't for him and he may be better off if he left the current organisation for a new job. The organisation is also better off because a demoralised, unhappy employee who doesn't have the right set of skills for the job is not a productive one.

Alternatively, other roles within the company may better suit the skills, talents, and aspirations of your colleague. If you and your colleague recognise this fact, then Performance Coaching can help the individual instigate discussions with the most appropriate people about a new role.

Part II

Does Your Face Fit?: The Personal Attributes of a Performance Coach

'Our boss used to be the cox for the
Cambridge University boat crew.'

In this part . . .

*I*n this part you start working out what it takes to be a really good Performance Coach. Discover the qualities and skills that make all the difference. Find out how to build a good coaching relationship, earn respect, and set out the ground rules. You also discover how to encourage people to become enthusiastic about making real change.

Chapter 4

Starting the Relationship with Trust and Respect

In This Chapter

▶ Getting on with people

▶ Finding ways of respecting people

▶ Setting out the coaching contract

▶ Making it work – together

Successful Performance Coaches all share a number of personal qualities such as respecting and seeing the best in people. These qualities help to build the relationship, enable you to gain credibility, and achieve a fruitful working partnership with your colleague.

This chapter is about getting started by putting some fundamental underpinnings in place for the Performance Coaching you intend to do. Certain attributes contribute directly to the success of coaching. We examine those attributes and ask you to determine how strong these qualities are in you. In order to engage constructively with people for the best outcomes, you may need to develop yourself first.

Building the Foundations of the Relationship

Few relationships click right away. You usually have a period of checking each other out, getting to know each other, and above all deciding to trust each other. This initial period is even more evident in coaching and contributes hugely to successful outcomes.

Getting to know you

Entering the Performance Coaching arena means developing a different kind of relationship, whether you and your colleague are meeting for the first time or you already know each other to some extent. In some ways, coaching may be easier if you and your colleague have no prior knowledge of each other because this knowledge may influence both of you, whether positively or negatively, prior to commencing the Performance Coaching process.

When Performance Coaches work within an organisation, it's inevitable that you and your colleagues have pre-existing relationships to some extent, especially if you're a manager *and* the Performance Coach. Table 4-1 shows the benefits and drawbacks of different types of relationships.

Table 4-1	Pros and Cons of Different Types of Relationship	
Relationship Type	**Pros**	**Cons**
No previous contact	You start the relationship with no prior knowledge, ideas, or expectations of each other that may get in the way of the Performance Coaching process.	You have to work hard to build a relationship and gain the depth and understanding of your colleague needed for the work you need to achieve.
Only know each other through hearsay	If you heard positive comments about the person, this may aid positive feelings towards your work together. If negative comments have been made, these may provide you with useful information about how your colleague is perceived. In both cases, remember that hearsay is opinion, not necessarily truth.	Positive comments may raise unrealistic expectations. Less positive hearsay may bring a negative expectation to the Performance Coaching process. Both parties may have to work harder to correct the impression that has been made.
Casual contact	You may already like each other.	You may already dislike each other!
Day-to-day professional contact	You have a realistic under-standing of each other's strengths and limitations.	You may have no liking or respect for each other.

Relationship Type	Pros	Cons
Professional contact as well as personal friendship	You know each other well and have respect and liking for each other.	You may find challenging a friend difficult for fear of hurting her feelings. You may find staying objective hard. Your colleague/friend may find it hard to take the coaching on board.

Trust me – I'm your coach!

Whatever the relationship you have with your colleague, you need to set very clear boundaries for the coaching work you're about to embark on. Make sure that your colleague is clear about what Performance Coaching with you entails and how it differs to any other type of relationship you have with her.

If you're very close to the person concerned, you may feel that what you can offer her is limited. Your feelings may influence what you can do. Think about whether you need to call in an external coach who can start afresh.

Fancy meeting you here

How do you both deal with situations when you bump into each other? What do you do and how do you behave towards each other if you find yourself at the same meeting? Your colleague may be more than happy for people to know that you're her coach. Or not. These kinds of encounters happen all the time, even if you just find yourselves going up in the lift together. Talk about how she wants to handle it before it happens.

Some organisations that use internal Performance Coaches normally have the individual work with a coach who is a member of staff who has little or no day-to-day contact with the individual concerned. In other organisations, Performance Coaching with close colleagues involves both parties acknowledging their relationship, discussing the boundaries, and setting a contract that takes all the above into account (the later section 'Writing the rules of engagement' has a sample coaching contract).

Either way can be successful for Performance Coaching. The key lies in discussing the situation openly, agreeing a code of conduct, and then behaving professionally.

Showing Respect

Respect is being able to stand back and not judge someone, simply accepting her as a human being. You may not like or approve of the way she does things. However, when you respect someone you see the *behaviour* and separate that from the *person*.

Think about it this way – you may read in the newspaper about people who have done dreadful things. Their *actions* have caused distress and may be pretty despicable. However, do you see beyond what they've done and wonder what may have caused them to behave in a certain way? What motivated them? Are they simply evil or were they driven to behave the way they did? Do they have good points as well as bad?

If you have children, you may love them but chastise them for their behaviour. You see beyond their behaviour to the whole person. Respect is the ability to see beyond what the person does to who the person is.

Being respectful while coaching

Respect is a fundamental underpinning of all coaching and cuts both ways. On the one hand, you want to be respected for your skills and results in coaching. On the other, you need to respect your colleague for coaching to progress. Few people set out to be disrespectful, but respect can be lost by a number of thoughtless ways, such as being inattentive or dismissive of ideas.

Showing respect means developing an accepting, empathic response to your colleague's feelings and experience. When you respect an individual you set out to avoid judging, advising, or ordering the person.

Accepting a person doesn't mean that you can't dislike some aspect of her behaviour. You don't have to like or approve of what the person does. Performance Coaching is about changing *behaviours* not about changing the person. As long as the person develops more effective behaviour, she can think what she likes. Often, when people change their behaviour, they end up changing the way that they think and modifying individual beliefs and ideas. However, change in thinking patterns is not always the case.

Avoiding judging people

Respect requires you to work at being *non-judgemental* – that is, not immediately imposing a value judgement on what you hear but leaving yourself open to consider ideas impartially. If you're judgemental, your colleague may pick up on your feelings and become defensive. She may find it harder to make the changes that are needed. Think about how you'd feel if you thought that someone didn't respect, like, or understand you. You probably wouldn't feel motivated to change – more like, 'why bother?'

Being judgemental usually points at some underlying beliefs about what people ought or ought not to do. Listen to your thoughts and notice when they may interfere with your really being able to hear what the other person is saying. When coaching you're working hard to see the situation through your colleague's eyes rather than filtered through your own views.

Becoming non-judgemental can be hard, especially because everyone holds many prejudices they're not even aware of. Think about some of the people you work with and consider who you respect and why. Who do you find it hard to like and why?

Some of the things that can get in the way of respecting a colleague are:

- ✔ **Moral judgements:** You may hold strong views about the way you believe that someone should behave at work or in her personal life. If your colleague holds a different set of values to your own, you may find yourself judging the other person and looking on her less favourably because of the lifestyle that she adopts.

- ✔ **Prejudices:** You may have grown up with certain views that were instilled into you about certain types of people and, perhaps without realising, you may hold views about groups of people that lead you to form judgements about them. If your colleague falls into one of these groups, you may find yourself stereotyping her and making assumptions and judgements about her.

- ✔ **Past history:** Knowing someone's past may colour the way you see that person. Not making judgements about someone is hard if you feel that she's behaved in a way that you've found unacceptable or contrary to your own code of behaviour.

- ✔ **Reputation:** If you've been told various things about your colleague, such rumours can influence the way you see that person and you may form judgements about her as a result of the hearsay.

Developing respect

Separating the 'person' from the 'behaviour' isn't always easy. As a Performance Coach, you can work on being non-judgemental of others and developing respect. You can increase your ability to be non-judgemental by:

- ✔ **Looking for good points:** Everyone has good points and focusing on these helps you to see that the traits you find difficult to accept are only one part of your colleague – and not the whole of her. Make a note of all the positive points your colleague manifests as a reminder.

✔ **Reminding yourself that everyone is a fallible human being:** Recognising and accepting your own imperfections makes accepting the imperfections of others easier. Making a list of your less-than-positive attributes can also help you to accept and become more non-judgemental of others.

✔ **Being open to finding out about your colleague:** When you understand what motivates a person to behave in a certain way, you can often develop a more accepting attitude of the person. You may still need to coach your colleague to change her behaviour, but understanding an individual's motivation certainly helps you become more respectful of your colleague as a whole person.

Your colleague may be very quick to find fault with people, doing so in a sharp and irritable manner that makes other people feel uncomfortable. However, you may discover that she feels passionately about producing a quality product and is a perfectionist who puts intolerable pressure on herself. In turn, this pressure manifests itself in the way that she behaves with others. When you understand the causes, you may find yourself feeling more empathic and, in turn, less judgemental of the person, even if you recognise the need for her to change her behaviour.

✔ **Using your empathy:** Being respectful and non-judgemental of another person is much easier if you can use your empathy to try to understand that person. Being able to see the world as the other person sees it enables you to gain greater insight and tolerance of behaviours that you may usually find less than appealing.

Not being judged gives a sense of acceptance and freedom. Being non-judgemental creates a climate where your colleague doesn't need to be defensive. Such an environment creates a sense of safety – your colleague is far more likely to be prepared to explore areas of difficulty and admit to failings and difficulties if she feels that she's not being judged. She may recognise the need to change but the acceptance you show makes it easier for her to think about the things she needs to change and how to change them.

In Performance Coaching, respecting your colleague creates an environment where change can take place more readily, which can save time and personal energy, making the Performance Coaching process far more productive for all parties.

Even Attila the Hun had good points – finding the best in people

Even the most difficult person has good points but these good points may be extremely well hidden by irksome behaviour. When coaching, you need to look behind these irritations and find the strengths that really make your colleague tick. In other situations, you can choose to be offended, irritated, or even totally disapproving of a range of behaviours. When coaching, you take a different tack.

When coaching, you often come across highly motivated people. They're not difficult people, but they may have really difficult ways. Colleagues often never see beyond this difficult behaviour. Finding even one thing you respect in any individual can switch your perception of her and make coaching possible. Actively recognising the blocks in your attitude and taking steps to shift them is vital in Performance Coaching. Façades and political games may encourage role-playing, flattery, and even deception in organisations. The respectful coach may be the only person who can hold up a mirror to colleagues with honesty.

Keeping free from external judgement, even – sometimes – from positive judgement, allows clients to recognise that they themselves are the real judges of their action, not you. Your role isn't to approve or disapprove of behaviour but rather to invoke your colleague's own balanced judgement. Coaching aims to keep putting control back in your colleague's hands. How rationally she judges her own achievements is important to sustain changes made through coaching. If, however, her judgement is overly harsh or complacent, you may need to prompt her to test the accuracy of her judgement.

Establishing the Ground Rules

An important factor in establishing trust is being absolutely clear at the onset about what all parties expect. Avoiding conflict by removing uncertainty and setting out ways of behaving together ensures that the coaching process gets off to a good and productive start. Establishing ground rules is one instance where you may be quite clearly directive!

Your colleague needs a clear understanding of what she's getting herself into. You can't assume that she understands the coaching process simply because quite a lot of organisations use coaching these days. Ensuring clarity is especially important if you already have a clearly defined relationship with the individual – if you're her line manager, for example. You need to clearly specify how your coaching role differs from your usual role.

For the Performance Coaching process to prove effective, you, as the Performance Coach, need to take account of two crucial aspects – confidentiality and establishing a coaching contract. These are perhaps the most fundamental building blocks to the whole coaching process.

Confidentiality

Confidentiality in Performance Coaching involves many of the same factors as confidentiality among friends. Your colleague may tell you things that she'd like to remain between the two of you. If your colleague isn't performing as well as she should, the Performance Coaching process can be hampered if she doesn't share the reasons for her behaviour with you. However, trust has to be earned and if your colleague thinks that you're going to tell other people or pass judgements, she's less likely to want to share this vital information with you.

Having said that, you need to take into account a number of legal issues. For example, employers have a duty of care towards their employees, and organisations have a range of policies that they adhere to. As a Performance Coach, you cannot offer *total* confidentiality to anyone. You might want to direct your colleague to the HR or legal departments or suggest she consults the policies if they're openly published.

This confidentiality conundrum poses a possible conflict for the Performance Coach who has a responsibility towards the individual, and a responsibility towards the organisation sponsoring the coaching, as well as legal considerations.

You can resolve these possible conflicts by ensuring:

- **Clarity:** Be clear with your colleague about what information remains between the two of you and what information you're obliged to pass on. This allows her to make decisions about what to disclose and the ramifications of any disclosure. For example, you'd be obliged to break confidentiality if she told you of illegal or fraudulent behaviour.

- **Outcomes:** By explaining that some aspects may be deemed as 'quotable feedback' such as the outcomes that are identified when you're setting the boundaries. Performance Coaching has specific aims and goals. Agree that progress will be reported back to key people such as those who suggested the coaching in the first place.

- **Process:** By separating the 'content' of what is discussed from the 'outcome', you can assure your colleague that what's discussed during your time together remains confidential between the two of you. So if a Performance Coaching goal was about becoming more assertive in meetings, you might report back to her boss on the advances made towards achieving that goal. You wouldn't mention that the focus of coaching had been on helping her to become more assertive by finding constructive ways to deal with the boss's difficult style!

Separating public from private

Julie met with her manager and performance coach Elaine to discuss the reasons for her missing important deadlines. During her first Performance Coaching session, Julie was very nervous and Elaine tried to put her at ease. Julie gave all kinds of reasons for why she'd been missing deadlines – colleagues hadn't provided her with the information she needed, and she'd had difficulties with the IT (information technology) system. Elaine suspected that there was more to the situation than met the eye and she reassured Julie that while certain company policies needed to be adhered to, she was prepared to separate the information that may be made available to others from that which they'd keep between themselves.

Reassured by this conversation, Julie explained that she was in the middle of a difficult divorce, wasn't sleeping, and was finding it hard to cope. With this information, her manager understood that Julie had a number of personal pressures as well as professional difficulties that were hampering her performance.

Elaine was able to help Julie consider ways to separate work-related aspects, such as IT, from those that were having a personal impact. Elaine was able to help Julie consider ways to scale down her workload and use the organisation's external counselling service to support her.

If Elaine hadn't reassured Julie that content relating to her personal circumstances would remain confidential, Julie may not have opened up to Elaine in the way that she did.

Writing the rules of engagement

When engaging in the Performance Coaching process, the individual being coached, and not the Performance Coach, drives the process. In other words, the coaching process is driven by the individual being coached. She must take responsibility for progress and commit to making it work.

You can ensure that your colleague is clear about the coaching process by creating a coaching contract, devised and agreed to by all parties – the corporate sponsor (your organisation), the colleague being coached, and the Performance Coach. Doing so minimises the possibility of misunderstandings and unrealistic expectations. The coaching contract becomes the vehicle by which the structure of the work to be achieved is documented.

The purpose of contracting is to:

- ✔ Ensure agreement on desired outcomes
- ✔ Clarify roles
- ✔ Define how outcomes will be achieved.

Your colleague is committing to:

- ✔ Actively engaging in coaching
- ✔ Working towards development
- ✔ Attending agreed sessions

You need to:

- ✔ Foster commitment to change and development
- ✔ Identify your colleague's goals
- ✔ Work with her to devise ways of achieving the goals

In the contract, you may want to include:

- ✔ **Coaching objectives.** Objectives define how the process is going to work. At the outset, you may want to take a brief from both the *corporate client* (such as the line manager to whom the individual reports and/or from Human Resources) and from the *designated client* (the colleague who you'll be coaching). These discussions form the basis for the initial objective of the coaching, as well as how you measure the success of the coaching.

- ✔ **Outcomes.** The coaching contract considers results that the manager needs to see and those that the coaching colleague wishes to achieve. You, as coach, synthesise these. At times you may need to take into account the possibility of a conflict of interests. For example, if you're an internal Performance Coach the kind of relationship you have with your colleague may mean that your loyalties will be torn. The contract also ensures agreement by getting everyone to sign off on the outcomes. Your colleague can now take control of the process having agreed to work on the outcomes identified.

- ✔ **Confidentiality and feedback.** The coaching contract needs to make a clear statement about confidentiality, its importance, what it means in practice, and the process for feedback, reviews, and evaluation. In addition, you need to share information with your colleague about duty of care and the fact that you need to discuss your colleague's progress with the corporate client.

- ✔ **Location and frequency.** Include details regarding the location of the coaching and number of sessions together with any additional items, such as whether you use psychometric tests (Chapter 7 has more about psychometric tests).

Figure 4-1 shows a sample coaching contract.

Administrative Details

Organisation Name:	Anywhere Anytime Ltd
Corporate Sponsor Name:	Jane Boss
Corporate Sponsor Position:	Head of Talent and Leadership
Coaching Client Name:	Michelle Money
Coaching Client Position:	Head of Financial Risk Management
Date of Initial Scoping Meeting:	8 May 2008

Coaching Objectives/Required Outcomes

To find ways of communicating more effectively with team members as well as facilitating such communication between team members
To improve the 'people-related' and 'emotional intelligence' aspects involved in managing staff
To improve personal work/life balance

Outcome Measurements

To identify and develop relevant people-related skills/strategies, such as trying out a variety of ways of communicating through verbal and/or written methods to enable more effective contact with team members
To devise mechanisms to understand the various team and personality type(s) based on internal psychometric testing and the similarities and differences of these types
To identify the strengths and limitations of team members while recognising the value of difference and the strategies concerned to maximise on the strengths and develop ways of helping individuals minimise their limitations
To identify and implement strategies to improve work/life balance, such as time management, delegation, and devising and implementing time saving systems

Number of sessions agreed: 6

Feedback Procedures

Information feedback with Michelle Money at the end of each session
Mid-point feedback at session 3 to Jane Boss from Michelle Money
Formalised feedback in written form at the end of the programme together with completion of the standard Evaluation Form.

Confidentiality: Recognising the need for discretion and confidentiality, all parties agree to take into account all aspects relating to the law and duty of care.

Additional agreements/details (if any): *None*

I agree to abide by the terms and conditions supplied to me.

Corporate Sponsor Name:	*Jane Boss*	Date: 10.5.08
Coaching Client Name:	*Michelle Money*	Date: 11.5.08
Coach Name:	*Anna Canhelp*	Date: 12.5.08

Figure 4-1:
Sample coaching contract

Working in Partnership

Working in partnership means working with your colleague in a way that is as transparent and honest as possible. It means checking out your understanding and seeking agreement, and it means including your colleague in decision-making, seeking her views and ensuring that they're taken into account. When you've entered into a tripartite arrangement (corporate sponsor, coaching client, and yourself), you have to take into consideration the needs of all parties because you're working in partnership with all of them.

When the coaching contract has been signed off, you and your colleague can set about the task of finding ways to achieve the outcomes listed. You're ready for action!

Chapter 5

Getting Your Hands Dirty: The Practical Skills of Performance Coaching

In This Chapter

▶ Realising the impact of communication
▶ Looking at body language
▶ Discovering the power of listening
▶ Asking the right questions
▶ Sharing the emotions

A number of basic skills underpin the Performance Coaching process. This chapter describes a range of techniques to ensure that you, as the Performance Coach, listen to and understand what your colleague tells you. We share a few sophisticated communication techniques that enable you to draw out the relevant information. The process of listening, clarifying, and understanding also helps you give colleagues a better and deeper understanding of the challenges that they face.

Letting Your Body Do the Talking

People tend to think that communication is about the words that you use and how you interpret them. However, you also communicate through *body language*, those non-verbal forms of communication expressed through body movement and your tone of voice. The way that you present yourself gives away a wealth of information about the way that you feel. Body language is largely unconscious and involuntary although certain aspects, such as choosing to smile, are under conscious control. As a Performance Coach, you need to use the information your colleague gives away in his body language to better understand the situation.

An incredible 55 per cent of communication is portrayed through body language, 38 per cent by your tone of voice, and only 7 per cent through the words you say.

If you're feeling anxious or defensive, you may cross your arms as if protecting yourself, or fidget. If you're feeling relaxed and comfortable you're likely to sit back in your chair, smile, and make slower movements. If someone says that he gets on well with his boss, but says it while casting his eyes down, with tight facial muscles, and with an edge to his voice, you may suspect that the claim is not the whole story.

As a Performance Coach, you need to watch all your colleague's movements and non-verbal clues all the time, as well as listening to what is being said.

Responding to non-verbal cues

Before you can respond to non-verbal cues in Performance Coaching, you need to know what you're looking for.

Peoples' bodies give away information all the time. Even when colleagues choose words carefully, they may not control the supplementary messages their bodies are sending out.

- ✔ **Eye Contact:** You usually maintain eye contact for about 60–70 per cent of the time. Any more than this percentage and you're probably staring, or gazing into your lover's eyes! Too much eye contact may make the other person uncomfortable and can indicate an aggressive challenge. Too little eye contact may give the impression of being timid. When Performance Coaching, your colleague may perceive you as more powerful than him, which may make him drop his gaze. He may find looking at you difficult, for a whole range of reasons that you need to explore. For example, your colleague may be anxious and find looking away easier than looking at you, or he may feel angry and looking away is a way of coping with these feelings. Demonstrating your attentiveness through constancy of gaze is vital. In the face of strong emotion, you can be respectful by dropping your eyes, showing that you're giving him privacy, or in the case of anger that you're not engaging. (Chapter 13 has more about dealing with anger.)

- ✔ **Facial Expressions:** The old saying that a smile is worth a thousand words says it all. People normally associate a smile with approachability. In contrast, facial tension such as rapid eye movement or biting of lips may be a sign that the person is feeling agitated or anxious. When coaching, watch for changes of expression that give you clues about what your colleague is really thinking. Be aware of your own expression. A frown may only mean that you're concentrating but may be interpreted as disapproval.

✔ **Posture:** The way that someone stands or sits says much about the way that he feels or the impression that he wants to make. If he stands squarely allowing an appropriate amount of *personal space* (the amount of space between him and you) then he's likely to be feeling fairly neutral. However, if he stands too close to you he may be feeling angry and wanting to invade your space, or if he's too far away he may be feeling anxious. As a coach, you want your posture to show that you're attentive, but not overwhelmingly. Sit in a relaxed and open manner, arms gently resting by your side, feet on the floor, and an attentive look on your face. Pay attention to shifts in your colleague's posture. The posture may reflect psychological discomfort about the topic in discussion (or maybe the seating is really uncomfortable!).

✔ **Gestures:** Gestures include everything from smiling or using your hands when talking to more formal gestures such as shaking hands, and they have social norms of behaviour associated with them. For example, if you meet someone for the first time in a business meeting, you'll probably shake his hand. If someone introduces you informally to a friend, you may simply give a slight nod and smile. How you greet your colleague in a coaching situation can set the tone for the session.

Unconscious gestures also give away information because they match the person's mood. If someone is nervous or disinterested, he may run his hands through his hair or pick bits of imaginary fluff off his clothes. Hand movements can also indicate mood. When someone experiences a strong emotion such as excitement or anxiety, his movements may become animated.

Look out for all these physical indicators in coaching because they're all sources of invaluable data.

Unlocking the secrets of the voice

Apart from the way a person expresses himself physically, the way he speaks – voice tone, pacing, and pitch – also gives you cues about his state of mind. In coaching, be aware of:

✔ **Tone:** You can tell a lot about what someone feels from the tone of his voice. Does the voice sound even and measured or can you hear a sense of irritation or anxiety?

✔ **Pitch:** The pitch of the voice changes when someone experiences negative feelings. You may notice that the person speaks in a higher pitch when anxious or when talking about a particular subject.

✔ **Pacing:** Speaking more quickly or slowly may indicate that someone has specific feelings about the topic you're discussing. For example, speaking too fast can indicate anger or excitement; you can ascertain which one he's feeling by assessing the individual's pacing, tone, pitch and, of course, body language. Shouting, frowning, or waving arms in the air can indicate anger, but if the same person were speaking more quickly but at a normal pitch while smiling, then excitement would be a more likely reason.

Hear, Hear! Using Listening Skills

By noticing inconsistencies between what your colleague says and how he speaks and acts, you can gain an understanding of how he feels. You also need to use careful listening skills while coaching.

Active listening means listening in a way that focuses entirely on what the other person is saying, confirming understanding of both the content of the message and the emotions and feelings underlying the message. Active listening ensures that your understanding of what your colleague is saying is accurate.

Attending

One of the skills of active listening is *attending*, which is the skill of demonstrating to your colleague that you're giving him your full attention. The acronym SOLER helps you remember attending skills:

✔ **Square.** Set up your seating arrangement so that you sit squarely facing the individual. Although your body is sitting squarely facing your colleague, aim to have your chair angled very slightly away from your colleague. Angling the chairs at 45 degrees around a small coffee table ensures that you have the right amount of personal space between you – close enough to feel warm and inviting but far enough away not to feel intrusive.

✔ **Open.** Use open body language, with legs uncrossed, arms by your side or rested on the arm rests, and face towards your colleague.

✔ **Leaning.** Lean forward slightly to show, non-verbally, that you're interested in what your colleague is saying.

✔ **Eye contact.** Maintain appropriate eye contact. As the coach, you do most of the listening, so you need to maintain eye contact for a higher percentage of time than your colleague.

✔ **Relaxed.** Sit in a relaxed pose, leaning forward slightly, to give the impression that you're professional and confident, which is comforting to your colleague.

Set out a room as if you were an external coach invited in to see a coaching client. If you're a manager who normally sees people in your office, create a space on the other side of your desk with two chairs and a coffee table and sit down in each chair in turn. Notice what it feels like to sit in each of the places. Is the seating conducive to good communication?

When you set out a space for coaching, ensure that:

- ✔ The chairs aren't too close together, because too close may intimidate your colleague.

- ✔ Other people can't see into the room. If that's not possible, change the way the chairs are positioned to provide your colleague with more privacy.

- ✔ No distractions are in the room that may divert your attention.

- ✔ You can see a clock, so that you can discreetly keep an eye on the time when you're coaching.

Listening to the end of the sentence

You may find yourself believing that you know what your colleague is going to say next and, in a bid to demonstrate your knowledge, you may not allow the person to complete his sentences. However, rather than thinking how understanding you are, your colleague may see your intervention as an interruption. An important skill of active listening is allowing the other person to fully complete what he's saying.

Using silence

Inexperienced coaches are often uncomfortable if a silence occurs in the coaching process. This feeling is often based on the idea that you have to fill the space to show your ability. However, people need time to reflect. Interrupting may hamper the coaching process and your colleague's need for reflection.

If a silence occurs, count to five slowly in your head before you fill it. You often find that the other person starts talking again. When you remain silent, you demonstrate that you respect your colleague's need to work matters out at his own speed. The reflection and the silence that accompanies this process are a legitimate activity.

Asking Different Types of Questions

An important skill of Performance Coaching is using appropriate questioning to help your colleague. Your aim is to allow your colleague to explore his situation in depth.

The *five* types of questions are:

- ✔ **Closed questions: 'Do you like her?'**

  Closed questions are good for helping people to focus. However, closed questions don't encourage people to open up because only a 'yes' or 'no' is likely to be the answer. The danger of using closed questions too frequently is that you may end up engaging in what seems more like an interrogatory conversation.

- ✔ **Multiple questions: 'Did you speak to John, how did he react, were you surprised?'**

  Multiple questions can be confusing. Your colleague may not know which question to answer and can feel flustered if he can't remember them all or know which one to answer first!

- ✔ **Leading questions: 'You work really hard, don't you?'**

  This type of question leads the person to the answer and is often used in court when a barrister wants a witness to give a specific response. Leading questions aren't useful in the coaching process, which is focused on the colleague's needs and not the coach's.

- ✔ **Hypothetical questions: 'What do you think he would say if you told him?'**

  This type of question can be a useful because you're asking the person to use his imagination. Doing so encourages him to think beyond his current situation and into the realm of possibility.

- ✔ **Open questions: 'What steps have you already taken to change your situation?'**

  Open questions help people to consider options. They're so important to the coaching process that the next section is devoted to them.

Using open questions

Open questions start with What, Where, When, and How. Answering an open question with a simple 'yes' or 'no' is almost impossible, so they really help people to open up. An open question requires the person to consider a range of factors surrounding the topic in question.

The only open question missing from the previous list is Why. Although Why questions are helpful, without the right intonation a series of Why questions can seem intrusive. However, if you use Why questions well and sparingly they can reveal a wealth of information. For example, 'Why do you think that you've stayed so long in your current role?'

Open questions encourage your colleague to:

✔ Think and reflect

✔ Give you opinions and feelings

✔ Take control of the conversation. When asking an open question, the coach takes a back seat as the emphasis is placed on the other person to lead the discussion into the areas contained in his answer.

Examples of open questions are:

✔ What do you feel like when your manager says that?

✔ What did you think people would say about you?

✔ Where do you think you can find that information?

✔ Where do you think you are now?

✔ How can things be different?

✔ How would you describe your situation now?

✔ When do you find yourself feeling anxious at work?

✔ When would you like to change career?

Table 5-1 shows the difference between open and closed questions.

Table 5-1	Open versus Closed Questions
Closed Questions	*Open Questions*
Are you happy with your current supplier?	What else might you want from your current supplier?
Do you want to change your job?	How do you feel about your job?
Do you like your colleagues?	What do you like about your colleagues?
	What do you dislike?
Do you think you've done a good job this year?	How do you think you've performed this year?

Asking motivational questions

Two of the main things that hold people back from achieving change are:

- ✔ Ambivalence
- ✔ Lack of resolve

This is the point at which the well-meaning amateur coach attempts to stiffen the sinews and encourage the colleague to believe he can do it. Nice to get the encouragement – but not always effective. Far more effective is to ask questions that lead your colleague to come to this conclusion himself.

Motivational questioning focuses on drawing out, clarifying, and resolving ambivalence in order to clear the way for action. *Reflective listening* is particularly useful, that is, playing back what you understand your colleague to be saying in such a way that he can hear it afresh and challenge it for himself. Here are some examples of using motivational questioning:

- ✔ **Building the resolve.** 'Are you saying that you're keen to develop in this area but you recognise that sometimes you hold back?'
- ✔ **Drawing out and reinforcing any statements about self-motivation and ability to change.** 'You also recognise that you have what it takes because you've come a long way already. On reflection, you recognise that careful planning has helped you achieve in the past.'
- ✔ **Measuring readiness to change.** 'I wonder what would make you want to change this now?'
- ✔ **Giving your colleague freedom of choice and self-direction.** 'How would you choose to approach this issue?'
- ✔ **Strengthening the desire to change.** 'Tell me about how the future will look if you make these changes.'

Table 5-2 shows examples of standard questions, which focus on problems, and their motivational equivalents, which focus on outcomes.

Table 5-2	Motivational Questions
Standard Question	*Motivational Question*
What is your problem?	What do you want?
How long have you had it?	How will you know when you've got it?
Whose fault is it?	What else in your life will improve when you get it?

Standard Question	Motivational Question
Who is really to blame?	What resources do you already have which can help you achieve this outcome?
What is your worst experience with this problem?	What is something similar you've succeeded in doing?
Why haven't you solved it yet?	What is your next step?

Be aware of any tendencies your colleague has to be negative because this will diminish motivation and interfere with him achieving his goals. Just as important is to ensure that you frame questions in the most motivational manner possible, without looking gormlessly on the bright side. Adopt an attitude of, 'Yes. This could be tricky. I can see how difficult it looks. So, how do we find a way through?'

Probing to Get to the Point

Probing, in a Performance Coaching sense, means accessing and exploring the unspoken or partly expressed thoughts, feelings, or concerns of your colleague in order to determine the really important issues that may lie just below the surface.

Examples of probing questions are:

✔ You mentioned your avoidance of speaking at board meetings. What's that really about?

✔ Where does this come from?

✔ What's behind that?

✔ What makes you say that?

✔ What else do you think may be relevant?

Bear the following points in mind when you're using probing techniques during Performance Coaching:

✔ **Earn the right:** In the initial phases of coaching, you need to listen respectfully, allowing your colleague to relax, confident in the knowledge that you'll hear him out. Only then, when he's convinced you've heard it all, is probing for more information appropriate.

✔ **Apply question style:** Exercise the range of questioning techniques explained in the preceding section and use particularly penetrating open questions to yield more information.

✔ **Remember that timing is all:** As with many aspects of good communication, timing is everything. *When* you choose to probe determines your success. Probe too early in the conversation and you're likely to encounter a stone wall of defensiveness and resistance, because your colleague won't be ready to think about it yet or believes he hasn't finished with a particular issue before you direct him into something else. Probe too late and you may have lost focus by disappearing into a cul-de-sac of detail about an irrelevant point. As the Performance Coach, you have to use your judgement about the best time to probe. For example, when you want to deepen your colleague's understanding of what may lie behind a particular point or when he seems to be expressing what you consider to be an excessive amount of emotion for the subject being discussed.

✔ **Apply the right pressure:** Probing is a stiletto-fine tool rather than a rubber mallet. Delicacy is essential. Pressure can range from tentative to quite firm depending on the circumstances. Most of the time you're likely to be tentative but if you've tried to be tentative and your colleague appears to be avoiding an important issue, you may need to take a firmer approach.

✔ **Get the non-verbals right:** Your tone of voice is especially critical when you're probing. Keep a neutral, interested tone with no hint of threat or sarcasm. Keep your expression alert and interested.

Table 5-3 shows examples of probing questions in response to a colleague.

Table 5-3	Probing in Action
Colleague	*Performance Coach*
I hate it when I'm late for meetings.	What's the worst thing about being late?
I have to do this because no one else will.	So, you're saying that it would never get done if you didn't do it?
I have to keep up this pace because I'm only as good as the last thing I did.	Who is deciding how good you are?
Everything is a mess. Nothing is going right. There's one change after another. I can't keep up.	It sounds like you feel out of control.
Nothing ever gets done here. It just gets snarled up in bureaucracy.	What examples can you think of where things did happen?
I know what my goals should be. I should be much more political in my dealings with people. That's the only way to get on in the business.	You're saying that becoming political is the only way ahead. Give me examples where people have done it differently.

Probing does not mean employing Gestapo-like tactics while shining a bright light into the eyes of your colleague. Probing in Performance Coaching isn't the same as questioning used in job interviews as a 'clever' way of catching someone out and getting to the real truth. If, in Performance Coaching, you have any suspicion that your colleague isn't telling you the whole truth or even admitting to the most important issues, this reluctance is probably more to do with the stage your relationship has reached in terms of trust and openness, rather than a deliberate intent to deceive.

When you start to hear someone's story or opinions, you may be tempted to jump to the conclusion that you know not only the rest of the story but also what the solution is likely to be. In the communication field, this jump is known as *premature closure*. You feel reassured that you know what the issue is and confident that you can handle it. However, by leaping on the first thing your colleague talks about and assuming that you've identified the real issue, you may prevent him from ever getting to the point he was really working up to. Be prepared to take your time and let the issues emerge.

Sounding It Out: Paraphrasing

When listening to people, a constant, complex stream of data comes at you. How do you manage, handle, retain, and acknowledge all that vital information? This situation is where paraphrasing becomes useful. Put simply, *paraphrasing* means restating something using different words to make it simpler or clearer. Paraphrasing doesn't mean repeating something parrot fashion.

By putting what you've heard into your own words and feeding them back, your colleague has the opportunity to hear them afresh. Listen carefully and choose your words well, and paraphrasing may lead to fresh insights in your Performance Coaching.

If you paraphrase in a haphazard, inaccurate fashion, you may set your colleague's teeth on edge. He may spend his time saying, 'Well, no, actually you got that wrong', which undermines the flow of your communication.

Table 5-4 shows the different purposes of paraphrasing, the rationale behind it, and examples.

Table 5-4	The Advantages of Paraphrasing	
Purpose	*Rationale*	*Example*
Proving you're listening	By being able to play back to your colleague what you've heard him say, you prove that you've been giving him the respect of truly listening to him.	'What I've heard you say is that you've worked very hard this year to achieve goals in both operational and interpersonal areas and now you're ready for more of a challenge.'
Checking for accuracy	By summarising back the key points that you've heard, you can check your grasp of what your colleague said.	'Can I just check, was I right in hearing you say that you'd been in your first role for three years and then your second for another two?'
Aiding your memory through rehearsal	You remember information if you have the opportunity to rehearse – imagine trying to memorise a phone number if someone keeps interrupting you. By putting the information into your own words, you lock the information into your memory banks effectively.	'Let me just run through this – you came from outside the company, were promoted in a short period of time, became the youngest ever manager here, and now you've set your sights on the next move?'
Seeking further clarification	Paraphrasing gives you an opportunity to seek clarification where information is confusing or missing.	'You told me about a number of problems within the team. We spoke of your particular difficulty with Fred and mentioned that morale was low. Can you expand on that?'
Allowing your colleague to hear what he's saying afresh.	Playing back someone else's words can shift their perception dramatically.	'You're seeing this new situation as very threatening because you doubt that you have the ability to carry it off, despite having done something similar for the last five years? Is that how it looks now?'

Table 5-5 shows examples of paraphrasing excerpts of coaching conversations.

Table 5-5	Paraphrasing in Action
Your Colleague	*Your Paraphrase*
It's been a pretty dreadful three weeks. Just when I thought I was getting the hang of the new role, head office sprang this new initiative. Some of it makes sense but I'm not sure that I'm confident about the way they're going to force it through. I just think it undermines my authority. Did they wait until I was in a position to do this? They didn't warn me that it was coming. My team is supportive but quite confused.	Just when you thought you were getting the hang of things, you were thrown by these new initiatives that have left you less confident and your staff unsure.
With this new job I've taken over responsibility for so many offices. I have to go on a road show and speak to really big groups. It is important that I set the right tone and get the message across. This will be the first time people will see me as the boss. I have to get it right. I feel very anxious and tend to prepare in immense detail and practise a lot but I've been told I come across as a bit boring.	Your job requires you to present to large groups in order to get things going but you tend to get anxious, over-prepare, and end up a bit boring.
Right now with the merger in the air, it's hard to know what to do. You can see that everyone is watching their back and jockeying for position. It's hard to know who's friend or foe and I still have to motivate the team and get the job done. I don't know whether I can trust my boss because I might be a threat to him if they're looking to lose people.	The merger is causing most people to think only of their own security. While you still have to keep the team working well, you're unsure how much you can rely on your boss.
She really is the most difficult person. No matter what I do she doesn't seem to want to be motivated. I've tried everything I can think of. She takes time off, resists responsibility, and comes to me for an answer on everything, so I end up doing it myself. I just can't tolerate that kind of person.	You've tried hard with her but she still doesn't perform. It's hard for you to respect her.

Challenging and probing are skills that can deepen both your knowledge as the Performance Coach and your colleague's understanding of his behaviour.

Reflecting Feelings

Reflecting in Performance Coaching means making a statement of the feelings or emotions you observe in your colleague. Reflecting demonstrates concern, helps build the relationship, and invokes empathy in you. It helps you clarify the exact nature of your colleague's feelings and gauge their intensity. It gives your colleague the chance to reconsider and modify his story. Reflecting is a vitally useful skill for responding to emotions detected in your coaching. Table 5-6 gives a couple of examples.

Table 5-6	Reflection in Action
Your Colleague	*Your Reflection*
John didn't give me the right information, then my computer developed a problem and IT couldn't solve it; my mobile went down, and to cap it all they cancelled my train due to a fault on the line – honestly!	Sounds like you felt pretty frustrated.
I know I have the right skills for the job and I have a good work record. However, I can't help but wonder whether I'm missing something and whether I do have everything they want for this new position.	Sounds as if you feel uncertain and apprehensive.

Challenging with Care

Challenging means actively engaging with your colleague to help him to reconsider the assumptions, beliefs, limitations, expectations, and behaviours he takes for granted and which may be blocking his progress. Challenging is an opportunity for him to test reality in order to expand his options through development. Challenging doesn't mean yelling, 'Oi, you!' at anyone!

Ensuring that you have the right to challenge

Consider the last time someone challenged you, in any setting – on the doorstep about your political affiliations or your religious beliefs; at work about your way of doing things; or even at home about your dress sense. How did that challenge impact on you? Did you welcome the opportunity to reconsider your thinking and adopt alternative ideas or did you become even more entrenched in your old thinking as you manned the barricades and fought back for the sake of your belief, habit, or choice of knitwear. Challenge isn't easy to accept. Challenge can be a dangerous tool to use.

Challenging yourself to hold back

A colleague was concerned about not achieving the top position in his firm. He had come second for the first time in his life and was finding it hard to bear as he considered his career options. He remarked on the fact that if he was fired he probably only needed £100,000 to live on after he considered all his expenses. He'd be able to get one of a dozen jobs the next day offering that salary (which was about a sixth of the salary of the job he'd failed to get). He said, 'It would be the shame of accepting anything at that level that would be terrible.' He then added guiltily, 'I know teachers only start on about £30,000.' (At the time a teacher's salary was actually £13,000.)

Where do you start with that? If you, the coach, think about your own income, or even harbour socialist tendencies, you may challenge him about social inequity; from a positive psychology perspective you may challenge him regarding the capacity of money alone to make him happy; or you may challenge his knowledge of salaries in the teaching profession. Each of these challenges would be about and for you, not him. The important challenge you need to make in this situation is about his automatic assumption that second place equalled failure.

Certain prerequisites make challenging more likely to be both palatable and effective in a Performance Coaching relationship:

- **Respect.** In the initial stage of the coaching relationship, you need to make it clear that you have total respect for your colleague. In turn, your colleague needs to find sufficient cause to respect you and value your opinion.

- **Trust.** Your colleague may test you early in the relationship, gauging how you handle less sensitive material before moving on to the more important. You earn trust as a result of the way you handle information.

- **Positive feedback.** Tell your colleague that you see his strengths and best qualities. Engaging in positive feedback can challenge your colleague's perception of himself.

- **Self-awareness.** Check your own emotions and determine what may be motivating you to want to challenge at any point. Is it more for your own ends than your colleague's? Are you feeling the need to score a point? Sometimes aspects of your colleagues' value systems, beliefs, and choices are different from yours but they may not be relevant to the coaching relationship.

Challenging before any of these aspects are in place is a high-risk option and may set you right back in your relationship.

Understanding the key skills of challenging

Columbo is an unassuming detective, unlike the many macho police heroes on television. In a grubby raincoat, he doesn't look much, but when you least expect it, in the most tentative manner, he'll explain a notion he had about how the crime had been committed. This always shows deep insight and with a gasp, the perpetrator admits all.

The Columbo approach has a few lessons for the style of challenging in Performance Coaching:

- Listening intently
- Observing minutely
- Thinking through the various theories
- Offering a tentative notion for your colleague to consider
- Being open to your colleague's response

Just as Columbo would modestly say, on the verge of exiting the room, 'Just one thing. It may be far fetched and I may be wrong but, hey, what do you think about this notion?', so you need to adopt a delicate approach to challenging that gives your colleague space in which to consider the notion you're offering.

An egotistical Sherlock Holmes, in contrast, would dramatically rip off the perpetrator's mask, browbeating him with, 'I see everything! I give you the truth!' Offer up any challenge in a contemplative rather than a confrontational manner. After all – you may be wrong!

Getting the timing right

Knowing when to challenge someone is a vital skill in Performance Coaching. Here are a few examples of when challenging is useful:

- **When your colleague holds a faulty assumption.** A faulty assumption means taking the information you have and assuming you understand what's happening when, in fact, you don't have all the information or evidence to back up that assumption. For example, your colleague is inveighing against the organisation for not promoting him as is his due. His belief is that the organisation is being unfair, even discriminatory. Yet he has already mentioned that his boss had advised him to attain a specific qualification or achieve further commercial experience. He has failed to do these things. During coaching, you can challenge this limited interpretation of the circumstances.

Seeing faulty assumptions in action

A colleague of ours was a senior manager in a traditional British industry. She described how difficult work was for her as a mixed-race American woman when the rest of the management were white British men. Surely she had a point, which we found easy to take at face value and so we started to explore appropriate ways of coping.

Then by chance we saw her addressing a personal assistant. In a completely humble, hand-wringing way with many a 'I'm terribly sorry' and 'if it isn't too much trouble', she made a simple request. Her body language said it all, as she shrank even further. We challenged her that, rather than factors of birth holding her back, her assumed subservience and lack of psychological stature and gravitas was doing the harm. Following a successful challenge, she worked to develop an assertive communication style with a firmness of conviction, which endorsed her ability and authority.

✔ **When your colleague has a contradiction.** A contradiction is where your colleague expresses one desire but his thoughts lead him to do something else. People are often unaware of some of the self-limiting thoughts and behaviours that you observe while coaching. At other times they perhaps subconsciously choose the limiting behaviour because doing so saves them from having to change. The actions they engage in may have a payoff and therefore your colleague may find it easier to maintain the status quo.

A colleague was experiencing a real crisis of confidence regarding his role as a board member of a large company. He doubted his ability to add value and to be as good as his peers. He said, 'I'm nothing special.' The challenge was: 'That's interesting – you win a scholarship to school, get into Cambridge University, leave with a first-class honours degree, and rise to the board – and yet it sounds as if you don't give yourself much credit. I wonder how many other people have managed to do the same. I wonder what qualities it took to make all that happen.'

✔ **When your colleague fails to honour commitment.** You've worked with your colleague to devise appropriate and relevant goals. But what do you do when your colleague keeps failing to achieve? Your colleague may have lots of good reasons for not having worked on the areas agreed – lack of time, for example, is always a reasonable excuse for most colleagues. Every now and then, however, you realise that something else lies behind the lack of progress. Your colleague needs your challenge in order to overcome the blockage.

You may simply ask, 'What is this really about?' or you may need to invoke the nature of your original agreement, saying, 'We agreed that this goal was important to you. Why do you think you aren't achieving results?' Use a contemplative rather than aggressive style to prevent knee-jerk defences. You may discover that the goal is too great, not relevant, or that a limiting belief is preventing him from even making a start. Or perhaps the goal was the wrong one in the first place.

✔ **When your colleague's thinking is downright illogical.** Often people make statements in coaching that they've never questioned, such as, 'You need to be nervous in order to present well.' A simple challenge here may be a gentle, 'Why?'

Sometimes that's all it takes to make someone start to challenge his own automatic assumptions and long-held beliefs. For others the challenge may take a few more steps:

Colleague: You need to be nervous to present well.

Coach: Why?

Colleague: Oh, but doesn't it make you perform better?

Coach: How can it do that? When you're calm you think more creatively, your memory works better, and you come across in a much more appealing fashion. Why would you choose to be tense?

Colleague: So you mean I don't have to put myself through this strain every time? I need to know more!

Challenging effectively

Table 5-7 shows statements and examples of ineffective and effective challenging.

Table 5-7	Ineffective versus Effective Challenging	
Statement	*Ineffective Challenge*	*Effective Challenge*
When I make up my mind, I don't change it.	That must be very limiting in life!	When has there been a time when you've wanted to change your mind?
It would be dreadful if I didn't get a good bonus this year.	Does money mean everything to you?	What real difference would it make?

Statement	Ineffective Challenge	Effective Challenge
I don't hold with these soft skills. Call a spade a spade, I say.	Are you saying that what I'm doing is a waste of time?	What situations can you think of where the people side of things matters?
This is how I've always done it.	And look where it's got you – right back to the same place!	Yet you're unhappy with the results. How might doing it a different way improve things?
I really can't see what I could get from coaching. I'm doing just fine.	You think so? Let me point out a few areas for improvement.	You may well be right. Let's look at what it will take to get where you want to be in the future.

You need to challenge carefully and sensitively to avoid irritating or offending your colleague. Challenging is never about scoring points – only about clearing blockages to further success.

Through a Glass Clearly: The Five Domains of Emotional Intelligence

Feelings are such a minefield. When you ask how someone feels, you may hear about a stew of emotions. Many people have long since lost the ability to identify, recognise, name, and deal with their feelings. Throughout your life, you're frequently told you don't feel what you most certainly believe you do. 'There's no need to feel like that' implies inappropriateness in your emotion and so you doubt your judgement. Some people say 'You make me feel . . .' when, in fact, no one has the ability to *make* you feel anything.

You make a choice about experiencing an emotion. Feelings are not inevitable; for example, you don't always have to get angry when dealing with difficult colleagues. Someone else may notice his colleague's bad behaviour but choose to stay calm, detached, and professional.

Emotions are a vital part of any human puzzle. If you ignore them, you only see a part of the picture. Yet many people are loath to draw attention to emotions even when they're rampantly visible. Emotions provide essential data when Performance Coaching. Improving your emotional intelligence and emotional literacy enables you to be calm in the face of messy emotion, to explore the sources of that emotion, its appropriateness, and how best to handle it.

Improving your EQ

While intelligence quotient (IQ) describes cognitive ability, emotional intelligence quotient (EQ) is hailed as a more accurate indicator of success in the workplace. In a nutshell, EQ means the ability to understand your own and other people's emotions and to use your understanding in a way that enhances communication with others. Emotions play a constant role in decision-making, relationships, and goal achievement. For coaching to be effective, you and your colleague need to strive towards greater EQ.

The five main aspects of EQ are:

- ✔ **Knowing your emotions.** Self-awareness, including recognising a feeling as you experience it.

- ✔ **Managing emotions.** Handling feelings so that they are appropriate is an ability that builds on self-awareness. For example, it's perfectly appropriate if your colleague is disappointed when, after investing time and energy in scoping a project, it doesn't get actioned. However, if your colleague's emotions spilled over into unhelpful anger it would be inappropriate.

- ✔ **Motivating yourself.** Emotional self-control, that is, delaying gratification and stifling impulsiveness, is an important part of EQ. People who are able to do this tend to be highly productive and effective in all they undertake.

- ✔ **Recognising emotions in others.** *Empathy*, the ability to imagine what it feels like to be in the other person's shoes, depends on emotional self-awareness and is the fundamental 'people skill'. Empathic people are attuned to subtle social signals that indicate what others need or want. Improving empathy leads to better teachers, salespeople, and managers.

- ✔ **Handling relationships.** Managing emotions in others is a skill. People who excel in relationship skills are social stars. They do well at anything that relies on interacting smoothly with others.

Recognising your own feelings

To be truly professional as an excellent Performance Coach, you need to be skilled in handling your colleagues' emotions in every situation. But first, you need to recognise emotions as *you* experience them, notice the impact they have on you, and manage them successfully. Honest self-awareness is critical.

This exercise helps you to become more emotionally literate. Picture yourself in situations in which you've experienced the emotions listed in the following table. Write down what you see, feel, and experience in your imagination. You don't have to tackle all the emotions. Try the ones you have most difficulty with.

Accepted	Disappointed	Lonely
Affectionate	Free	Loving
Afraid	Frustrated	Rejected
Angry	Guilty	Repulsed
Anxious	Happy	Respectful
Attracted	Hopeful	Sad
Belonging (in community)	Hurt	Satisfied
Bored	Inferior	Shy
Competitive	Intimate	Superior
Confused	Jealous	Suspicious
Defensive	Joyful	Trusting

Now you've described how you feel when you experience the emotions, you have a wider range of words, phrases, and statements both to describe your own emotional states and to identify emotional states in others. Listening to your own emotions is a prelude to listening to the emotions of others.

Recognising others' feelings

After you've become more aware of the ranges and nuances of your own feelings and the impact they have on your morale, behaviour, and relationships, you can turn your attention to the emotions your colleagues are experiencing. Simply asking, 'How do you feel about that?' isn't always effective. Many people have spent a lifetime denying that they feel anything at all. Some people have a resistance, awkwardness, even embarrassment about the very word 'feel'.

A group of quite traditional senior managers jokingly talked with us about the 'only four letter f-word we *can't* say'. Somehow, however hard they tried to ask about a colleague's feelings, the words just died away on their lips. Facts are so much easier to focus on. The responsibility falls on you as Performance Coach to become adept at observing and recognising the emotions others display.

Reading emotions

An important Performance Coaching skill is checking for congruence between the body language, non-verbal clues, and spoken language of your colleague. Here's how:

 ✔ **Watch his body language.** What posture has your colleague adopted, and how genuine is his facial expression? What emotion do you think you perceive?

Remember not to jump to conclusions – he may only look tense because the air conditioning has turned the room into a fridge! (To find out more, see *Body Language For Dummies* by Elizabeth Kuhnke.)

✔ **Listen to his tone of voice.** Does he say he's delighted to have this opportunity, but his voice is flat or fearful? Always comment on such a mismatch. If you know the person well, you know what range of emotions he tends to express. Is his tone of voice consistent with his normal style?

✔ **Check his vocabulary.** Is his choice of words appropriate, exaggerated, or diminished? One person describes a Sunday night as being 'when the shroud descends'. The graphic nature of that language alerts you to explore his feelings about his career, being alert for depression, stress, and a lack of job satisfaction.

Listen while someone talks about an important and emotional experience. Try to identify as many emotions as you can, even in a short conversation. Do only one thing: *Name that feeling!*

Don't take over the conversation, but make small interjections, naming as many emotions as you possibly can. Gauge all the different nuances from 'You were slightly miffed' through to 'You were absolutely livid'. Table 5-8 shows an example of naming feelings during conversations, with the emotion in italics.

Practise naming emotions in your head if doing it out loud is inappropriate – when overhearing conversations on the train, for example. You probably notice that in everyday conversation, people sometimes ignore an emotion as big as a barn door, focusing on irrelevant facts in preference.

Table 5-8	Naming that Feeling
Your Colleague's Story	*Your Response*
When I first started to ski I wasn't sure how I'd cope because I'd never done it before. It was amazing to master the basics so quickly and be whizzing downhill.	You were a bit *anxious*.
	You really worked hard (this implies your appreciation of their need to do a good job).
	You were *exhilarated*.
The boss called me through to her office. I didn't know what to expect but she wanted to tell me how much she appreciated my work and that she felt I'd go far.	You must have been a bit *apprehensive*.
	I bet you were *thrilled* at her feedback.
	You must have felt so *proud* of yourself.

Your Colleague's Story	Your Response
I couldn't believe it! When I got there they had no record of me in the diary. I made all that effort and they hadn't even bothered to keep note. I want them as a customer but I could have told them where to go right there and then. I was very reasonable and agreed another meeting. Actually we ended up having quite a good chat.	You were *furious*.
	You felt *frustrated* after all your efforts.
	You just felt like telling them off (this implies that the person was frustrated).
	You really worked to keep calm for the sake of the business (this implies the person felt anger or frustration but was able to deal with it).

Be careful when you reflect someone's feelings when you're Performance Coaching. If you come across as judgemental, this can have a negative effect. You don't want to cause your colleague to react to you with denial, anger, guilt, or violence! A bad reaction undoes any trust and relationship-building.

Table 5-9 shows ineffective ways of reflecting feelings – avoid them at all costs!

Table 5-9	Ineffective Feeling Reflection
Coach	*Likely Colleague Response*
You're in denial.	No I'm not.
You're really despairing.	Oh no! I knew it was bad but I had no idea it was so bad. I can't go on.
I can see that you're very defensive.	I don't know why you should say that.
You feel really ungrateful about your bonus.	Oh, do you think so? – how awful!
You're so angry. You could just fire him right now.	You're so right. I'll go do it now while I'm furious!

Effectively reflecting feelings means gently shining a light on and naming the emotion you see your colleague experiencing. You give him the chance to take stock and rethink – for example, from feeling despair to feeling just a bit down. If you're able to demonstrate to the person that his behaviour was quite normal in the circumstances and that you understand how difficult a situation is and the feelings attached to it, this can change the individual's feelings.

Some people may not have recognised that they're experiencing certain feelings, and so end up acting on them without considering consequences. By drawing your colleague's attention to what the emotions are, you give him the opportunity to deal more effectively and professionally with situations. Table 5-10 shows examples of effective feeling reflection.

Table 5-10	Effective Feeling Reflection
Coach	*Likely Colleague Response*
I wonder if you've realised how strongly you feel about the situation.	Do you think so? I thought I was coping fine but now I realise I'm not happy about the way things are.
I can see that you're a bit down about the way work has been.	Yes, lately I just haven't enjoyed it as much.
When I offer feedback, I notice sometimes you feel as if you're being got at.	I suppose I do take things very personally and think the worst.
When you were telling me about how good your bonus was, you sounded a bit fed up.	Yes, they did give me a lot of money but I still don't feel they recognise my contribution to the company.
You're quite irritated by the way he's behaving. What's that about?	Yes, I was furious earlier but actually I'm just irritated. I suppose I need to be calm to deal with it.

Chapter 6

Advancing Your Skills: The Magic of Motivation

In This Chapter

▶ Stirring people up

▶ Getting change in your sights

▶ Communicating well

▶ Getting through it

*C*onsider these questions:

✔ Why do you get some things done but not others that you profess to
   want just as much?

✔ Why are you really effective at some times in your life but not others?

✔ Why does motivation seem to be such an elusive thing?

✔ Why are other people not the same as you?

Is motivation down to planetary alignment and so beyond your control? Or is
there a way to harness motivation and achieve more of what you really want
and help others to do the same through Performance Coaching?

Despite brilliant analysis of issues during coaching, lengthy discussion of
possible goals and approaches, and clear knowledge of what to do and when,
people don't always change. You know lots of things that you 'should' be
doing or would quite like to do – yet they just don't happen. Who wouldn't
say that they want pleasant homes, fit and healthy bodies, excellent relationships, and a high level of efficiency and productivity at work? (Well, maybe
quite a few people, but they're unlikely to be reading this book!) This chapter
considers the importance of that extra magical component – real motivation.

Getting People Excited

How many people do you see grinning and skipping their way into work, enthusing about the day ahead, keen to face the challenges? Maybe some people are far too cool to let their enthusiasm show, but the reality is that much of the time people have to use real effort to engage with the day ahead. Any single day is likely to be good and bad in parts, yet people often require grim determination to get through.

In this section we work out what actually motivates people to get enthusiastic – that's the key to accelerating and maximising the rate of change through coaching.

Remembering they're not all like you

A pitfall you may encounter when coaching others is to unwittingly assume that what motivates you is likely to motivate someone else. That's unlikely to be the case. Think about it – your colleague's upbringing, life experiences, professional history, physical makeup, age, gender, and race, to name just a few variables, may be different from yours. A safe premise is to start with the assumption that you can't make assumptions about anyone else. What motivates another person is unlikely to be the same thing that motivates you. Using the wrong motivators can turn people off quickly, effectively, and for a long time.

One thing's for certain: Everyone is different. On the one hand, this fact appears to make Performance Coaching more tricky, but on the other hand it means that when you work out what makes an individual tick, you're much more likely to produce really dramatic progress because you understand her personal motivators.

What gets you out of bed in the morning?

Start with yourself. What motivates you to get out of bed in the morning? What's the first thing that springs to mind? Possible answers may be:

- ✔ I need to pay the bills.
- ✔ I want to get my teeth into that new piece of work.
- ✔ I like being my own boss.
- ✔ People are depending on me.

From the mouths of babes

One day, when my (Averil's) daughter was little, she asked the question that hits most mothers in the pit of their stomach: 'Mummy, why do you have to go to work?' I replied, 'Well, I need to earn the money to make sure that we can buy food, live in a nice house, and afford the things we need.' She looked quite satisfied with that and we almost left the subject there. However, as soon as I'd spoken, I knew it wasn't the entire truth. I added, 'Actually, I also go

to work because I love what I do. It's so interesting working with people every day, and every day is different and exciting. One day I hope that you have a job that gives you just as much fun.'

My first response had probably been justificatory, excusing myself for leaving my adored child. The second was the truth and I hope I inspired her to settle for nothing less one day in her own career.

> ✔ I hate laziness.
>
> ✔ I don't want people doing things without my input.
>
> ✔ I've just thought of a new way to do something.
>
> ✔ Someone may take my designated parking space.

After your first reaction – which may be a conventional response, think more deeply about the question and consider what other factors contribute. Shallow motivators are those that give a here-and-now buzz, such as a financial bonus. Deeper motivators are those that add meaning and purpose to life, like believing that people matter and being motivated to be honest and helpful because of this belief.

Understanding what motivates you to work hard at something that gives you insight into yourself.

Realising that you have many possible motivators can help you to see where you're going wrong if you're finding motivating others hard. Be really honest with yourself.

Considering career drivers

A *career driver* is the force inside you that determines what you need and want from your working life. Drivers give energy and direction to your career. They can change over time. For example, when you have a huge mortgage, a young family, and high demands on income, monetary reward and security may loom large, but they subside as you become more comfortably off. Other people may still have these career drivers long after they become well off. Here's a list of career drivers:

✔ **Monetary reward.** Money is the currency of business and the most widely used motivator. Although people are unlikely to turn down the offer of a pay rise, in many instances you may as well save your money if the purpose is to increase motivation. Wealth alone may motivate but more often the lifestyle choices that money supports – good living and desirable possessions – are the real drivers. However, insufficient money, or a salary not in line with colleagues', has a considerable capacity to dissatisfy. The key for people motivated by money is to clearly link development with opportunities for material reward.

✔ **Power and influence.** Some people are driven by the opportunity to have control over people and resources in order to make things happen at every level in their organisation. People who aren't given power often take it anyway if power is what motivates them. The ferocious personal assistant or doctor's receptionist who protects the boss from all comers may be searching for some of the power their role otherwise lacks. The key for people motivated by power is to help them find a way of getting power in an agreed and productive area.

✔ **Search for meaning.** An increasing number of people want to feel part of something bigger than themselves that has an intrinsic value. The key here is to link their role to the larger vision of the organisation as well as perhaps for society as whole.

✔ **Expertise.** People with specialised knowledge are driven and defined by their expertise. Often specialised professionals with a high level of qualification in a particular area become quite demotivated if asked to take on less-specialised projects. The key is to help them engage their expertise in any new activity.

✔ **Creativity.** People motivated by creativity are always looking for a new, better way to do things. They love being innovative and can easily be stifled by having to play within the rules at all times. The key is to help them find specific work areas where they're challenged to innovate. In coaching, for instance, they'll come up with many more options for how they can change than you can think of!

✔ **Affiliation.** Some people are driven by working really well in conjunction with other people. They spark ideas and draw their energy from the group around them. Isolate them and they start to wilt. The key is to help them ensure that they keep engaging with their teams and peers in a relevant and constructive way.

✔ **Autonomy.** People driven by autonomy are independent, needing to make their own decisions and take responsibility and blame if necessary. Coaching is likely to be successful because it enables them to make their own choices and decisions.

✔ **Security.** People driven by security can find change hard because their ideal environment provides a solid and predictable future. As constant change tends to occur in most organisations and long-term certainty is hard to give, the key is to help them focus on what underlying security they have, such as their own talents, and how development can help them.

✔ **Status.** People driven by status seek recognition, admiration, and respect for what they do. The outward trappings of status can be important – titles, perks, and receiving the kind of respect given to those of a high status. The key is to help them find ways to get the respect they desire.

Looking at deeper motivators

On a good day, what do you anticipate with most glee? Understanding motivation is about recognising what makes an individual feel enthusiastic. Contemplate the following questions yourself so you really understand the impact of motivation on your own actions and then use these questions in Performance Coaching to really understand how to motivate your colleague effectively:

✔ What gets you going and makes you feel enthusiastic?

✔ What makes you move mountains and strive to be the best you can be?

✔ Who and what energises you?

✔ Who and what de-energises you – the people or situations that make you feel drained and less enthusiastic?

✔ Who or what motivates you?

✔ Who or what demotivates you?

✔ Who have you motivated through your actions or words?

✔ Who have you demotivated through your actions?

✔ What is your vision for how you'd want things to be?

After you work your way through these questions, both alone and during coaching, you'll be much more familiar with the range of motivators available to you.

Playing to people's strengths

Many people are unclear about what their key strengths are. Instead, they pour a lot of time and attention into improving their weaker points rather than building on strengths. People aren't equally gifted in all areas and although through coaching they can expand their range of talents and achieve much more of their potential, people never change their spots entirely. Time and time again, you see people who are terrific in one area having to bend themselves out of shape to work in another.

A strong connection exists between people's strengths and their job satisfaction. Think of the last time when you were so engaged with a task that you lost track of time, you were neither hungry nor thirsty, happy nor sad. This state is being in *flow*. Being able to work in flow is closely linked to happiness, and differs from person to person. If you ask a range of people to describe these flow experiences, a finance director may describe designing the perfect spreadsheet with no interruptions, a coach may describe being utterly focused and in tune with her client, and so on. How often are people able to operate in flow in the workforce? All too often you have no opportunity to focus for any length of time or the work you have to do fails to engage you in any deep way.

If you can discover and truly play to people's strengths, you improve their work satisfaction, overall enjoyment of work, and success. Of course, everyone has to do things that play less well to strengths but by using key strengths, the task becomes more palatable.

Mary's key strength is working with people. As a consultant, she is in her element. Clients bond with her, remain loyal, and refer more work. She barely realises that what she does really is work, happily working long hours to complete a project. However, she has a business to run. Put her in the office with a tax return to do or invoices to chase up and she's in trouble. Concentration goes. She drinks too much coffee and allows herself to become distracted. Enabling Mary to use her strengths meant that she sorted out her tax issues by going to meet real tax people – they do exist but they were a bit surprised at someone wanting to come and talk to them in person. Mary argued her case face to face and got them to explain how she should code aspects of her business. She had fun while achieving a result. Similarly, when payments of invoices were delayed, Mary knew the name of the person in the accounts department, where they came from, and how they'd just moved house. Invoices somehow ended up being paid more swiftly and Mary became more interested in sorting them out when she used her tremendous people skills more than her weaker administration ones.

Signature strengths

Here's the list of strengths defined by Christopher Peterson and Martin Seligman in their huge tome *Character Strengths and Virtues: A Handbook and Classification* (Oxford University Press). The strengths they discuss were chosen by studying every culture and creed to determine the universal virtues and the strengths that emerged from those virtues. You can use this table to begin to consider the idea of strengths and how these can impact on an individual's motivation.

This Strength	Contains these Attributes
Wisdom and knowledge	Curiosity
	Love of finding out new things
	Judgement
	Ingenuity
	Social intelligence
	Perspective
Courage	Valour
	Perseverance
	Integrity
Humanity and love	Kindness
	Loving
Justice	Citizenship
	Fairness
	Leadership
Temperance	Self-control
	Prudence
	Humility
Transcendence	Appreciation of beauty
	Gratitude
	Hope
	Spirituality
	Forgiveness
	Humour
	Zest

Being your best

Think of a time or situation when you performed at your absolute best. This may be when you chaired a meeting, gave a presentation, or completed the marathon. Try to think of a complete incident and write down the story, with a beginning, middle, and an end. Don't generalise, but describe the incident in detail. Afterwards, go back through and work out all the strengths you were using. You may surprise yourself. Don't take these abilities for granted! This self-knowledge is invaluable when contemplating how to overcome problems and deal with any situation. Use this exercise when you start coaching someone so you can both be clear about the specific strengths the coachee can draw on.

1. Write a 300-word Positive Introduction about one concrete moment in time of yourself at your very best.

2. Review the Introduction and ask

    What strength does this illustrate?

    Is it a signature strength?

    Do you use it often?

    Where do you use it?

    What is the effect of this strength on you?

    What is the effect on others?

    Does this strength get you into trouble? If so, why do you still use it?

People can easily identify their strengths when you explore them together using these questions. You may see their faces light up as they talk about their strengths, even if they modestly discount them. One of the most interesting questions to ask is that final one. People often beam as they say, 'Yes, of course it gets me into trouble but I just wouldn't be me if I didn't do that!'

Understanding your strengths means that you can decide how to use them to advantage. If your colleague has a strength of wisdom, how does she use this at work to make her better at what she does? Equally, if your colleague is unhappy at work, then it is possible this is because she is not using her best strengths. Individuals are likely to be most productive, motivated, and happy in a role that uses their natural strengths.

Aiming for Change

The change you're aiming for when Performance Coaching isn't a Jekyll and Hyde affair, creating a whole new different and potentially frightening version of the person you're coaching. Instead, you're accessing the full potential of that particular person, taking into account her drivers, motivation, and strengths. The change you aim for involves accessing the best someone has to offer, building on those talents, and finding ways of helping her succeed, aligned with her own wishes and the goals of the organisation. That is the recipe for dramatic transformation.

Part of motivating people to change and improve is encouraging self-knowledge and giving constructive feedback.

Discussing Feedback

As a Performance Coach, giving feedback is an essential motivational skill. Here are some tips about giving feedback:

- **Be descriptive rather than judgemental.** Give feedback in clear, simple, and specific terms, ensuring that you reflect accurately what your colleague said.

- **Ensure that you give praise or criticism relating to performance in behavioural, not personal, terms.** When coaching you need to focus on the *behaviour* and not the *person*. What your colleague is doing rather than who she is is the important focus point. Look for evidence to support any observations you make so that your colleague gains an understanding of how her behaviour impacts on success and performance as well as on other people.

- **Be supportive and encouraging, not authoritarian.** Coaching around feedback is a supportive activity where you encourage the individual, considering what positive impact change will bring.

- **Encourage participants to contribute their views.** Coaching is a two-way process, which means encouraging your colleague to state her views.

- **Be careful when comparing your colleague's behaviour with that of others.** You may find it helpful to encourage your colleague to consider someone who is successful at a particular behaviour she finds difficult. This type of intervention encourages your colleague to 'model' useful behaviour. However, don't *compare* your colleague to that person because doing so may demoralise the individual rather than promote change.

- **Restrict feedback to what your colleague can absorb in one sitting.** Everyone has a limit on how much information they can absorb at one sitting. Check in with your colleague and pace the coaching feedback session to ensure that your colleague isn't becoming overloaded.

Giving positive feedback

Feedback is such a powerful tool in the workplace that it seems quite extraordinary how underused it is. Because most people are unused to consistent, specific, and productive feedback, training them to get the most out of it can take a while.

Great piece of work! Well done for your part! Good for you! Hearing any of these comments is great but they aren't really the most effective form of positive feedback. Instead, effective positive feedback contains much useful information about:

- ✔ **Characteristics of the person.** 'You're such an organised, detail-focused person.'

- ✔ **Strengths used.** 'You used your influencing skills really effectively.'

- ✔ **Specific behaviours that made the difference.** 'When tempers flared, you stayed very calm, concentrated on the facts, and waited for people to calm down.'

- ✔ **Actions that were most effective.** 'You organised the team and kept everyone on task, but I think the most important thing was the way you kept motivation so high.'

Positive feedback is effective when carefully thought through and genuinely delivered. However, your colleague may still think, 'You're just saying that.' If this is the case, be more effective by asking your colleague to give herself positive feedback. Ask her:

- ✔ What do you think went especially well?

- ✔ What do you think you did best?

- ✔ Which of your strengths were most important in your success?

- ✔ What will you remember to do again in a similar setting?

Asking questions like this internalises the feedback, building your colleague's confidence in her own skills and making her more likely to be effective in the next situation.

Conferring constructive criticism

People find it hard enough to give and receive positive feedback, so you can bet they're not brilliant at the trickier stuff. When criticism is required, people either pussyfoot around and drop hints or go for the complete character assassination technique. Neither approach works too well in Performance Coaching! Instead, give your colleague clear feedback about where she's going wrong and back it up with guidance about what can improve her performance.

FENOmenal feedback

When you need to give constructive criticism, consider facts, effect, need, and outcome (FENO). Table 6-1 shows the issues you need to delve into and some sample feedback.

Table 6-1	Using FENO to Give Feedback	
FENO	*What You're Exploring*	*Sample Feedback*
Facts	Where did your colleague go wrong?	*When you failed to meet your deadline . . .*
Effect	What was the effect (including emotional impact)?	*. . . the team felt very let down because they were depending on you so they could meet the deadline.*
Needs	What exactly needs to happen in future?	*In future, you need to be clear about negotiating deadlines and keeping people posted about any delays.*
Outcome	What are the benefits?	*That way, the team can feel really confident in you.*

Try to put any negative feedback into a succinct, straightforward statement that gives your colleague clear options for improvement. If you need to, ask questions at each stage to elicit what your colleague thought the impact was and what the best action would be rather than giving them your ready-made solution.

Take a look at Chapter 7 to find out about eliciting feedback from other people in the company in the form of 360-degree feedback.

Motivating people with feedback

An amazing thing you discover when you coach is that people often lack self-knowledge. This lack may be a modest inability to express what they know about how great they are, but sadly is more often because any feedback they have received has been scant and negative. People may not have a solid view of their strengths, limitations, preferences, and successes, which is extraordinary when you think of how much assessment and appraisal is carried out at school and further education.

In Performance Coaching, one of the key tools you have is the opportunity to give immediate feedback. This immediacy can be tremendously motivating because many people toil away feeling unnoticed most of the time. Effectively, what you're doing is holding up a mirror to the coachee so that she can see what she's like and what effect she has in the organisation.

How and when you give feedback is critical. Being too blunt can traumatise someone. Feed back too soon and she won't trust you enough to take it on board. Feed back too tentatively and she won't hear it. If the feedback is too negative, the positive change just won't work!

You need to give feedback in a positive manner. For example, perhaps your colleague gave a short seminar on a particular topic and showed you the delegate feedback forms. She scored highly for presentation and clarity of thought. You can reaffirm this by saying, 'it certainly seems as if your colleagues valued your input and the rating scores they've given certainly confirm this'.

There are no hard and fast rules about when to give feedback. However, the times it can be most helpful are when the feedback reinforces positive changes, when your colleague may be doubting her ability and you remind her of positive events as a way of challenging this thinking.

Table 6-2 shows areas that you can cover when giving feedback, and a few examples.

Table 6-2	Examples of Feedback
Areas for Feedback	*Example*
How we're doing.	We seem to be working well together. I notice that after we've discussed something, you take it on board and start to make changes right away.
What's working.	It strikes me that when you plan your professional interactions in advance, they go so much better.
What isn't going so well.	Several times now when we've agreed targets, you haven't made any progress. This isn't what we'd agreed.
How your colleague comes across.	Although you say you're excited about this, your manner – the way you avoid eye contact and your tone of voice – give me a different impression.
What your colleague's strengths are.	You're meticulous in everything you do. You're thorough. You follow through and you ensure the best quality.
What you need to focus on.	Your focus has tended to be on your technical skills. You tend to want to develop those but seem more resistant about developing your influencing skills.
How much your colleague has achieved.	You've come a long way in executive meetings. I can see real improvement in the way you look assured and field questions from the senior people.

Too little, too late

A senior, highly able client felt undervalued by her organisation because she never received any feedback or recognition for achieving the really extraordinary results that had transformed the business.She had, of course, been paid huge bonuses over the years but, as far as she was concerned, that just didn't count as feedback. In fact, little did the company realise, but she'd saved those bonuses to give herself a 'running away fund'. By now she could afford not to work for two whole years. Finally, a new boss arrived in the company, perceived her talents, and offered her promotion. At exactly the same time, she was headhunted externally for one of the top jobs in her field and accepted the offer. Who knows what a little timely feedback would have done for the company?

Be aware of issues that may interfere with effective feedback:

- ✔ You may have little practice in giving feedback.

- ✔ Your colleague may have little practice receiving feedback.

- ✔ You may feel embarrassed at being direct and personal.

- ✔ You may worry about how your colleague will receive the feedback.

- ✔ You may pull your punches (using hints rather than straight talk) with both positive and honest critical feedback.

A powerful and effective experience is to always ask your colleague to critique herself before you give her feedback. Remind her to give you the positive first because otherwise she may start with self-criticism. Training her to recognise what she did right, what strengths she used, and how she can do so again, means she's better equipped for next time. A benefit of this approach is that because she has to work out her strengths for herself, they're more likely to stick. If you point out her strengths, she can always discount the positive as you being nice to her!

If you ask someone at the end of a day to tell you how things went, she's most likely to give you a list of what went wrong, what's unfinished, and what could have been better. This description is often quite an unbalanced representation of a day that had good, bad, and maybe even ugly in it, but probably was not uniform. To combat your colleague focusing on negatives, ask her questions such as:

- ✔ What went right today/this month?

- ✔ What did you do to make that happen?

- ✔ What aspects of your behaviour/strengths/personality played a part?

Chapter 7 covers passing on feedback from the organisation to the person you're coaching.

Are We There Yet?

Remember what setting out on a long journey was like as a child – fine for a while, then when the novelty wore off, pretty boring? Games like I Spy distracted you from how long the trip was taking. Performance Coaching can sometimes be a little bit like a long journey, with you or your colleague wondering if she's moved at all because progress seems to be so slow. It can be motivating for everyone when change and development are rapid and exciting, but coaching isn't always like that. Keeping someone working away at changes she may need to practise for a while demands more than a child's game to distract from the possible tedium.

I spy changes

Think back to when you started driving. You couldn't imagine being able to steer, indicate, and change gears all at once. Before long, you were doing all that while carrying on complex conversations (but not, of course, on your mobile phone these days!). This confusing effect of perception means that you quickly forget what you were like when you started a new activity and so cannot see how much progress you've made.

When colleagues become frustrated by the speed of their progress, you need to help them see exactly how far they've come in order to encourage them to continue striving. Regularly review your original findings and where your colleague has moved to now in order to measure and celebrate achievement. Your colleague may find it useful to ask other people what changes they've seen in her.

Delaying gratification

Everyone's experienced times when, no matter how hard they work, the change just doesn't happen and won't for some time. What keeps people striving with no immediate reward? The capacity to delay gratification is an essential component of self-motivation. Being able to keep working at something, knowing that the results will come eventually, has been strongly linked with success. People who give up because they don't get something right or don't get what they want the first time, are likely to fall well short of the desired outcome.

Everyone has varying degrees of capacity to delay gratification in different settings. If you've ever studied for exams, you chose to revise rather than read the latest novel or go out partying, so you know that you're capable of delaying gratification. When coaching, simply giving support is often enough to keep someone pursuing a demanding goal.

Positive feedback about the effort being made rather than just the end results is vital. Instead of waiting until you can say, 'Well done, you made it,' say 'I can see how much effort you're putting into achieving your goal. That kind of determination will get you there in the end.'

Chapter 7

Equipping Your Coaching Toolkit

In This Chapter
- ▶ Solving problems quickly
- ▶ Finding your personality type
- ▶ Pulling together to give feedback

ime to roll up your sleeves and get stuck into some theory. Don't worry, you don't have to be Einstein to grasp the concepts. This chapter considers a number of problem-solving models and gives some insight into ways of understanding your colleague's personality.

Introducing the Seven-Stage Problem-Solving Model

You can use a *seven-stage problem-solving model* to successfully hold the coaching process together.

Presenting individuals with a problem-solving model to follow may seem at first glance to stifle their creativity, but thinking things through in a structured and systematic way actually encourages creativity. In addition, you can use this model as a way of providing individuals with a structure for both professional and personal goal-setting.

Table 7-1 shows the seven-step problem-solving sequence and accompanying questions that you can coach your colleague to ask himself at each step.

Table 7-1	The Seven-Stage Problem-Solving Model
Steps	*Questions/Actions*
1. Problem identification	*What's the problem/challenge I'm facing?*
2. Goal selection	*What do I want to achieve?*
3. Generation of alternative ways of proceeding	*What can I do to achieve my goal?*
4. Consideration of consequences	*What are the pros and cons of the course of action I propose?*
5. Decision-making	*What am I going to do?*
6. Implementation	*Doing it!*
7. Evaluation	*What worked and why? Do I need to amend my action plan?*

When your colleague becomes adept at using the seven-step model, he may want to use a shorter model to quicken the problem-solving process. Shorter models of problem-solving are usually used for rapid processing of a problem in order to deal with a crisis or make a quick decision.

With a shorter model – PIE – deliberation is exchanged for speed, so your colleague may experience a less satisfactory outcome.

The *PIE model* provides a quick solution when forced to think on the spot.

- ✔ Problem definition: What needs to be achieved?
- ✔ Implement a solution: Let's do this.
- ✔ Evaluate outcome: How did it go and what can I do differently?

For example, at a meeting it became clear that the discussion was leading towards an attack on internal communications. Using the PIE model can provide clarity of thought in potentially heated circumstances. In this case, your colleague was able to quickly pen a scribbled note to himself while he was listening to other people's comments:

- ✔ **Problem definition.** Heading James off when he starts to discuss systems and communication.
- ✔ **Implement a solution.** Highlight the implementation of the new intranet as a way of communicating more effectively.
- ✔ **Evaluate outcome.** People agreed that the changes in the pipeline should make a difference. I turned a potentially negative situation into a positive one.

Whether you choose the seven-stage problem-solving, PIE, or devise your own problem-solving model, the underlying structure combined with a flexible approach to coaching ensures the most professional approach.

Testing, Testing

Recognised, reliable, well-validated, and appropriate questionnaires or tests can be useful during Performance Coaching. Without claiming that these tests are tablets of stone, the information gleaned from them can be extremely helpful in opening up discussions about preferred behavioural styles and behaviours. Well used, tests enable you to:

✔ Develop insight

✔ Discuss personal characteristics

✔ Discover strengths

✔ Determine preferences

✔ Define development areas

✔ Distinguish differences in people

Here, as an illustration, are a couple of well-known instruments and a few thoughts about their usefulness in Performance Coaching.

Using the Myers-Briggs Type Indicator (MBTI)

The *Myers-Briggs Type Indicator (MBTI)* is one of the most used instruments in Performance Coaching. Based on the classificatory system of psychiatrist Carl Jung, it categorises individuals into basic personality types. Jung explained the four main categories, and Katherine Briggs and Isabel Myers, a mother and daughter team, went on to use the work of Carl Jung to develop one of the most well known of all the psychometric personality tests.

✔ **Energy:** Do you derive your energy from the world outside you or from your own inner world? For example, do you gain energy when you're with people and need the stimulation of others, or are you someone who's happy with his own company, gaining all the stimulation you need from your own thoughts?

✔ **Perception:** Do you prefer to gain your information through facts, examples, and in very down-to-earth ways, or do you prefer to use your imagination and focus on the big picture?

➔ **Judgement:** Do you prefer logic and reason, using your head to make decisions based on facts, or do you tend to be more heart-driven, looking to your values to help you make decisions?

➔ **Action:** Do you prefer to follow a well-developed plan of action based on facts or do you prefer to leave your options open and have a flexible approach?

Table 7-2 goes into more detail on each of these areas. Reflect on this information to give both yourself and your colleague greater insight into the many differences between people.

Table 7-2	Myers-Briggs Types
Type	*Traits*
Energy	
Introversion	Thinks first, then acts
	Needs regular time alone to recharge batteries
	Internally motivated. Mind is sometimes so active it's immune to the outside world
	Prefers one-to-one communication and relationships
Extraversion	Acts first, thinks later
	Needs interaction with the outside world or feels cut off
	Usually open to and motivated by the outside world of people and things
	Enjoys wide variety and change in people and relationships
Perception	
Sensation	Mentally lives 'now', attending to present opportunities
	Uses common sense and creates practical solutions
	Memory recall is rich in detail of facts and past events
	Prefers using past experience for decision-making
	Likes clear and concrete information; dislikes guessing when facts are 'fuzzy'

Type	Traits
Intuition	Always thinks about the future, attending to future possibilities
	Uses imagination and creates new possibilities
	Memory recall emphasises patterns, contexts, and connections
	Prefers using theoretical understanding for decision-making
	Comfortable with ambiguous, fuzzy data and with guessing its meaning
Judgement	
Thinking	Instinctively searches for facts and logic before making a decision
	Naturally notices tasks and work to be accomplished
	Easily able to provide objective and critical analysis
	Accepts conflict as a natural, normal part of relationships with people
Feeling	Instinctively employs personal feelings and impact on people when making decisions
	Naturally sensitive to people's needs and reactions
	Naturally seeks consensus and popular opinions
	Unsettled by conflict; has almost a toxic reaction to disharmony
Action	
Judging	Plans many of the details in advance before moving into action
	Focuses on task-related action and completes meaningful segments before moving on
	Works best and avoids stress when ahead of deadlines
	Naturally uses targets, dates, and standard routines to manage life

(continued)

Table 7-2 *(continued)*

Type	Traits
Action	
Perceiving	Comfortable moving into action without a plan, or plans on-the-go
	Likes to multi-task, have variety, and mix work and play
	Naturally tolerant of time pressure; works best close to the deadlines
	Instinctively avoids commitments which interfere with flexibility, freedom, and variety

Myers-Briggs can be an excellent tool for helping individuals gain an understanding of their personality type and the personality types of others. For example, many so called 'personality clashes' in the office are simply the meeting of two very different personality types. When each person understands that the differences are based on the ways each person thinks and acts, this information often makes it easier each to appreciate the pros and cons of the other's personality type.

In addition, your colleague may gain a greater understanding of why he behaves in a certain way in certain situations and you can use this information to develop the strengths of his personality style while developing ways of minimising the less desirable aspects.

Putting yourself to the test

Try out any tests yourself to determine which work best for you and give you the type of insights that you and your colleague can find most useful. Some organisations charge for their tests but let you try the test for free or for a nominal sum. Some tests require that you train in their administration first. You need to decide:

✔ Does the test give useful information?

✔ Is the data provided in a user-friendly form? Some people like numerically presented data such as graphs and grids, while others would rather have a candid narrative.

✔ How do you feel when completing the test? Does it irritate you? Is it too long? Does it seem valid or a bit bonkers?

✔ How do the answers to the test make you feel? If you think, 'Wow – that's so like me! I'm proud of having these characteristics and, yes, I can make those developmental changes,' then you're on to a winner!

What shape are you?

Psychogeometrics are one way of understanding your communication style and were developed by Dr Susan Dillinger. Psychogeometrics are fun to do but can also produce just as good results as the highly sophisticated tools. Try them yourself by following these steps:

1. Look at Figure 7-1 and choose the shape that you like the most. Choose quickly and without thinking carefully.

2. Choose the second shape you like the best.

3. Read the analysis in Table 7-3 and see if the description fits you.

4. Think about the impact of having two shapes working together, such as a box and a squiggle.

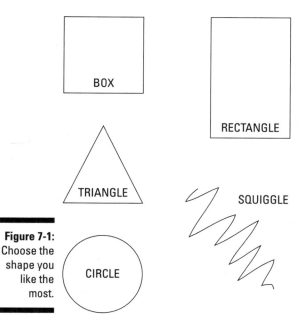

Figure 7-1:
Choose the shape you like the most.

Table 7-3		Shape Indicators		
Box	*Triangle*	*Rectangle*	*Circle*	*Squiggle*
Traits				
Organised	Leadering	In transition	Friendly	Creative
Detailed	Focused	Exciting	Nurturing	Conceptual
Knowledgeable	Decisive	Searching	Persuasive	Futuristic
Analytical	Ambitious	Inquisitive	Empathic	Intuitive
Determined	Competitive	Growing	Generous	Expressive
Common words used				
Logistics	Interface	Unsure	Lovely	Experiment
Deadlines	Escalate	Consider	Gut level	Challenge
Allocate	Jargon	Maybe	Comfort	Create
Policy	Thrust	Delegate	Team	Develop
Efficiency	Return on Investment	Options	Co-operate	Conceive
I did it!	You do it!	Why?	No problem!	What if?
Male appearance				
Conservative	Stylish	Erratic	Casual	Sloppy
Short hair	Appropriate	Changeable	No tie	Dramatic
No facial hair	Expensive	Facial hair	Youthful	Dirty
Female appearance				
Understated	Tailored	Erratic	Overweight	Varied
Navy, grey, or brown clothes	Manicured	Extreme	Feminine	Artistic
Thin	Briefcase	Unusual	Faddish	Fat/Thin
Office style				
Every pencil in place	Status symbols and awards	Disorganised mishmash	Homelike and comfortable	Messy, bleak, or dramatic
Body Language				
Stiff	Composed	Clumsy	Relaxed	Animated
Controlled	Jaunty	Nervous	Smiling	Theatrical

Box	Triangle	Rectangle	Circle	Squiggle
Nervous laugh	Pursed mouth	Giggle	Full laugh	Sexual cues
Precise gestures	Large gestures	Flushed face	Excessive touching	No touching
Personal Habits				
Loves routine	Interrupts	Forgetful	Easy-going	Spontaneous
Always prompt	Early arriver	Nervous	Joiner	Interrupts
Planner	Joke teller	Late or early	Sloppy	Disorganised
Precise	Fidgety	Outbursts	Socialiser	Daydreams

Tools such as questionnaires and tests can enhance insight, leading to more sophisticated and professional behaviour but be careful about their use and misuse. Play with them and use them as a discussion starter, but don't take them too seriously!

Check the British Psychological Society website at www.bps.org.uk for more information about questionnaires.

Seeing the Value of 360-Degree Feedback

A great coaching tool to help your colleague gain feedback is the *360-degree feedback exercise*.

The purpose of 360-degree feedback is to help people to understand their strengths and weaknesses, and to contribute insights into aspects of their work that need professional development. 360-degree feedback means employees receive performance feedback from their manager and between four and eight peers (all reporting staff members, co-workers, and customers), plus a self- assessment. In many self-assessments, people score themselves more harshly than others would. However, those with an overinflated view of their abilities provide a higher score for themselves than their colleagues would. This method gives an opportunity to look at the scores and comments to see how closely they match, and feedback on the differences to your colleague. You may even find that the reason you're coaching an individual is because a 360-degree feedback exercise highlighted areas that need work.

If a smaller company is unable to conduct their own 360-degree feedback, they can link in with an external provider. You can find external providers through your Human Resources Department.

Discuss with your colleague how best to present the request for feedback. You can simply send out a questionnaire with a note:

> 'Donald is planning the next stage of his development. He would really value your feedback. Please answer the following questions. Information will be fed back to Donald anonymously.'

Part III
Applying Performance Coaching

'The performance coach
seems to be a success.'

In this part . . .

It's almost time to turn you loose! Equipped with the Performance Coaching basics you can begin to look at applying them. Use your skills to attract and retain talent through good career development, drive successful organisational change, and develop high performing teams.

Chapter 8

Getting the Best: Talent Management

. . . .

In This Chapter

▶ Finding your talent

▶ Hanging on to your people

▶ Knowing what talent looks like

▶ How the type of organisation affects talent

▶ Thinking about tomorrow

. . . .

*I*n this chapter we consider the role that Performance Coaching has in what's termed *talent management.* Talent management involves those people who are today's successful leaders or the successful leaders of the future. These people are the ones who are likely to reach senior positions within the organisation, guiding its future and its place in the market.

Studies show that organisations that are good at managing their talent achieve better business performance compared with their peers. What's more, the organisations that are most successful at managing talent ensure that all their managers are explicitly accountable for creating a talent pool for the organisation as a whole. These organisations treat talent management as a critical source of competitive advantage.

How Performance Coaching helped a top banana

Will was the Divisional Director for a leading investment bank. Having been recruited into the 'talent programme', he was seen as a potential leader but was struggling to progress to the next level.

A major restructuring programme had been announced and Will's team was halved in size. This downsizing put pressure on the remaining staff to perform at exceptional levels. Will was a perfectionist and keen to satisfy both his customers and his colleagues, as well as to grow his own personal reputation. He had been successful in all of his roles but his self-belief was starting to erode and he was now questioning whether he was starting to plateau.

Will's manager offered additional support to help him through these challenges by giving him a number of Performance Coaching sessions.

In the initial meeting, as part of the Behavioural Contracting process (refer to Chapter 3), Will identified areas of self-development, including his leadership style and self-confidence (in particular his upward influencing), and his management skills, particularly his presentation skills, delegation, time management, and chairing meetings.

Through coaching, Will recognised that he had high standards and expected everyone to live up to his own standards, which led to a couple of problems. Firstly, his staff never believed they were good enough and as a result motivation had started to decline among key players within the team. Secondly, his overly detail-conscious and people-friendly approach meant that he dictated how his staff should resolve problems. This failure to enable his team to work out the options and the solutions for themselves meant that his staff weren't able to progress and grow. The team became over-reliant on Will and his volume of work increased.

During the coaching sessions, Will realised that by adapting his own style to address how others viewed things, he was able to explore options with them, helping them to see the world differently. As a result he found that he enabled his colleagues, his senior managers and his team to adapt their behaviours, and in many cases he adapted his own behaviours.

The whole process took approximately six months but, by the end, Will was earmarked for a further promotion and was offered further development through his enrolment on a Director's Development Programme. The organisation had protected its initial investment in Will and he was back to being highly motivated.

Fighting for Talent

Organisations are experiencing an increase in demand for top talent, yet the supply of able people to the potential workforce is reducing dramatically. According to the Employers Forum on Age, the number of people in the age group 35–45, traditionally the age band from which a large proportion of business leaders are drawn, is set to fall by 17 per cent in the UK by the year 2012. In the United States and Western Europe the scale of the reduction is similar. One key factor is that the so-called baby-boom generation are now well on the way to retirement. Figures show that, in 1999, the percentage of people under the age of 18 was 36 per cent and that it is set to fall until about 2020. However, the percentage of people of retirement age is likely to increase.

The talent population is also more mobile today than ever before. Long gone is the concept of the 'job for life' career model. Employees now vote with their feet. Having spent money on recruiting and training individuals, losing this investment, together with the intellectual capital and creativity that each individual brings, can have significant effects on the productivity of an organisation.

We live in a global marketplace and many organisations recruit from this 'world talent pool'. You only have to visit any university campus to see the ways in which organisations try to sell the advantages of joining them to the students.

The real challenges to attract, motivate, and retain talent are likely to increase in momentum. In the light of such changes, Performance Coaching continues to be one of the main tools that organisations look to as part of their overall talent management strategy.

Ask your colleague to see herself from four different perspectives as a way of opening up her understanding of what impact her style and behaviour have on others. Ask your colleague to see herself from the perspective of:

- ✔ The team
- ✔ The boss
- ✔ Customers
- ✔ Herself

Encouraging Talent

High talent is different from high performance. If you're a leader of industry you're a high performer, but not all high performers go on to be leaders. Perhaps you have the most wonderful personal assistant who is a high performer but she won't have any impact on business strategy.

Consider the following (rather philosophical) questions:

- ✔ What do the most talented people do that makes them successful?
- ✔ What does 'good' look like within your organisation?
- ✔ How do you measure potential talent?

Talent-spotting is a bit like identifying the next Rembrandt!

The following sections further explore how Performance Coaching can help with talent management.

Determining your strategy

Talent management concerns the present and future needs of the business. What types of people and skills are required to fulfil important roles and meet the challenges of remaining competitive? Organisations spend time, energy, and money considering what their vision is for talent, people management, and objectives. Succession planning (figuring out who is to replace the top managers when they leave, and beginning their development process) is also a key factor. Many companies have downsized over the past decade and having the right people to provide continuity has become important. Ensuring that such individuals are in place and are being trained and developed to take over when the time is right is crucial. This is most effectively achieved through Performance Coaching at all stages.

Identifying talent

Having taken time to consider the business needs and plans for the future, the next consideration is where to find the leaders of tomorrow. Some individuals may move from the 'high performance' category into a talent pool after the company recognises their value and ensures that they achieve their potential through Performance Coaching. However, this route is unlikely to supply all the talent required by an organisation. Recruiting people with the potential to fulfil such needs is important.

Attracting talent

After your company has identified talented people, you need to think about what is likely to attract such individuals. With so many organisations on the lookout for talent, you need to carefully consider what extras your organisation needs to have in place to stand a chance of recruiting such people. The types of packages on offer often reflect the shortage of talent and the competitive nature of recruitment. Many organisations now actively promote their Performance Coaching as part of their commitment to those they are trying to recruit. Coaching is a perk of the job and a sign of an organisation's commitment to ensuring that employees are developed as well as supported. Candidates are sophisticated and keen to ensure that they progress at work as quickly as possible. To this end, Performance Coaching is like coaching athletes – an activity that can hone the skills that the individual already has. Many leaders have had coaching or continue to have coaching at different times in their careers.

Retaining talent

After recruitment, your organisation has to consider how to ensure that it holds on to its people, and avoid talented people being headhunted.

Money alone doesn't necessarily keep people in their jobs! Even the most talented individuals require help in refining and developing the skills they need to support their true potential. Organisations can use Performance Coaching to address both refinement and development. Coaching helps individuals to develop skills that can help them to accelerate their professional and personal development. If employees aren't happy, in the longer term they may look for a job in an organisational culture that they find more personally rewarding. Organisations known for the coaching and development they make available to their personnel can more easily attract and retain employees than companies that don't.

The Chartered Institute of Personnel and Development (CIPD) state that managers need to develop their capability to identify and manage talent and that this means developing their skills in coaching people.

When thinking about using coaching to retain staff and colleagues, especially during times of change and upheaval, consider:

- **What strengths does the individual demonstrate and how can you tap into these strengths?** Working with you as the Performance Coach helps your colleague to identify her strengths and how to best use these skills. For example, your colleague may be tenacious and this tenacity can help her stick the course in times of upheaval.

- **What aspects of work motivate your colleague? How can you as the Performance Coach use these factors to motivate change?** Using your coaching skills, identify aspects that motivate your colleague. Try to use this information as leverage for change. For example, if your colleague enjoys being challenged, use this knowledge as a way of encouraging her to see changes at work in this way.

- **How does overcoming challenges position your colleague for future gain within the organisation?** Using your coaching skills, you can help your colleague to see potential promotions to aim for.

Coaching the leaders of tomorrow

If your organisation is thinking about the leaders of tomorrow, you need to:

- Devise the types of talent profiles you need.
- Identify the people with the potential to match the profiles.
- Work out a process for developing the individual's skills.
- Manage that individual while she's in the organisation.

As the Performance Coach, you find that you employ your Performance Coaching skills most in assisting individuals to live up to their potential.

Measuring the Impact of Company Culture on Talent

An organisation's *culture* is the collection of values and goals that drives a company. A company's culture influences the way that employees interact with each other and with people who interact with the organisation.

Management may try to determine a *corporate culture* by imposing their own values, objectives, and standards of behaviour on the organisation. This varies from one organisation to the next: a large bank's culture may focus on prudence and integrity, while a new advertising firm has a culture that fosters creativity and style. Ideally, issues of culture are transparent and openly discussed and agreed with employees. However, all too often the culture may simply have grown up through tradition and may not always be constructive.

Another organisation may want to develop a *people-centred culture*, seeing its employees as its greatest asset, and setting up a range of coaching and training systems that support individuals. Such an organisation may recognise that while financial reward is important in attracting individuals, money is only one part of a much bigger picture, with job satisfaction and a sense of purpose also seen as factors that retain staff.

In contrast, another organisation may hold on to a *command and control culture*, believing that money alone keeps people. Such an organisation may pay extremely well but have the expectation that employees need to work excessively long hours and that job satisfaction is more a luxury than an essential part of success.

If you work for an organisation that subscribes to a command and control culture rather than a people-centred one, your organisation is unlikely to see much value in Performance Coaching. Any coaching they do is likely to be of a performance recovery nature. Talent in this kind of organisation is acknowledged through the pay packet alone.

Organisational culture has an effect on the success of talent management strategies. Organisations are more effective if they encourage active leadership by managers and coach people to 'go the extra mile'.

Think about the following questions:

- ✔ **What is the culture of my organisation?** Is it competitive, nurturing, or people-centred?

- ✔ **How does the company's culture affect people?** Is the culture motivational, stressful, or does it encourage people to be loyal?

- ✔ **Is the culture open to change?** What avenues do you have to change the negative aspects and encourage the positive?

Organisations across the world take talent management seriously, with dedicated programmes for recruiting and retaining staff. The need to secure talented individuals has made organisations take a long hard look at who they are, what they do, and what they need to do now and in the future.

Mapping your company's position

Mapping the needs of the organisation is a key factor in ensuring that the talent recruited actually meets such needs. Consider:

✔ **Where are we now?** Establish your current market position.

✔ **Where do we want to go?** For example, you may want to increase your profile and profitability by 50 per cent over five years.

✔ **What resources do we need?** Identify the people, resources, and systems that you need.

Chapter 9

Managing Change

. . . .

In This Chapter
- ▶ Seeing change in a positive light
- ▶ Living through change
- ▶ Dealing with stress and finding support

. . . .

Change is an integral part of corporate life, yet research suggests that only half of all business transformation programmes meet their short-term targets, and even less actually achieve their long-term goals. Charles Darwin said, 'It is not the strongest that survive, or the most intelligent, but the ones most responsive to change.' In this chapter we consider the impact of change on organisations and on individuals, and how you, as Performance Coach, can help to smooth transitions.

Coping with Changing Times

Whether you like it or not, change happens! Change impacts on individuals as well as the organisation as a whole. As a Performance Coach, you need to understand the impact of change and what you can do to mitigate the negative effects.

Can't live with change; can't live without it

More change has occurred within the corporate sector in the past hundred years than has ever happened before. The emergence of new markets, improvements in technology and working practices, outsourcing, the changing economic climate, and women's increased role in the workplace are just some of the developments. High-performing organisations are adept at sensing changes in their environment and altering their strategies to accommodate them without compromising performance. Transition occurs along a continuum, sometimes slowly and sometimes much more quickly. Organisations that adapt to internal and external changes have a much better chance of performing well than organisations that don't.

Most organisations start as small concerns, with a few people and scarce resources. As they begin to accomplish their original targets and goals, they need more people and more money. This growth brings new requirements for better ways to communicate, make decisions, and work with various markets.

Change and survive

Research by the Chartered Institute of Personnel and Development (CIPD) suggests that most change initiatives fail and that over 40 per cent of them don't deliver their bottom line improvement objectives.

Many change initiatives fail due to:

- ✔ A lack of highly visible senior executive sponsorship – if the people at the top are unclear about the transition or don't seem to support the initiative, this transmits itself throughout the whole organisation.

- ✔ Line managers being poorly trained in change implementation, so people don't know what's expected of them or what they need to do.

- ✔ A lack of reward and recognition for success – individuals are treated like a cog in a wheel and don't feel valued.

- ✔ Inadequate communication and explanation of what needs to be achieved and why, while allowing total flexibility in how change is achieved.

- ✔ Outdated policies, systems, and processes that are barriers to achieving the vision.

- ✔ Not enough budget or resources to undertake the change.

Corporate strategies need to be in place to ease the process and when these strategies are absent or inadequate everybody feels the negative impact of change more keenly.

In an ideal world, change is handled professionally:

- ✔ The organisation provides employees with timely information to enable them to understand the reasons for proposed changes.

- ✔ The organisation ensures adequate employee consultation on changes and provides opportunities for employees to influence proposals.

✔ Employees are aware of the probable impact of any changes on their jobs. If necessary, employees are given training to support job change.

✔ Employees are aware of timetables for changes.

✔ Employees have access to relevant support during changes.

So, for an organisation to embrace change effectively, you have a duty of care to ensure that managers are behaving constructively. The main route to this comes through:

✔ Involving people in the decision-making process

✔ Developing commitment throughout the organisation

✔ Recognising and rewarding people adopting new behaviours

✔ Encouraging employee-led initiatives

✔ Empowering individuals by explaining the relevance of change

✔ Dealing promptly and honestly with dissenting or resistant behaviour through feedback and coaching

No real shortcut exists for gaining commitment from people. Although inspirational speeches at annual conferences may get people fired up to be 'simply the best', it's the day-to-day attention to them, through good communication, that's most likely to bring them with you. You may try to win the hearts and minds of people so they want to commit to changing their behaviours in alignment with the business needs. Or, on the other hand, if you can get people to change their *behaviours* successfully, *attitudes* follow when the individual sees that participation is personally relevant. Feeling powerful, people move towards making change work for the sake of the organisation.

On a personal level, even the smallest change can bring about a dip in confidence and competence. When the change affects a larger team or a whole organisation, the impact can be to significantly undermine performance and profitability. However, when handled well, the dip can become a mere blip, and performance levels improve to new and greater heights.

Cutting Costs and Speeding Up the Process with Coaching

Coaching is one way that organisations can cut the cost of the impact of change. Demotivated employees are less productive than motivated ones. People need time to settle in to what are often new roles or existing roles with new responsibilities. New IT systems take time to get used to. New teams may be formed of people who have no experience of working together.

The more quickly the team discovers how to work together, the more effective their collective and individual output is.

Coaching your colleagues or team coaching can help people adjust more quickly. The quicker the adjustment, the smaller the cost to the company, and the happier and more productive employees become.

For managers, the ability to use coaching skills and act as a Performance Coach is also a way of getting to know new staff members and their strengths and limitations quickly. By understanding these strengths and limitations, you can assist colleagues to adjust to the new situation.

Managers are just as susceptible to all the emotions and difficulties that face any employee following a reorganisation. If you're a manager as well as a Performance Coach, you can use coaching skills to your own advantage as well as for the good of the others. The skills that you help your colleagues to develop can often be of benefit to you too.

Coaching through Change

People facing change often experience a number of emotional stages over a period of time, as shown in Table 9-1. The period of time a person takes to adjust is based on how welcome the change is, the impact on the individual, and his prior emotional state. For example, someone who was stressed prior to a change may find adjusting harder than someone who was calm. Individual circumstances are all different, so it's possible for someone to skip over some of the stages in the transitional process shown in the table.

Your colleague may be going through a variety of transitions because of multiple changes in his life. You may be unaware of life changes outside of work, such as ageing or ailing parents or changes in marital status, but these changes outside work may all interact with the changes going on within work. Remember too that you may be going through transition yourself at work, so be sensitive to your own needs.

Table 9-1	The Stages of Change
Stage	*Reaction*
1. Relief	Enjoying the end of a long period of uncertainty and instability. People may have found events stressful and knowing that that period has ended brings emotional relief.
2. Shock, immobilisation, and loss	A sense of numbness and lack of emotion

Stage	Reaction
3. Searching and denial	A search for new ideas about what to do next. Sometimes this means a period of blocking out the reality of the situation
4. Anger	An intense, all-consuming emotion where the person blames others, or perhaps themselves, for what has happened.
5. Depression, self-doubt, and inertia	Feeling intense sadness, self-blame or guilt, and lethargy. These feelings may have no rational basis. For example, your colleague may blame himself for not spotting a situation earlier when, in fact, no one could have done so.
6. Acceptance	Accepting the reality of the situation
7. Testing options	Considering realistic and feasible career options
8. Searching for meaning and self-awareness	Accepting the changes and feeling more optimistic
9. Integration and renewal	Adopting of a new and more positive lifestyle at work

In Performance Coaching, understanding the stages of change can enable you to assess how your colleague is coping with the transition and provide options for helping him speed the process towards integration and renewal (Stage 9) where possible. Coaching can help individuals understand the impact of change and also provide ways in which to minimise the associated emotional and practical implications.

Understanding the impact of change

Becoming familiar with the stages of change in Table 9-1 can help people to understand that the feelings they experience are quite normal. You can share the stages of change with your colleague and ask questions such as:

✔ Which stage do you think you are at now?

✔ What obstacles do you feel you're facing?

✔ What do you think you need to overcome these obstacles?

Taking control of negative thoughts

Negative thoughts = negative feelings = negative actions.

Psychological research shows that negative thoughts lead to negative feelings that lead to negative behaviour. For example, someone may think, 'It's my fault, there's no point in trying to fix things because I've blown it'. This thought may lead to a feeling of depression, which, in turn, may lead to your colleague not actively seeking to take control of the day-to-day things that he could change. When you coach, you need to be on the lookout for this type of thinking and use your coaching skills to help your colleague to think more realistically about the situation he faces.

Remind your colleague that mistakes are a fact of life. Encourage your colleague to take action to correct any mistakes where possible and to profit from them. This encourages people to adjust to the settling-in period that changes bring.

Part of accepting and getting the best out of change while minimising the difficulties means recognising the ways in which your colleague may limit himself or make matters worse by the thinking style he engages in.

Different thinking styles

The way people see situations is often coloured by their own perceptions and the kinds of 'filters' they apply to their experiences. For example, one person may see a particular situation at work as positive, whereas another may see the same situation as negative. How can both be right? Seeing a situation realistically means being able to stand back and evaluate what is really happening.

The following sections explain the three most common negative filters that people apply.

All or nothing

People may see things as merely right or wrong, good or bad, successful or unsuccessful. This kind of 'all or nothing' thinking means that it becomes hard to recognise that many shades exist between the two extremes. Use your coaching skills, especially your Socratic open questioning (refer to Chapter 5) to ask questions such as:

- ✔ What good things have happened because of the change?
- ✔ What opportunities does the change offer you?
- ✔ What opportunities does the change offer your team?

By getting your colleague to look at the positive sides of change and transition, he can develop a more balanced view of the situation.

Catastrophising

People often make situations worse by seeing them as the end of the world, rather than as a short-lived setback. *Catastrophising* means using exaggerated words such as 'terrible', 'nightmare', 'awful', and so on to describe situations. Using extreme emotional words only increases negative feelings.

Coach your colleagues to focus on:

✔ How the situation at work really is

✔ Using replacement words such as 'difficult' rather than 'awful'

Use open questions to get your colleague to reconsider his terminology.

Here's an example of how the coaching conversation may go:

> **Coach:** When you say 'awful', what do you mean by that?
>
> **Colleague:** It's really difficult having a new team and us not knowing each other and how we can work together.
>
> **Coach:** It sounds like you're saying that things have changed, you and your team don't know each other as well as you'd like, and that this is proving a challenge for you?
>
> **Colleague:** Yes, that's just what I'm saying.
>
> **Coach:** When you think of things as being a challenge rather than being awful, does it make you feel better or worse?
>
> **Colleague:** I've never really thought about it, but now that you've said that, it feels better.

Mind-reading

People often make assumptions about situations based on their perceptions rather than the reality of what's happening. They mind-read what other people are thinking or feeling. For example, Anita comes into the office and her colleague Jane doesn't speak to her. Anita's immediate reaction is 'Jane's really off with me today, can't think why. We're all under pressure so no need to take it out on me!' Anita spends the rest of the day avoiding Jane.

When Anita speaks with you, try to identify the assumptions that she's making and the conclusions she's jumping to about Jane's behaviour. Get Anita to check how realistic her thoughts are.

> **Coach:** What makes you think that Jane is upset with you?
>
> **Colleague:** Well, she didn't even look at me and I think she thinks I'll get her job when we reorganise!
>
> **Coach:** What kind of relationship do you two normally have?

Colleague: Quite good usually.

Coach: If your relationship is normally quite good, I wonder if there may be other reasons for Jane's behaviour?

Colleague: Well, Jane has been under a lot of pressure.

Coach: How was she with other people that day?

Colleague: Now that I think about it she was the same with everyone.

Coach: So I wonder if she was off with you or perhaps just preoccupied with her own issues?

Colleague: You may have a point.

Don't blame everything on transition! Blaming everything that goes wrong on the impact of the change is easy but not always useful. For example, someone who was struggling with effective communication prior to the change taking place is likely to continue to struggle after the change. Part of Performance Coaching is helping individuals to recognise that the issue concerned is an ongoing one rather than one brought about because of the change.

Asking useful questions

You may find the following questions useful when coaching for change.

- How do you know that the information you have is accurate?

- What's happening at work for you at the moment?

- What other factors are relevant?

- What is the other's person's perception of the situation?

- What have you tried so far?

- How do you feel about the feedback you've received?

- What can you do to change the situation?

- What alternatives to that approach do you have?

- Would you like some suggestions from me?

- What are the benefits and pitfalls of these options?

- Would you like to choose an option to act on?

- What possibilities for action do you see?

- What are the next steps?

- When will you take the next step?

- What may get in the way?

- What support do you need?

- How and when will you enlist the support you've identified?

- How can we overcome the obstacle you've identified?

Helping Colleagues Make Use of Their Support Systems

Everyone needs support in life. Support takes many forms, from your treasured possessions that give you a sense of comfort to the feelings of wellbeing and self-worth you get through support from others. You can often take these things for granted until you face a major change, or your support systems are threatened or taken away.

When coaching people who are experiencing change, you may want to focus on the people, hobbies, leisure activities, possessions, or pets that are supportive to the individual. Although these things aren't necessarily work-related, they're all anchors in someone's life. Individuals often manage change better when their life is in balance – after all, work is important but work isn't the whole of a person's life.

When your colleague (and yourself, of course) faces change and challenge, encourage him to think about the resources at his disposal and how he can draw support from them. The following list shows some examples of support resources.

- ✔ **Yourself:** Characteristics you can rely on, such as an easy temperament, a sense of humour, and resilience.

- ✔ **People:** You can benefit from secure professional and social relationships, taking time to see people, and talking things through.

- ✔ **Thoughts:** Constructive thinking – by thinking about what you can do, how you can do it, and challenging unhelpful thoughts as well as visualising the new situation in a positive light – can help.

- ✔ **Activities:** Engaging in enjoyable aspects of work, and having outside interests.

- ✔ **Meaning:** Recognising that the change has a positive purpose and seeing where the transition fits in the big picture.

Understanding Stress

Dealing with change can be stressful for some people. If you want a simple way to understand stress, think in terms of the demands made of people and the resources people have to cope with those demands. Even when the demands made are balanced by an individual's personal and organisational resources, that person experiences a certain amount of pressure. Pressure is motivating and some people thrive on a considerable amount. However, when individual resources are unable to cope with the demands, the person begins to feel stressed. The more that's asked of someone and the fewer resources the person has, the more stressed the person is likely to become.

Stress is a biological response that releases stress hormones into the bloodstream. The body's 'fight or flight' response is a survival mechanism and can be helpful. However, the things we're stressed out by are unlikely to be life-threatening and yet our bodies respond as if they are. In the long term, prolonged exposure to stress hormones is debilitating.

As a Performance Coach, you need to be able to recognise the symptoms of stress. As some of these symptoms are ones that only your colleague is likely to know about, having a list of these in the shape of a handout that you can give to your colleague is a way of helping that person decide which seem relevant.

Physical signs of stress include:

- Palpitations (erratic heartbeat)
- Pain and tightness in the chest
- Indigestion
- Breathlessness
- Nausea
- Muscle twitches
- Tiredness
- Vague aches or pains
- Skin irritation or rashes
- Susceptibility to allergies
- Clenched fists or jaw
- Fainting
- Frequent colds, flu, or other infections
- Recurrence of previous illnesses
- Constipation or diarrhoea
- Rapid weight gain or loss
- Irregular menstrual pattern in women

Emotional signs of stress can include:

- Mood swings
- Increased worrying
- Feeling
    - tense
    - drained
    - angry
    - guilty
    - cynical
    - apprehensive and anxious
    - helpless
- Loss of confidence and self-esteem
- Lack of concentration, and withdrawing into daydreams

Behavioural signs of stress can include:

- Becoming more accident-prone
- Poor work quality and time management
- Increased smoking, consumption of alcohol, or dependence on drugs
- Over- or under-eating
- Irregular sleep pattern; difficulty in getting to sleep and waking tired
- Loss of interest in sex
- Withdrawing from supportive relationships
- Irritability
- Taking work home more and being too busy to relax
- Not looking after oneself

If your colleague is stressed beyond your ability to help (by encouraging him to use support systems, and using other advice in this book), you can refer him to a specialist stress coach or your occupational health department.

Discovering how to get the most out of life using the least energy is the aim of good stress coaching. As a Performance Coach, you may find yourself helping your colleague decide what issues to place with his manager to consider. For example, if your colleague has to report to two managers, both of whom require more work than he can manage, then your job is to help your colleague consider how to effectively present his case. This is an organisational rather than individual issue that needs to be addressed.

Individuals can find new ways of turning unhealthy stress into healthy pressure. For example, if your colleague has a perfectionist thinking style your role would be to assist him to recognise this, challenge his thinking style, and devise a more appropriate thought process to stop him from stressing himself. Taking away the stressful event is not always possible or desirable (your colleague may hate giving presentations but doing so is part of the job). Instead, help the individual become more resilient and able to cope, using an individually tailored stress management technique.

Chapter 10

Following the Organisational Life Cycle

In This Chapter
▶ Growing up in the organisation
▶ Surviving the down times
▶ Thriving in the boom times
▶ Levelling out

*I*n this chapter we examine the role of Performance Coaching throughout the life cycle and changing business cycles of organisations. We look at the stages of development within the organisation and how these can influence the focus and need for Performance Coaching. We also consider the impact of external market forces on Performance Coaching such as in times of recession.

Understanding the Organisational Life Cycle

Organisations, like people, come into being, develop, and eventually die. Each stage of development has particular challenges, needs, risks, and opportunities. Understanding these stages can give further insight into the most effective use of Performance Coaching.

If employees can meet and survive the challenges at each stage, the organisation extends its life. Overall, the aim is to reach and maintain the phase where the organisation is in its prime. This phase is when the organisation is at its fittest, healthiest, and most profitable. After passing through this phase, rigidity and bureaucracy may overwhelm the enthusiasm and entrepreneurialism of earlier stages, causing the demise or stagnation of a formerly successful business. Figure 10-1 shows a simplified version of the organisational life cycle:

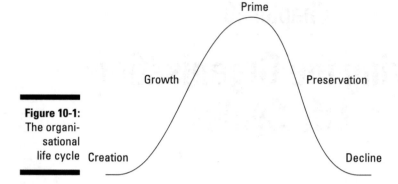

Figure 10-1:
The organi-
sational
life cycle

Performance Coaching can contribute to the overall goal of keeping the business alive by coaching the right things at the right time.

Table 10-1 shows ideas about what your company may face at different stages of the cycle.

Table 10-1	Organisational Life Cycle Needs	
Stage	*Challenges*	*Potential Areas for Coaching*
Creation	Focus on sales and survival	Entrepreneurial thinking
	Commitment to common purpose	Energy
	High energy	High sales focus
		Creativity
Growth	Too many priorities	Consistency
	Lack of focus	Professional management
	Going beyond the vision of the company's founder	Administration
Prime	Less entrepreneurialism	Flexibility
	Potential for stagnation	Innovation
	Loss of competitive edge	Growth

Stage	Challenges	Potential Areas for Coaching
Preservation	Procedures rule	Bureaucracy
	No innovation	Hierarchical behaviour
	Traditions emerge	Celebration of ritual
Decline	Internal systems take over	Overhauling the system
	Original purpose lost	Revisiting the vision

Growing up is hard to do

When an organisation is new, work life is exciting and scary but people know exactly why they are there and how much they count towards success. Everyone wants growth but it's easy to forget that success changes every-thing. If you're coaching through these growth stages, you need to help people deal with the human aspects of growth as much as the financial or operational considerations. Consider the following questions when tailoring your Performance Coaching to the stage of the organisation:

✔ How do you keep that feeling of belonging?

✔ How do you keep people excited about change?

✔ How do you keep the stories and good traditions alive?

✔ How can you be organised without becoming too bureaucratic?

✔ How can you help people grow up into bigger roles as the business grows?

✔ How can you keep people fresh and creative?

We were working with a professional services company that had started small – just a charismatic boss and three other people who felt like they really belonged. The early days of the company had been a lot of fun – like being on a roller coaster. The excitement and challenge were great. The company experienced its ups and downs, but through all their effort the company prospered. Now the company employed 150 employees and sales had risen to £40 million.

The original group were now in authority positions, managing teams of their own. Alasdair, the entrepreneur who had started it all, was now Chief Executive but was still operating as he always had: doing everything himself, micromanaging, and driving people mad. His explosive energy was legendary and those who knew him well knew that his bark was worse than his bite, but they still avoided crossing him. New managers were bringing new, different experiences and ideas but Alasdair and the older managers were resisting. Staff became disillusioned. The business suffered. Sales started to fall. Growth became less certain.

We used Performance Coaching to help navigate this difficult growth phase:

- ✔ Performance Coaching for the new managers focused on working within the established system, understanding its ways, and building on the original energy. They had to inject new ideas with respect for everything that had already been achieved, to avoid the longer-serving staff feeling threatened and becoming defensive and resistant.

- ✔ Performance Coaching for the established managers emphasised their need to achieve a higher level of professionalism in the way that they managed people for success. Another goal was to keep the energy levels high by using inspiration from those early days.

- ✔ Performance Coaching for Alasdair concentrated on helping him to understand his team and find ways of motivating and inspiring them. We coached him to free himself up from the administrative duties that he'd had to shoulder as the business grew but were now stultifying his high energy. By growing his team so that they can drive operations, he's now free to do what he does best – seek out new opportunities that continue to keep the company alive.

All too often creativity can go out of the window when a company rapidly grows in size – as if a bunch of creative children suddenly feel they have to stop playing and start pretending to be grown-ups. Overnight the focus turns to systems and procedures. Meetings that were once exciting and produced innovative thinking can suddenly become boring and the attendees passive. People who were good, productive performers are promoted and become untrained, uncoached managers, and the risk is that they fearfully try to contain the very behaviour that may keep entrepreneurial spirits alive.

Creating the best blend

When I (Averil) visited Jerez in Andalusia I went on a sherry tour at one of the well-known producers. The tour was really enjoyable, giving a feel for the industry and its fascination with perfecting the whole range of sherries. One aspect of the painstaking production process struck me particularly forcibly: the Solera System. Barrels are placed with the oldest wine at the bottom and more recent wines stacked on top, as shown in Figure 10-2. The topmost level is the nursery wine. After a specified time, a portion of the oldest sherry is drawn off and bottled; this amount is replaced from the younger barrel above; that barrel is topped up from the one above it, and so on. In this fashion, you keep the true, traditional flavour of the sherry but enliven it with the fresh young spirit.

Like the Solera System, companies need to find ways to keep everything fresh while not losing the worthwhile traditions and shared knowledge that are central to an excellent organisation.

Achieving this balance between old and new in an organisation requires:

- ✔ Respect for the parts played by both the old and the new
- ✔ A clear understanding of the quality of the organisation's brand
- ✔ Constant vigilance to ensure that the organisation reflects quality in everything it does

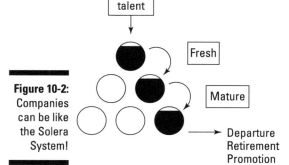

Figure 10-2: Companies can be like the Solera System!

What goes around, comes around

The organisational life cycle model shown in Figure 10-1 isn't really a *cycle* but a normal distribution curve or an inverted U. However, this shape implies an inevitability about the eventual death of the organisation! Waiting to die isn't a particularly good business option. That outcome has to be averted by effectively employing, developing, and coaching people.

For most people, doing what they've always done feels comfortable and safe but may constitute a slippery slope. It may fall to you, as Performance Coach, to be the person to:

✔ Highlight the risk of falling into destructive habits such as complacency, assuming success is a given, or allowing rivalries between departments that need to co-operate.

✔ Challenge blinkered thinking along the lines of 'the old ways are the best ways'.

✔ Enable colleagues to test out new ideas and refresh their thinking.

As Performance Coach you can hold up the mirror to reality and ask colleagues to view the situation from a range of perspectives so that keeping working practices fresh remains a constant goal.

In any organisation, individual divisions and departments may all be at different stages of their growth. Birth, life, and death can co-exist in a continual cycle of life. Plainly put, the organisation may need to use certain parts to stimulate the others.

If you can create cross-fertilisation of ideas between departments and divisions, you have a better chance of re-energising and vitalising the organisation through many 'life cycles'. Performance Coaching options include:

✔ Encouraging individuals to broaden their networking within the company to expose themselves to new ideas

✔ Organising co-coaching between different departments

✔ Initiating group coaching to continually engage with the challenges happening throughout the organisation and to pool ideas and resources

Being Prepared for a Recession

While you're keeping track of your own organisation, sensitive to its constantly changing needs at each stage of growth, external factors go and mess it all up with a downturn. What can you do? Sit quietly and wait it out? Hide behind the sofa? At such a time, Performance Coaching may seem like a logical budget cut, but that is just the time to invest in it!

The United Kingdom has experienced continuous overall economic growth since the 1960s. Despite recessions the trend has remained upwards. As a result, assuming that business cycles may be a thing of the past is tempting, especially for blind optimists. Sadly, recessions are a fact of business life. Although better economic management may have made the cycles less extreme, you can't be complacent. The average duration of business cycles is 5–8 years from one peak to the next. Be prepared, rather than surprised into making foolish or costly mistakes, especially where manpower and talent are concerned.

Performance Coaching has an enormous contribution to make, at each stage of the cycle, to ensure that the company achieves the best outcomes by having the best people doing the best job they can at the right time.

When companies recognise that a downturn is inevitable, making the wrong choices is a real risk. Panic can lead to damaging decisions, such as choosing to lose talent that may have taken years to acquire, cutting costs dramatically, and even changing the nature of products on offer. Development budgets are cut and key people begin to feel dissatisfied because their growth is restricted.

Alternatively, the company may avert its gaze and wait until the recession passes, hoping for the best. This attitude is suitable if you're an ostrich but not if you're a professional manager.

Adopting the brace position

Most companies manage to weather recessions. The majority of executives also attest that a downturn gives opportunities to improve business. Some managers advocate that recession is the perfect time to innovate, create new markets, and buy in staff cheaper than in the boom times. However, the results vary hugely. While some companies never get back to their previous strengths, others capitalise on conditions and use the opportunity to get ready for the next upswing. Business advice, which must shape Performance Coaching, insists:

- Examine the costs of the organisation and trim excess but never cut what enables the business to operate.
- Keep the business structure sound.
- Have a well-thought-out plan to cut excess staff.
- Use the time to develop people within the organisation.
- Be ready to hit the ground running with the best talent as soon as the upturn appears.

Cutting costs and restructuring may be justified for many organisations but only at the same time as considering future growth and being ready to move forward in pursuit of that growth.

Finding that old wartime spirit

Adversity can cause people to combine their talent and pull together to make the best of hard times. In the worst of times, people can self-destruct through blame, fear, and confusion. If the organisation or team has an affirmative, positive, and encouraging style, the chances are that you find the former behaviour. If your organisation has a tendency to blame or scapegoat, you're likely to be rewarded with the latter. All that positive stuff about people being your most valuable asset comes true right now. By harnessing all that intellectual and emotional capital, you have a much better chance of getting through the toughest challenges.

If you're reading this book during a recession, this next bit may really irritate you, but now is not the time to start planning to survive a recession. You need to do that during the good times. Areas of preparation include conservative financial management, strategic planning, and narrowing your business focus to key areas. Most companies eliminate excess spending and reduce costs but this alone is insufficient to improve the chances of good performance.

A study that analysed what the winners of the last recession got right discovered that those who pulled ahead of their competitors gained a lasting advantage. Making short-sighted decisions about people during a recession can have a disastrous impact on a business with effects that last right into the next upswing.

Here are a few Performance Coaching tips for planning ahead with people:

- **Constant scanning.** A downturn shouldn't be able to creep up behind you. Coach people to constantly scan for a recession and align development planning and recruitment so people can ensure that they're carrying out the right roles to the level required.

- **Managing talent.** A recession can be just the incentive to focus on developing people from within rather than hiring from outside. The basic maths on talent management is easy when you consider the cost of recruitment and induction. Encourage managers to look after home-grown talent and gear people up to be ready to leap into action at the first whiff of improving markets. Having in place a positive plan for keeping people growing in their jobs through the difficult times is a real inducement for employees to stay put when they may consider leaving in the hope of finding a more secure future.

- **Sustaining the culture.** In hard times you can't afford to lose or dilute a carefully achieved corporate culture of shared values. Coaching people to keep the faith during the hard times through maintaining the culture keeps the organisation in a state of readiness to bounce back when given the chance.

- **Developing leadership.** Grooming talent for the top jobs ensures that you have a return on all the investment made so far.

I don't do failure

James is the Managing Director of the UK division of a construction company that had been performing better every year. Then the housing market in the United States started to suffer and the impact on the UK division was potentially enormous. Faced with an imminent UK downturn, James was also under pressure to shore up the US results. For the first time in his career, everything wasn't on an upward trajectory. James started to see himself as a failure and felt stressed. He began to suffer from headaches and stomach upsets. All these things happened just at the point where he had to be at his most effective. The company needed him to be on top form to take them through the difficult time.

The following processes helped his coach determine where to start with Performance Coaching:

✔ The most important aspect was self-blame. Challenging James's interpretation of his own failure was critical. Times were hard. The economy had changed. The demands of his new role were tough. None of these things added up to his being a failure. The coach asked him to reflect: What were the strengths that he had brought to this role? Did he still have them? Could he still use them?

✔ The next emphasis was on shifting James's perspective from being highly 'me'-focused back to being task-focused. Instead of agonising over 'where did I go wrong?', he needed to shift his thinking to, 'What will it take to make the best of this situation?'

✔ His coach also looked at the way that James was behaving. His negative thinking had led him to shoulder all responsibility and to work harder and harder. He was protecting his team from the worst at the time when he needed them to perform at their best. Instead of disappearing into a fog of gloom, locked in his room each time the monthly results came out, through coaching he realised that he needed to be functioning as part of his team. So James called the team together when the results were due each month so they could examine the results and immediately brainstorm constructive action together to turn the situation around.

✔ **Redeploying people.** How can you use talent in as positive a manner as possible? Normal career options can be limited. How can you keep people fresh by coaching them to use their talents in other parts of the business? Performance Coaching can help people to become more flexible and adaptable.

✔ **Managing performance.** During a recession it's critical that people work fully to their strengths, with regular reviews, rewarding feedback, and opportunities to grow in the job.

✔ **Career progression and succession planning.** At a time when predicting the future may be tricky, you still need to coach people to help create a vision of what their next steps can be – even if these steps are somewhat in the future.

✔ **Recognise problems early.** Doing an ostrich impersonation at this point doesn't help. Keep track of any small problems that may turn into major problems if undetected and unresolved. Challenge complacency and thoughtless optimism. Don't let people wait to see if things get better. Encourage action.

✔ **Use opportunity.** Adversity can provide opportunity. When things are going well, people are less assiduous at looking for ways to improve. Now is the time to coach creative thinking.

Riding the Wave of Expansion

Good though it may feel when the market picks up, you need to avoid the panicky hire-and-fire trap that companies can fall into.

You're also at risk of losing all that lovely talent that you nurtured, coached, and built up during the tough times now that more money is swilling about and carrots are being dangled in front of your key players.

Organisations throw money at people although money alone is not a sufficient motivator. People form an emotional attachment to their company given any opportunity. Central to that bond is the question of whether the company is committed to helping people develop their careers.

One day you know everyone's name and life story, the next, the place is full of strangers! What worked in the early days may not be feasible when the organisation grows bigger. Rapid growth is a dangerous stage because you risk losing the humanity and originality of the company. As part of your Performance Coaching, encouraging networks and strong team bonds can help keep the shape of the organisation intact. Research estimates that you can know everyone in an organisation until staff numbers reach between 100 and 150. Beyond that, people belong more to their department than to the organisation as a whole. A sense of belonging, knowing you're valued, and identifying good, clear opportunities in the future can do much to counter the financial lure of other companies. The tendency to pay over the odds in an attempt to do well by talented employees is a waste if these other factors aren't catered for first.

Growing companies run the risk of becoming swiftly bureaucratic in order to cope, thereby changing the nature of the company. As a result, some people may vote with their feet if working for a large bureaucratic organisation was never their intention or desire.

Coaching during recession: Margaret's story

Margaret had hand-reared her department over the years. She always made a good case for new personnel, and resources had been available. She liked having a big team but was not always good at managing performance as tightly as she needed to. When it became clear that the markets weren't going to get better, she realised that she was going to have to thin out her department. When she thought about each team member, she became quite agitated. They all had dependents or were such nice people. How was she to do such an appalling thing to them and their families? She turned to coaching for help.

✔ The first task in Performance Coaching was to help her focus on assessing her team. When she reviewed each case, Margaret realised that she had, in the past, been a bit remiss in her feedback. Some people were underperforming in their roles but their appraisals didn't reflect this underperformance. Performance Coaching helped her focus on assessing who was performing well and who would contribute most effectively through these challenging times.

✔ Although Margaret was now clear about who she had to let go, she was still avoiding the difficult conversations. Her coach encouraged her to consult with Human Resources and to be clear about the correct process.

✔ Performance Coaching focused on the actual form of words she would use with her staff and on how to cope with her own emotions and those of her staff. Through rehearsal and role play, Margaret prepared to handle these conversations as professionally, empathically, and effectively as possible.

✔ Margaret needed to handle the issue of morale. Her coach encouraged her to think about how to inspire the reduced team to get back on track. She decided to communicate openly about how she had decided on the rationale for the cuts, leaving them in no doubt that she'd chosen them to stay because she needed their skills. She instituted more interactive team meetings focused on moving forward and being as creative as possible in the face of the new challenges.

✔ Margaret realised that her rather bland feedback system had failed everyone in the past and that she needed to be more robust in her own coaching of people for higher performance – using both successes and failures as an opportunity to raise performance.

The team knew they'd be given chances for advancement as soon as the upturn came but also knew now that Margaret would have very clear ideas about the performance she required from them.

As the organisation grows, it needs to design a more sophisticated talent management process. The ideal is to catch the company at the optimum time and design a scalable process that accommodates growth. Coaching managers to be consistent in their talent management process across the company ensures a rapid integration following mergers and acquisitions. Also, growing talent internally has the benefits of being cost-effective and ensures that the soul of the company remains intact at critical stages.

Getting Back to Normal: Performance Recovery

Performance recovery (getting the business back on track after hard times) is not an occasion for wallowing in soul searching but an opportunity to grow and benefit from the experience. You may have to have difficult conversations with people to get to the real core of issues and take action on them.

Frequently, problems aren't solved because people

- ✔ Don't want to criticise other people or working practices.
- ✔ Don't want to admit to mistakes.
- ✔ Are concerned about hurting others' feelings by pointing out errors.
- ✔ Think that ignoring a problem can make it go away.

Any Performance Coaching intervention has to be results-focused, and set clear goals, including salvaging the self-esteem of all involved, rebuilding professional reputations, and impacting on economic performance. See Chapter 3 for more about setting goals.

Assessing what went wrong (without blaming)

Stop the blame! If you want to get to the root of the issues causing a dip in performance, people need to trust your ability to analyse the reasons for the poor performance with them, without it turning into a witch-hunt. You need to stop those involved punishing themselves for long enough to start building repairs. At the same time, you want to benefit from the problem so that you can avoid it another time. This approach applies to individuals, teams, departments, and whole businesses.

Performance Coaching questions to ask include:

- ✔ What do you know about what went wrong?
- ✔ Why do you think this happened?

✔ What could have been done differently?

✔ What difference would that have made?

✔ How can you spot early warning signs sooner?

✔ How could you have changed the outcome?

The point of asking these questions and analysing the answers is to ensure that the bad experience is put to use as an educational tool. By understanding how the person, team, or company got where they were, they can choose not to go there again and you can begin to clarify what it would take to get over it and move on.

Remembering that when one door closes another one opens

If your colleague has trouble moving forward, letting go, and starting to act to repair the situation you may need a process to get her going. When people experience a setback or disappointment, they predict that they'll feel bad for a long time. When something good happens, they predict that the good thing will make them happy for a long time too. Neither is accurate. Some people take longer to get over things. Others are able to say 'Bygones' and start moving forward.

You want people to be cognisant of any part that they played in things going wrong, but moving on has to be a priority. You can help people move on by reviewing their past responses to dealing with company downturns.

Ask your colleague:

✔ Think of times when you felt as if a door closed for you.

✔ How did you feel?

✔ How did you get going again?

✔ How long did it really take?

✔ How does this make you view the current situation?

Take time to really explore and be respectful of your colleague's responses at each stage. Don't hurry her along, making light of how bad it felt at the time. As in all coaching, ideally your colleague has the 'aha!' experience herself, realising that the bad time did pass and that she did survive. This is always so much more effective than a platitudinous 'it'll get better' from you. So take your time getting to question 5. Table 10-2 shows a worked example.

Table 10-2	Moving On
List times when you felt as if a door closed for you	I didn't get that new job I applied for.
	I wasn't chosen to give the quarterly presentation.
	My department failed to meet its targets.
How did you feel?	It felt like the end of the world.
	I felt second-rate.
	I didn't think my career would amount to much.
How did you get going again?	Well, I suppose I just got on with things, kept at it, and then got another chance.
	I tried again and some things went right.
	Something else just cropped up.
How long did it really take?	It felt like eternity but, looking back, I suppose it was a couple of months.
	They asked me to speak at the next quarterly meeting so I had time to prepare and I could watch how the Quarter 1 guy handled the meeting so it didn't really take that long.
	It did take quite a while overall, but I began to see results pretty soon so that helped me to get back on top of things.
How does this make you view the current situation?	Well, I guess it feels pretty bad right now but I just need to start again and it will get easier.

Becoming resilient and having a plan

When issues seem insurmountable and people believe failure is inevitable, rigor mortis sets in. You can't afford to let people linger in a downward spiral of helplessness and negativity. You have a job to do! While respecting your colleague's feelings, process what happened and move on to a plan.

Research in positive psychology shows that if people are resilient they can draw on positive emotions when they face setbacks and can profit from the experience and become stronger. Being part of a strong, positive team fosters resilience but if this situation does not exist, your role as Performance Coach is especially critical.

The process is a bit circular really because in order to be resilient you need to exercise the positive emotions, such as optimism, hope, and enthusiasm that:

- ✔ Fuel psychological resilience
- ✔ Broaden attention and thinking
- ✔ Undo lingering negative emotions that slow down progress
- ✔ Build personal resources

We encourage you to coach along these lines after any setback, but coaching in this way when everything's going well is like putting money in the bank. Building a personal model of resilience stands people in good stead for the tough times, enabling them not only to bounce back much faster but much further each time. Don't start from a setback! Start long before!

Table 10-3 shows questions to ask when using the opportunity of failure to coach someone. These questions get your colleague moving on to the planning stage.

Table 10-3		Moving On to Action	
Initial Questions	**Answers**	**Performance Coaching Questions**	**The Plan**
Describe a time when you felt as if a door closed for you.	I didn't get that new job I applied for.	What can you deduce from that? Why do you think you didn't get the job? How can you get some evidence about whether it was the interview or your skills or experience that let you down? How can you remedy that?	I need some Performance Coaching in interview skills.

(continued)

Table 10-3 *(continued)*			
Initial Questions	*Answers*	*Performance Coaching Questions*	*The Plan*
How did it feel?	Like the end of the world.	How can you recalibrate what you're feeling? (That is, assess and adjust the strength of the interpretation.)	It's not the end of the world – more a bit of an earthquake!
		Can you reframe statements of your emotions? For example, rather than thinking 'the end of the world', would 'this is a setback' be more appropriate?	I have coped before. I will cope again. Talking it through is a good start.
How did you get going again?	Well, I suppose I just got on with things, kept at it and then got another chance.	How have you got over such let-downs in the past? What actions can you take now to move forward practically and emotionally?	I realise that, in the grand scheme of things, it made me unhappy, but it isn't the end of the world.
How long did it really take?	It felt like eternity but, looking back, I suppose it was a couple of months.	How long do you need to deal with this? How can you speed that up?	When I look back it's amazing how quickly I've got over things that I thought at the time would wreck my life!

Initial Questions	Answers	Performance Coaching Questions	The Plan
How does this make you view the current situation?	Well, I guess it feels pretty bad right now but I just need to start again and it will get easier.	So, how is your situation looking now?	I want to get started asking for feedback, looking for ways to improve, and preparing for the next interview.

Ask your colleague to summarise her plan, rather than summarising for her. This summary is called *affirmation of intent*. When someone asserts, 'I am going to do X, Y, and Z', she has a greater chance of following through and actually doing what she intends. Make this summarising, such a small thing, into a big habit.

Chapter 11

Managing Careers

In This Chapter

▶ Understanding values

▶ Coping with a new job

▶ Making a good first impression

▶ Taking care of personal resources

*I*n this chapter we consider the ways that Performance Coaching operates throughout all the stages of an individual's career development. You can help colleagues get a sense of achievement from working life by encouraging them to put in thought about their current jobs while planning for the future. Making an impression and letting people know what you're good at is as important as being able to do the job. Managing the work-life balance is crucial to long-term success, and this chapter gives you tips on coaching people to achieve balance.

Stepping Out on the Career Path

Careers require attention in the same way as pot plants do – neglect them and they start to wilt. The most promising and talented of individuals may find that a lack of planning or understanding of what really matters when it comes to designing and implementing a career plan can lead them to take the wrong path or slow down career progression. As a Performance Coach many of your colleagues may talk to you about a variety of issues connected to their current or future career aspirations.

Looking where you're going

Your colleagues may need help in thinking about their current positions and how to make the most of them. Although they need to focus on what's happening today, today soon becomes tomorrow. Planning ahead is crucial because it ensures that your colleagues remain energised and enthused about the positions they already hold as well as being clear about what steps they need to take to make the next career move.

People who set clear plans are more likely to give their best and achieve more. Managers often only focus on the current position the person holds. However, by helping colleagues to consider the future, the quality of their work and enthusiasm for their current position can be maintained and even heightened. Performance Coaching contributes both to heightened current performance and to the fulfilment of longer-term ambitions.

The potential here is for a win/win scenario for everyone:

- ✔ For the manager, who has a more motivated employee
- ✔ For the organisation, which gains a better worker
- ✔ For the individual, who develops a heightened sense of personal satisfaction at work

Help your colleague to consider his career in relation to short-, medium-, and longer-term goals. Here are a few specific steps and questions for your colleague:

- ✔ **3–6 months ahead**
  - Start small – what changes can you make to ensure that you're meeting your current work commitments?
  - What short-term goals can you easily achieve that also help move you towards the longer-term goals? Use the Behavioural Contracting Model (refer to Chapter 4) to include tangible goals.
- ✔ **6–12 months ahead**
  - What new skills do you need/want to acquire?
  - What new ideas would you want to develop and share with others?
  - What changes do you want to make?
  - What do you need to do to make the changes happen?
- ✔ **12 months onwards**
  - Design specific plans that you know will take more than a year to achieve.
  - Be realistic and break your ideas down into specific goals.
- ✔ **3–5 years ahead**
  - Consider where you'd like to be in the next 3–5 years, including your life beyond the company. Devise work goals with the whole of your life in mind because one set of aspirations can affect another.

Encourage your colleague to discover all the training, coaching, and mentoring opportunities available within the organisation. Coach your colleague to think about the relationships that he needs to cultivate in order to meet success. Networking can be the key to future positions.

Understanding personal strengths and limitations

If you want your colleagues to have successful careers, you need to help them to identify and make the most of their strengths and minimise the impact of their limitations. Many people focus on improving weaknesses; however, truly successful people know what they're good at and do as much of it as they can.

To help identify strengths, ask your colleague questions such as:

- ✔ Which skills come easily to you?
- ✔ Which skills do you need to improve?
- ✔ What do you know that you do well?
- ✔ What do others recognise that you do well?
- ✔ What gives you a sense of satisfaction?

Having considered strengths, turn to limitations. Limitations are sometimes hard for the individual to see. You, as the Performance Coach, may know your colleague's weaknesses all too well. You can simply tell him, but the most successful form of Performance Coaching is where you help people identify limitations for themselves. Ask your colleague to contemplate any area of weakness himself before launching into an analysis of the perceptions others may have. Bring in the perceptions of others (from appraisals, for example) a little later in the process.

To help your colleague identify limitations, ask questions such as:

- ✔ What are the things that you find hard to do?
- ✔ Which tasks do you find yourself putting off?
- ✔ What are the things you do only because you 'should' do them?

In most cases, people have some accuracy in their self-awareness. Sometimes, however, people have a bit of a blind spot to their faults or, at the other extreme, they're too self-critical. In both instances, you can use others' feedback to help them adjust their perception to a more accurate level.

Playing to your strengths

Morag was finding aspects of her role in management quite challenging. Unlike many of her colleagues, she was really excellent in dealing with people. Where she fell down was in attention to some of the more technical aspects of financial management. Morag knew the standards she needed to attain in order to advance in her career but found motivation hard when the subject wasn't particularly interesting to her. Her heart really wasn't in it. We worked with her to think about how she could use her strengths to tackle this lack of motivation. Using all her interpersonal skills, she engaged with the people involved, formed strong relationships, and found herself much more fascinated by the topic when seeing it through others people's eyes. Her new-found interest and enthusiasm also ensured that the team were eager to perform well.

Fred, on the other hand, was appalling with his people. He did and said quite inappropriate things, unchecked by any forethought. When he realised that one of his major strengths was a love of learning, he used this strength to approach the situation from an intellectual standpoint. By reading up and understanding theories about how people behaved and how to manage them, his behaviour improved dramatically. He realised that he'd been held back by his assumption that you had to be naturally 'good with people' to be proficient at that side of management!

Developing a career plan

You can begin to help your colleague to develop a career plan by plotting the steps between his current situation and his longer-term plan. Focus on strengths and assist your colleague to set goals that play to those strengths. Areas that require development need to be addressed. However, research suggests that individuals are likely to fare far better if they focus on using their strengths in overcoming difficulties, and work on limitations as a secondary issue.

If your colleague has many limitations with regard to his current role, he is probably not in the right career or position and is unlikely to do well in the longer term. He is likely to become disheartened, with little work satisfaction. In this case, use your Performance Coaching skills to help him discover and work to his strengths in a different role.

When setting goals, help your colleague to create the image of the person he wants to be and the career he wants to have. Questions to ask your colleague include:

- How do you want to be perceived by others?
- What kind of career do you want to have?

- How good do you need to be?
- How much money do you want to make?
- What type of job title do you want to have?

When you've explored these questions and found answers, you can begin to help plot the steps between who your colleague is now and who he wants to be.

As you plot the route for your colleague to take, decide on deadlines for achieving or revising the goals (Chapter 3 has more on goal-setting).

What Really Matters to Me?

Helping your colleague to identify personal values is an important part of a successful career plan, wherever he is on his career path. The word 'value' in relation to a career refers to how your colleague feels about the work itself, as well as how he perceives the contribution the work makes to society. Most people who pursue work that's in line with their values are successful in their careers and gain a greater amount of work satisfaction than those who do not.

You can divide work values into two groups:

- **Intrinsic:** Values that relate to a specific interest in the work itself or to the benefits that the work contributes to society.
- **Extrinsic:** Values that relate to the favourable conditions that are linked to career choice, such as earning potential, location, and all other external features.

For people to feel satisfied with their work, most have to find a degree of personal intrinsic value in it.

The following is a list of intrinsic personal values that are important to people in their careers. Ask your colleague to explore personal and work values, rating each value listed on a scale of 0–10 (0 = not important and 10 = very important). Add any other values that your colleague considers essential.

- **Expertise/specialist competence:** Seeking a high level of accomplishment in a specialised field.
- **Power/influence:** Being responsible for people and resources and being accountable for work done by others.
- **Search for meaning:** Doing things that you believe to be valuable for their own sake, that are worthwhile, and contributing to society.

- **Creativity:** Initiating and carrying out new ideas
- **Affiliation:** Cultivating close and meaningful relationships at work
- **Autonomy:** Being independent and making key decisions for yourself
- **Security:** Creating a solid and safe future

After your colleague has identified the values that are important to him and has rated each out of 10, you can use your coaching skills to explore how his current position and future aspirations fit with these values.

For example, Jill had begun to feel restless despite liking the business, the people, and the money. When she did the previous exercise, she discovered that expertise was very important for her. When she first joined the company, she had resolved many tricky issues and revelled in the results she achieved. Now everything was ticking along well and she was experiencing an element of boredom. Coaching encouraged her to seek new projects and she began to work in a more consultative role where her expertise was highly valued.

After you've explored these intrinsic values, list your colleague's *extrinsic* values. Certain factors may limit opportunities. For example:

- If someone is very settled with family and friends providing a strong support system, he may be very unwilling to move away to gain vital experience elsewhere.
- If someone's lifestyle demands a high income, whatever other values concerning meaning he may have, this may not be the time to reduce income and work for a charity .

Completing the values exercise provides the basis for future work. Some people gain insight into why they're dissatisfied with the work they're doing and can focus on the changes they need to make to redress the situation. The company also gains value if they can keep a talented individual by simply moving him to an area of work to which he's better suited.

Excelling During the First 100 Days

The first few months in a new position are a crucial time in most jobs. The key achievements to aim for in this phase are to:

- Make the right impression
- Become comfortable in the new role
- Deliver what is expected
- Establish the most effective types of working relationships with superiors, peers, and direct reports

Some people make the mistake of focusing solely on the work, thinking they'll be judged by results. If fact, the way you fit in with people, the culture, and your way of doing things is just as important as instant results, if not more so.

Receiving Performance Coaching is now quite common, especially for senior executives, as a way of helping people settle in as quickly as possible. Time is money, so apart from the obvious benefits to your colleague, the organisation gains financially.

Managers who coach also have a role to play in ensuring that new staff settle in as quickly as possible. If you're coaching internally, you may have invaluable information that can help your colleague to get up to speed quickly. This may involve helping him to recognise and understand aspects of the culture that aren't immediately obvious to the newcomer, especially the less formal traditions that form bonds – from cakes on birthdays to where people eat their lunch.

Ta-da! – Making the right impact

The new person has to find out and understand the culture of the organisation as quickly as possible. Part of your Performance Coaching role is to encourage him to think carefully about the initial impact he needs to make to position himself to best advantage. You can help your colleague settle in and pave the way for success by getting him to consider how to make the right impression at every stage. When creating an image, consider whether your colleague:

✔ Needs to appear decisive early on, or is it more appropriate to spend time listening?

✔ Has certain expectations that he wants to create. You can help your colleague to ensure that he can live up to the expectations later on.

Hitting the ground running

The first few weeks in a new job can be quite traumatic. The new organisation is unlikely to have the same methods as the old one. This is particularly true if someone has moved from a large organisation to a small entrepreneurial company or from the public sector to private.

People have to deal with the new situation and may well make a few mistakes on the way. Anticipate this reality and use your Performance Coaching skills to help your colleague to settle in more easily and perform better for the business.

Your role as Performance Coach is to act as a guide through the complexities of a new position, new working relationships, expectations, and demands. You can function as a sanity check for your colleague and ensure that he's reading new situations right.

In this way you ensure that people begin their journey by making a successful contribution to the organisation while encouraging a sense of professional and personal satisfaction.

You have a number of key factors to consider, which we cover in the following sections.

Getting to know the way things work

As a Performance Coach you can encourage your colleague to find a mentor or sponsor who can provide some of the 'softer' information in the new workplace, such as a historical perspective ('how we got here'), who the leading characters in the firm are, and the best way to tackle difficult situations. Encourage him to use existing networking skills to cultivate useful contacts both inside and outside the organisation. Other people who have recently joined the company may also provide useful insights for your colleague.

Finding your way around

During the first crucial days, encourage your colleague to discover more about his job by asking questions and observing how the system works. Areas for consideration are:

- **Corporate strategy.** What does your colleague need to know to understand the mission and corporate strategy?

- **Corporate culture.** What are the values and attitudes of the organisation and how can he adapt his individual working method to fit in with these values and attitudes?

- **Organisational goals.** What does your colleague need to do to find out about goals or statements of intent in areas such as client service, product quality, and market positioning?

- **Products and services.** Whatever his role, your colleague needs to know the range and market position of products or services that affect the organisation's performance.

- **The hierarchy.** Encourage your colleague to establish answers to the following questions:

    - Who sets the pace?

    - How are decisions made and who makes them?

    - How are problems solved?

    - What is the real power structure?

✔ **Communication systems.** In what ways can your colleague become familiar with both the formal and informal communication systems and any organisational jargon?

So, what am I meant to be doing?

The selection process should have given your colleague an insight into his responsibilities and the reporting structure. However, initial impressions from interviews are rarely fully accurate or complete. Encourage your colleague to clarify:

✔ His precise responsibilities

✔ The expectations of his manager and any other senior staff whose objectives he'll be supporting

✔ Budgetary and management responsibilities

✔ The structure of the department and its place in the organisational hierarchy

✔ How his function or department is perceived within the organisation (is it held in high regard, and if not, why not?)

✔ Lateral lines of responsibility and liaison

✔ Key internal customers and suppliers with whom your colleague needs to establish effective working relationships

And how am I meant to do that?

The organisation probably operates some kind of performance review system, and has a series of objectives for your colleague. Your colleague needs clear parameters and targets to channel his contribution effectively. If he isn't given any specific targets in the initial period, you can encourage him to agree with his manager regarding the following:

✔ Key job functions where he'll make a significant contribution

✔ A series of regularly reviewed, measurable objectives, such as how he'll contribute to the overall profitability and development of the department and the organisation as a whole

✔ The measurement criteria used (so that your colleague can check that performance targets are realistic and achievable)

If your organisation doesn't set objectives or targets, help your colleague to set a series of goals to work towards (Chapter 3 has more about setting goals).

Considering training needs

Encourage your colleague to identify any further training needs he may have as early as possible. Help your colleague investigate any technical training as well as training in management and interpersonal skills. Encourage him to draw up a comprehensive training plan that addresses his needs and acts as a framework for personal development.

Balancing Life and Work

Part of Performance Coaching at different stages of people's careers is helping colleagues to find a work-life balance, which is no simple task. Consider:

- ✔ Spending more time at work than at home means that people can miss out on a rewarding personal life.
- ✔ Spending too much time at work creates the possibility of becoming stressed and even burned out if the situation is sustained.
- ✔ If people are experiencing challenges in their personal life, concentrating on work can be difficult.
- ✔ Some people may work longer to avoid difficulties at home.
- ✔ Lots of people enjoy their jobs so much that putting in long hours is no sacrifice.
- ✔ Some people feel they have no choice about the way they work.

One thing is certain: each person needs his life to be balanced in slightly different and unique ways.

Look at me – the plates are all spinning

People used to work eight to nine hours, Monday to Friday, with clear boundaries between work and home. However, the world has changed and, unfortunately, the boundaries have become blurred for many workers.

Performance Coaching helps individuals to realise that working long hours isn't necessarily a badge of honour but may be a disaster waiting to happen. If your colleagues can find ways of balancing the demands of work with the human need for relaxation, family, fun, and hobbies, then they are likely to perform consistently better at work than those who don't make time for 'life'.

Being willing to arrive early and stay late every day may help you keep on top of your workload. However, Table 11-1 shows the possible consequences associated with excessive working and the coaching you can provide to a colleague to break the cycle of overworking.

Table 11-1	Consequences of Overworking	
Aspect of Overworking	***Consequence***	***Performance Coaching***
Fatigue	An individual's ability to think decreases with fatigue, which means that your colleague is less productive and may make mistakes. These mistakes can lead to injury or the need to repeat work, and negatively impact his professional reputation.	Help your colleague to appreciate the consequences of fatigue and recognise the false economy of working long hours. He may end up doing more in fewer hours!
Family	Your colleague may miss out on important events, which may harm relationships with partners, family, and friends.	Help your colleague to appreciate that a good life outside work supports the ability to withstand the stresses of the working environment.
Friends	Friends are a key part of your colleague's support system. But spending too much time at the office makes it difficult to nurture those friendships.	Help your colleague recognise the importance of external support networks.
Expectations	If your colleague works extrahours as a general rule, he may be given more responsibility. This can create a never-ending and increasing cycle, causing more concerns and challenges.	Performance Coaching can help your colleague appreciate that a human being can't function like a machine and that everyone has limits.

Sometimes working overtime is important – a choice you can make to adjust to a new job, new boss, or to pay your bills. Sometimes you can't avoid overtime, but you can manage it.

A bridge too far

When coaching, having a range of statistics available can be helpful to enable your colleague to understand the impact of working too hard and for too long. Work-life balance is a concept that people may understand intellectually but find hard to accept on an emotional level, believing that working at 110 per cent all the time leads to career success.

✔ The Confederation of British Industry (CBI) estimates that over 360 million working days a year are lost due to stress-related illnesses.

✔ The Web site www.NetDoctor.co.uk undertook a survey that suggested that one in three people felt life to be less than worthwhile, while one in ten thought they'd be better off dead.

✔ It costs the UK £3 billion a year for the psychiatric treatment of stress-related illnesses.

✔ Sleep difficulties are one of the most common symptoms of stress.

✔ 70 per cent of the 4,000 annual suicides in the UK are people suffering from depression and 15 per cent of people experiencing depression go on to commit suicide.

✔ 1 in 10 people suffer from panic attacks, which are a common stress-related symptom.

Getting out of the comfort zone

Juggling the demands of career and personal life isn't easy. For most people, doing so is an ongoing challenge. Here are a variety of ways that you can help your colleagues to maintain the balance between stretching themselves to achieve the best at work, and maintaining a healthy mental, emotional, and physical life:

✔ **Keeping a log.** Encourage your colleague to keep a diary of everything he does for one week. Include work-related and non-work-related activities. As a result, he may see a way to cut out or delegate activities that he has control over but doesn't enjoy. If he doesn't have the authority to make such decisions, encourage him to talk to his manager.

✔ **Taking advantage of your options.** Help your colleague to understand what facilities and benefits the organisation offers. Encourage him to make the most of these, such as using the gym and counselling services.

✔ **Communicating clearly.** Encourage your colleague to communicate clearly and limit time-consuming misunderstandings.

✔ **Fighting the guilt.** Help your colleague to remember that having both a family and a job is okay and that both require *attention* but not always *perfection*.

✔ **Nurturing oneself.** Explore the possibility of your colleague setting aside time each day for an activity that he enjoys.

✔ **Setting aside one night each week for recreation.** Help your colleague to discover enjoyable activities that he can do with others.

✔ **Protecting days off.** Encourage your colleague to schedule some of his routine chores on workdays so that his days off are more relaxing.

✔ **Getting enough sleep.** Help your colleague understand that nothing is so stressful and potentially dangerous as working when sleep-deprived. Productivity is affected and mistakes can be costly.

✔ **Bolster your support system.** Encourage your colleague to develop a close working relationship with at least one co-worker to talk with during times of stress.

Chapters 16 and 17 have a cornucopia of ideas you can use to help people become more confident and successful in these areas.

Chapter 12

Getting the Best Out of Your Teams

In This Chapter

▶ Mining the qualities of the team

▶ Accentuating the positive

▶ Building the strengths

▶ Minimising the weaknesses

*I*n some organisations, improving team effectiveness is often dealt with by providing an annual Team Building Awayday. The day is spent on an activity – cooking together, climbing ropes, building bridges, pretending to be spies and so on – that allegedly makes the team more effective. While these activities may be fun, often not a great deal of thought is given to just what and how much change has been achieved and how sustainable any benefits are. Awaydays and other team training have their advantages, but Performance Coaching offers *daily* opportunities to raise levels of performance and commitment in individuals and the team as a whole.

In this chapter, we consider how to best apply Performance Coaching to teams. We outline the ways in which Performance Coaching can greatly enhance team effectiveness and productivity, and how to increase a team's strengths and reduce its weaknesses.

Delving Deeper into Teamwork

The word 'team' is used fairly indiscriminately for any disparate group of people who happen to be working together on a common project. We were once introduced by a Managing Director to her team of 39 people at one of their regular and strikingly ineffective meetings. Her team found that actually functioning as a team was impossible, and the MD was able to simply impose her decisions on everyone in the way she always had. Total restructuring of the organisation was an essential first step before we could work on this team's performance.

Team working means ensuring that everyone's ideas, talents, and contributions are considered and when working with a group of 39 people this becomes a mammoth exercise. Too many people were in the mix and no structure was in place to decide what ideas were good, which needed reformulating, and which needed to be dumped.

The team works!

Although most people generally assume that teams are a good thing, in certain instances they can actually be destructive. Members of some positively toxic teams out there seem to work actively against each other. Perhaps more insidious but less obviously dangerous is the team where group consensus has become so ingrained that truly appalling decisions can be made without team members even noticing. Just because a group agree doesn't mean the decision is the right one – group consensus can come about because people are too afraid to disagree or because simply going with the flow can be easier than really thinking through the decisions to be made.

So, what distinguishes a real team from a random group of colleagues who sit near each other and attend the same meetings? Here are the basics of a real team:

- **Small group of people:** Keeping the group small may seem obvious: small teams are more effective than large teams because communication tends to be tighter and relationships more developed. On the other hand, with each addition to the team you get a wider range of skills. Teams consisting of between five and ten people seem to work best.

- **Agreed joint purpose:** Perceptions are shared and people are clear that the purpose of the team is fully congruent with the aims of the organisation.

- **Clear, defined goals:** Teams can pull apart if consensus isn't clear regarding which goals the team are pursuing.

- **Requisite complementary skills:** These skills vary according to the purpose of the team, whether the team is permanent or coming together for a specific project.

- **Knowledge of and respect for each other's strengths:** Even where people have worked together for a period of time, they need to sustain their recognition and understanding of each other's skills.

- **Constructive way of working together:** A good team works well together to maximise the team's output. This means listening to each other's suggestions, sharing information, taking time between meetings to reflect, researching information when necessary, and deciding on common aims.

Coaching individual team members

In a team functioning below par, you often find at the root of the problem:

- ✔ Lack of respect for members of the team and their contributions.

- ✔ Low confidence – people fear being wrong and therefore don't say what they feel.

- ✔ Poor communication between members of the team, especially when explaining their points and asking for feedback.

- ✔ Destructive competition, where, rather than working together, individuals believe that they have to have their ideas accepted at all costs, whether or not the idea is a good one.

Group dynamics are fascinating and determine the efficiency of the group in performing as a real team. When things aren't going well, people become defensive. They're unlikely to feel comfortable being honest with their peers. On the other hand, they may use such an opportunity as licence to go for the jugular and let rip in an extremely destructive fashion. The team or group leader needs to ensure that everyone has an opportunity to express opinions.

With a dysfunctional team, start by coaching each member of the team individually. Doing so gives each person the opportunity to speak with no holds barred about their grievances and resentments. By giving people the opportunity to have their point of view listened to respectfully, acknowledged, and incorporated into team coaching, you:

- ✔ Allow your colleagues to relax a bit and trust you to ensure that their issues will be addressed.

- ✔ Reduce their need to resort to difficult and challenging behaviour to make them feel they've been heard.

- ✔ Are able to help each individual to develop her own Personal Development Plan with regards to the group. This is where each member of the group works out what she needs to do to develop the skills required to be an effective team member.

- ✔ Can coach them in behaving constructively and confidently within the group.

Only after providing individual coaching can you move on to coaching in a group format with any hope of achieving positive and constructive outcomes.

Starting to team coach

Before you start to team coach, ensure you consider all the practicalities such as arranging a meeting room or off-site location, how many sessions you need, and how long the sessions need to be. If you're the team manager, you need to consider your role and how team members may respond to you. For example, will team members clam up because you're their manager? If this is the case, we suggest you ask all team members for their opinions to counteract this.

Certain factors contribute to the success of any team. Table 12-1 shows the key attributes of successful teams and the questions and focus for coaching, although specific teams may need different emphasis on each of the components.

Table 12-1	Coaching for a Great Team		
Key Attributes	*Questions to Consider*	*Issues*	*Performance Coaching (PC) Focus*
Engagement	How involved is everyone? Does everyone seem to be as focused and committed as each other? Do you hear from everyone in the group?	Differences in personal style, a sense of belonging, and excitement about the challenges can leave some people cold while others are truly engaged.	Increase understanding and respect for different styles by pointing out how these different styles add value and how the team can learn from these. Explore different ways of encouraging each team member to contribute. Think about each member of the team and what she can contribute to the subject matter. Ensure you draw that person out by asking questions you know she can answer about the topics in question.

Key Attributes	Questions to Consider	Issues	Performance Coaching (PC) Focus
Directness	Are all opinions aired? Do people hold back because of the risk of conflict? Do team members fear retribution from others?	Look out for a lack of trust, fear of the consequences of conflict, or lack of assertiveness.	Draw people out when you can see they're holding back. Work specifically on developing trust within the team by ensuring that each person is validated for their contribution. You can, for example, ask other team members what they believe the strengths of an individual team member are. Coach people in expressing their dissent without aggression. Build the confidence of less assertive people by asking their opinion and validating it.
Focus	Are goals and values truly shared by each eam member? Is the team moving forward together with purpose?	Divisions can lead to unhelpful competition between team members and waste time.	Ensure that the basic goals and values of the team and the company are aired and shared by all. Build support even in the face of some disagreement. Explore and dissolve any cliques that have formed by asking different people to work together.

(continued)

Table 12-1 *(continued)*

Key Attributes	Questions to Consider	Issues	Performance Coaching (PC) Focus
Flexibility	How open is the team to change and new circumstances? How welcoming and absorbing is the team to new members? Does the team constantly review how it needs to change in order to meet new goals?	Rigidity and an attitude of 'we've never done it that way before' can seriously limit the team's adaptability to constantly changing circumstances.	Encourage the team to take stock of changing demands. Coach the team to question how things are done, not only attending to *what* gets done. Help people get to know each other quickly and positively by asking individuals to share their achievements during the past 12 months.
Ownership	Does everyone share responsibility for the results of the team? Do different people step into leadership roles at different times?	In a truly confident team, people take charge and assume responsibility by making sure that they speak up when they've something to say and support other team members.	Developing leadership abilities Reviewing the sense of power in the team

Now that you have a general overview of the team, you need to make decisions about priorities of focus by assessing key areas of team working.

In Table 12-2, rate the team on each of the issues with 1 being poor and 5 being excellent. Assess them again after the Performance Coaching process so that you can see where improvements have been made. When you have this information you can make a decision about how to share it with the team. For example, you can discuss the findings at the next team meeting or send out a breakdown of the information via e-mail.

Table 12-2	Team Performance				
Team Performance	*1*	*2*	*3*	*4*	*5*
Clear objectives					
Good decision-making processes					
Agreed guidelines about team behaviour					
Trust, co-operation, and support					
Constructive conflict – people have the confidence to dissent					
Clear roles, responsibilities, and leadership					
Sound relationships with other groups					

Identifying Strengths and Weaknesses in Team Roles

When teams are operating at their very best, they benefit the business in a number of ways. The best teams:

- Enhance performance
- Achieve goals
- Engage people
- Develop quickly
- Co-operate effectively
- Are responsive, flexible, and adaptable

When you're Performance Coaching teams, ensure that:

- ✔ Individuals have insight into and confidence in their own strengths.
- ✔ The team recognises and respects the different talents that others bring to the group.
- ✔ The three attributes of flourishing teams are in place:
    - Positivity
    - A questioning style
    - Openness to outside ideas
- ✔ You as coach and all team members become skilled in handling difference, difficulty, and communication within the team.

Your goal, as a Performance Coach, is to turn a randomly collected group of people into an effective team by maximising strengths and minimising weaknesses. If you know each person well already, you may have an idea of everyone's strengths and weaknesses but you may find it worthwhile to assess both personal and team strengths. Assessing team strengths is useful for:

- ✔ Equipping individuals to improve their self-knowledge
- ✔ Comparing individual preferences with actual team demands
- ✔ Enabling the team to recognise and respect the strengths in the group
- ✔ Considering how they can best work together
- ✔ Checking for any gaps in the strength of the team

Using Belbin Team Roles

The Belbin Team Roles method is one of the best-known instruments for assessing teams. During a research period of nine years, Dr Meredith Belbin studied the behaviour of managers worldwide in a set of complex team circumstances. Using a range of tests, she identified nine clusters of behaviour that she called *team roles*. Belbin defines a team role as 'a tendency to behave, contribute, and interrelate with others in a particular way'. Each role has defined strengths and a few 'allowable' weaknesses.

When assessed, most people have a number of preferred roles that they use in different situations. Few people only have one. Take a look at the Belbin Team Types in Table 12-3 and see if you can recognise any of these team roles.

Table 12-3	**Belbin Team Types**		
Belbin Team Role	*Contribution*	*Strengths*	*Weaknesses*
Plant (the person who comes up with ideas)	Solves difficult problems	Creative, imaginative, unorthodox	Ignores the details, ineffective communicator, preoccupied
Resource investigator	Makes contacts and explores opportunities	Extrovert, enthusiastic, communicative	Over-optimistic, loses interest after initial enthusiasm
Co-ordinator	Clarifies goals, makes decisions, delegates	Mature, confident, makes a good chairperson	Manipulative, offloads personal work
Shaper	Drives to overcome obstacles	Challenging, dynamic, thrives on pressure	Offends people, easily provoked
Monitor evaluator	Makes accurate assessments, sees all options	Serious, strategic, discerning	Low drive, unlikely to inspire others
Team worker	Builds connections without conflict	Co-operative, mild, perceptive, diplomatic	Indecisive under pressure
Implementer	Turns concepts into action	Disciplined, reliable, conservative, efficient	Inflexible, slow to respond
Completer finisher	Delivers high quality on time	Painstaking attention to detail, conscientious	Worries too much, poor delegator
Specialist	Provides special knowledge and skills	Single-minded, self-starting, dedicated	Solely technical focus, narrow contribution

Do you recognise yourself in any of these team roles? Understanding your own preferences is useful and it also helps team members to recognise others' strengths and how they feel about them. One team member may be a high 'completer finisher' but you perceive her as boring and nit-picking. You may be a creative 'plant' and as a result your behaviour irritates the life out of your average 'monitor evaluator'. Team respect starts by understanding difference and its relevance to the task in hand.

Coach your colleagues to think for a moment about the people they have difficulty dealing with. Ask:

- ✔ What qualities in another person do you find difficult to handle?
- ✔ Why?
- ✔ Do you have those attributes as well?
- ✔ Are you completely different to the other person?
- ✔ Can you see the other person's talents being useful sometimes?

So, what are you good at?

Knowing your preferred team role is useful but remember that the roles reflect a snapshot in time. With development, application, or effort, role preferences can and may have to change according to demands of life or work. Also, at times you may have no choice but to play a certain role – most often because no one else in the team has taken that role. Don't use your test results as an excuse to be rigid in your team!

Make name cards with each team member's preferred team roles on them. In meetings, the team can refer to these cards when discussing issues or deciding actions. You can make a chart of team roles so people can check the best person to go to for help or so they can remind themselves not to expect particular strengths in certain of their team mates. By using these name cards or charts in a number of meetings, you help team members to understand the concept of playing to strengths rather than expecting the same behaviour from everyone.

Here are a few Performance Coaching questions you can use with the team:

- ✔ What are your main team strengths?
- ✔ Where are your weaker areas?
- ✔ Who in the company has these weaker areas as their strengths?
- ✔ How can you use their strengths to add to yours?
- ✔ What type of behaviour tends to irritate you?
- ✔ How can you make use of these irritating behaviours to produce a better outcome?
- ✔ How's the balance in the team?

Sometimes people jump to the conclusion that you need one of each team role to make the perfect team. That's neat but bears no resemblance to the reality of teamwork. Decide what talents, skills, and roles the team needs according to the purpose and goals of that particular team. Assess who's best placed to ensure success by playing their role well for each goal.

The following classification in Table 12-4 may help assess whose roles are be best suited to accomplish whatever the team needs to do:

Table 12-4	Team Roles	
Action-oriented roles	*People-oriented roles*	*Cerebral roles*
Shaper	Co-ordinator	Plant
Implementer	Team worker	Monitor evaluator
Completer finisher	Resource investigator	Specialist

Get people working out each other's strengths and good ways of working together by asking each team member to 'make a date' with each of the other team members to do something that uses both people's particular strengths. You can have fun with this 'dating' as a team-building opportunity outside the working day or you can apply it to the working tasks at hand.

Ali was highly sociable while Bill was rather brave. They elected to try karaoke together, thereby using both their strengths. Their work version of the date was to join up to do a bit of cold calling together, because they now felt they could depend on each other's strengths to tackle a challenging situation.

What can't you do?

We talk a lot about strengths but what if the team has a gaping void right where performance needs to be? Is it appropriate or cost-effective to spend time and money shoring up weaknesses through more extensive coaching? In the short term, coaching may be essential to get the work done, or the project finished, but as Performance Coach you need to be observant about the impact the coaching has on team members. People can carry out roles in which they're not strong. However, you need to consider the long-term consequences of people in a team not being suited to the role they're in:

✔ How long is the individual or the team required to perform in this way?

✔ What effect does doing a job she's not suited to have on her and the team's motivation?

EXAMPLE

The sales team that couldn't . . . but did

We were asked to work with a team of lawyers who weren't developing the business successfully. Most of them couldn't even say the word 'sell' without looking as if they'd drunk vinegar. They were experts, specialists, cerebral types. Sales people, they thought, were outgoing, sociable, and made connections with many people, so selling simply wasn't for them. However, they needed to bring in new business, so something had to be done. The lawyers needed coaching to enable them to carry out roles with which they weren't initially comfortable.

Coaching took the form of:

✔ Encouraging the lawyers to use their 'completer finisher' skills to keep closer track of actual and potential clients on a database

✔ Building teamwork by coaching them in 'plant' behaviour – creativity and problem solving – which they used to consider how to find new clients.

✔ Coaching in 'resource investigator' roles and skills to ensure that they expanded their network of potential new clients and felt comfortable and skilled in a range of networking settings.

At no point did they change from being lawyers into double-glazing salespeople, but quietly, in their own 'specialist' style, they successfully built the business.

✔ How does the rest of the team regard her?

✔ What reward is there for working in this way?

✔ What extra coaching does she need to be able to carry out her job more successfully?

Minimising Team Weaknesses

By encouraging strengths, you're already minimising the possible limitations of the team. By encouraging openness, participation, understanding, respect, and the pursuit of clear goals, you're well on the way to success. An important tool to wield with discretion when you're identifying weaknesses in the team is your role as an objective observer. Standing back and analysing the way that the team is working means that you're a source of invaluable feedback about what the team achieves and the means by which they achieve it. Be sensitive as to whether this feedback is best given to the group or to individuals requiring personalised attention in order to minimise disruption to the functioning of the team.

Table 12-5 shows examples of the trickiest team members to deal with.

Table 12-5	Dealing with Difficult Team Behaviour	
Team Member	*Behaviour*	*Coaching Strategies*
The Mega-neg	When you say, 'Is the cup half empty or half full?', she says, 'What cup?' She sees the downside of any new idea and deflates enthusiasm in the team.	Ask your colleague to consider the upside if ideas worked, and if she's ever experienced a situation where she thought something wouldn't work but it did.
The Silent One	She's physically present but never takes part beyond offering one-word answers to direct questions. You have no idea what she thinks, or even sometimes what she does . . . or why she comes to work at all.	Ask your colleague open questions such as 'what do you think about these ideas?', and 'How would you tackle this issue?' Make a point of asking your colleague to comment on the ideas mentioned.
The Stress Carrier	She seems to enjoy fanning the flames, getting everyone panicking at worst-case scenarios.	You may need to ask your colleague what her rationale is for her fears and then discuss these with her and perhaps the group.
The Devil's Advocate	Just when you're getting somewhere and resolution is in sight, she starts challenging all over again.	Be assertive and explain that decisions have been made, and recap the basis for the decision.
The Talker	You just cannot shut her up. You can see people losing the will to live but the Talker just keeps going.	Remind the group that they don't have endless time and while you'd love to talk more, you have to limit the amount of discussion on any individual topic.
The Big Bully	The Bully isn't an obvious thug. She just knows everyone's weak point and strikes to rob confidence and make people falter.	You can discuss the ways in which people interact and ask that the group only make positive statements.

(continued)

Table 12-5 *(continued)*

Team Member	Behaviour	Coaching Strategies
The Pleaser	She agrees with every new idea even if it's diametrically opposed to the last one she liked. She gets away with murder because everyone knows her intentions are good.	Ask each person in the group to decide what course of action is best, and give a rationale for this. Doing this forces your colleague into having to decide on and defend a position.
The Angry One	She has simmering resentments from the past that threaten to erupt all the time. She loses patience about the smallest things and regularly takes offence.	Depending on how verbal and disruptive your colleague is, you may need to have a quiet word with her during a coffee or lunch break. Point out her behaviour and how it's affecting the group. Offer to discuss her feelings with her.

Labelling the *person* as difficult is easy, but we're actually referring to difficult *behaviours*. No one is a difficult person – but some people have difficult ways! This realisation makes a difference to the way you feel about the individual and to the way you handle her.

Some highly motivated people put a lot of energy into the task but have simply got the wrong idea about how best to go about it. As a result they get little reward for their efforts, and so they act in even more challenging ways.

As Performance Coach, you need to help your colleague see the impact of her ways but also look for ways to help her get what she wants at work.

Useful questions to ask yourself are:

✔ **What does this person do?**

- She interrupts others.
- She goes back to things you thought were settled.
- She doesn't listen to others' points of view.

✔ **What does this person want?**

- To be heard.
- To win the point.
- To have her own way.

✔ **What can you do?**

- Try to see beyond the difficult behaviour to the needs that are motivating the team member, and work out which needs you can fulfil.

Ensuring Effective Communication

So, you know what everyone's strengths and weaknesses are. The team recognises that each member has different strengths and has respect for individual talent. But is the team working well together yet? This section covers what else good teams need.

Being clever isn't good enough!

You can have the smartest people gathered together and yet not achieve your goals. What else does it take to create high-performing teams?

Research by psychologist Dr Marcial Losada in 1999 analysed all communication within 60 teams. She found clear distinctions between high-, medium-, and low-performing teams on several scales, as shown in Table 12-6.

Table 12-6	Team Communication Styles
Attribute	**_Action_**
Positive and negative points made by individuals	For every negative point made, flourishing, high-performing teams made 2.9 positive points (2.9:1 ratio). This ratio clearly distinguished them from the poorer-performing groups.
Inquiry versus advocacy	High-performing groups tended to use questions to draw people out (inquiry) rather than telling them what to do (advocacy) – a coaching approach.
Self-interest versus interest in others	The most successful groups didn't isolate themselves but welcomed and were open to contributions from outside the team.

The implications for Performance Coaching are clear. Build positive styles of communication, encourage a coaching style of communication between the group members, and develop an openness and confidence to seek external ideas and contributions. The positive emotions engendered by this style of behaviour clearly distinguish flourishing from languishing teams.

Seeing the blind spots in communication

When you first start to drive a car, you find out where the blind spot is. You can never overlook the blind spot or you're be in trouble.

A psychological term that rolls off the tongue is *reticular activation,* which means that seeing one thing can make seeing the other impossible. Where are the blind spots in the team? Whose blind spots are they? What blind spots do you have yourself? Teams have to be aware that consensus can become such that you all see the same thing – even when it's not there. Tunnel vision – ignoring all contradictory data and doing as you have done before – can be dangerous. Teams need to have a safe environment in which to have discussion, argument, and disagreement in a grown-up fashion without team members becoming either scared or overbearing.

Coaching Teams: A Case Study

As a Performance Coach you need to constantly broaden your range and develop a repertoire of techniques to use with the team at different times. This section describes one intervention where we, as coaches, operated in a variety of ways.

We were called in to work with the board of directors of a medium-sized consultancy. The company had been doing well, but had started to flounder. To the naked eye, you would have sworn that the main purpose of the team was to destroy the company as quickly as possible while making everyone's life a misery. The two original founders, Fred and Angela, acted like an unhappily married couple – overly familiar and openly disdainful. Angela would brush threads off Fred's jacket while she was attempting to make a serious point. Fred would hide in his office sulking when Angela was having an emotional outburst. Every now and then, they would argue in the middle of the open-plan office. The rest of the team acted like disturbed children – seeking attention and avoiding responsibility.

Where to start? We began with the following strategies:

✔ **Get them alone.** One-to-one coaching interventions were essential to find out where each individual stood in this situation and to give them the chance to take control of their future performance. Coaching sessions – which all focused on the future goals of the company – were essential for setting the scene before joint sessions were conceivable. We could see a lot of goodwill for each of the founders, but a great deal of distress about what had been happening. No one felt they were actually part of a team. Each person felt alone, unappreciated, and undervalued.

✔ **Start with the positive.** We analysed the strengths that each individual brought to the team and presented them to each person in the initial group coaching session. The strengths were celebrated. We invited everyone to comment positively on their own and others' strengths. Other factors emerged in the discussion, such as the fact that those people who were most in conflict seemed to have strengths in common. They recognised that they'd been competing for positive attention which was in short supply. We also concentrated on how they could work together to combine their strengths.

✔ **Build a code of conduct.** We asked the team to discuss and agree a code of conduct that reflected how they wanted to be treated. Each point was examined and discussed. The team produced the final code of conduct and each person pledged not only to abide by the code but also to respectfully draw it to the attention of others if people deviated from or broke the code. Inevitable slip-ups were to be treated as such, rather than interpreted as deliberate and malicious attempts to pervert the group, as they'd previously been regarded.

✔ **Don't wimp out on the tough stuff.** As Performance Coaches, we couldn't gloss over the bad stuff and had to have the tough conversation exploring what had been going wrong, why it had happened, the impact on the business, and how the future would be different. This conversation could have been a deeply humiliating process for members of the group so we ensured a lightness of touch and even a sense of humour. Most importantly, if we'd tried to *tell* them how bad they'd been, the team would have become defensive. So we helped them to review, explore, and reflect on their previous behaviour before easing them on to focus on moving the business forward.

✔ **Look from the inside out.** When people lack confidence, they tend to be pretty self-obsessed, asking questions such as 'How does this make me look?' and 'How can I reduce others' importance to make myself look good?' Resolving the personal issues in a group by discussing how feelings can get in the way of working effectively freed the members up to focus on running the business more efficiently. The team could discuss the lack of clarity and that the role definition for the two founders had contributed to their issues. They could now move on to a logical, less emotional discussion about how to restructure the roles without bruising egos.

We operated in a range of different ways at different times to guarantee effective outcomes. This flexibility requires constant process review and creativity to come at the issue from different perspectives.

Avoiding the Pitfalls

You face a number of risks when you work with a team as the Performance Coach. Look out for pitfalls. Where can you go wrong? Following are a few common missteps:

- ✔ **You're my best friend.** You just can't help it. You like some of the team members more than the others. When difficult members demonstrate annoying behaviours, you begin to feel the way they do. You may end up being sucked into letting that partiality show. The answer? Remain professional. Take time to see the situation from all points of view and regularly check yourself for bias.

- ✔ **Here! Give it to me.** Before you realise it, you're taking over, carrying out tasks that team members should be doing themselves. On odd occasions it may seem appropriate for you to contribute in this way, but is it getting out of hand? The answer? Coach the team to take the activities back.

- ✔ **Am I invisible?** You simply don't make any impact. The team continues as if you weren't there. You need to ensure that they take you seriously. The answer? See if you're being too tentative. Are you pulling your punches? Is it time for a bit of tough love?

However good your intentions, and thorough your Performance Coaching, at times you may have a difficult and intransigent team. Your role is to offer support and encouragement whenever team members find the situation particularly difficult. You can continue to coach towards team cohesiveness and excellence but also have to spend a lot of your time coaching individual team members in how to cope with the difficult behaviour to ensure that the team's goals are met.

Part IV
Troubleshooting in Performance Coaching

'This is the failed performance coach ward'

Part IV

Troubleshooting in
Performance
Coaching

In this part . . .

However skilled you become at Performance Coaching, problems can crop up and, of course, people usually account for most of the issues. You need to be able to deal confidently with a whole range of scary emotions – your own and other people's. You'll also need to be able to deal with difficult behaviour too.

In this part you also find information about how to handle organisational issues such as negativity, change, and uncertainty. And last but not least, you discover how to keep out of trouble with the law!

Chapter 13

Coping with Difficult Situations

In This Chapter

▶ Understanding anger
▶ Coping with distress
▶ Dealing with people who don't get on
▶ Blaming others
▶ Keeping it in the family . . . or not?

*I*n this chapter, we consider a range of difficult emotional situations that you may have to deal with when Performance Coaching, and we share the strategies for dealing with them. Although most people like to think that they behave in a totally reasonable and rational manner, especially at work, it's almost impossible not to experience negative emotions at some point. You need to understand these negative emotions and to consider how to make them work for your colleague within the Performance Coaching process.

People vary as to which emotions or situations they find difficult. Some people can cope easily with someone who cries but may find dealing with an angry person difficult. Another person can deal with anger but may feel extremely uncomfortable around someone who's crying. You need to be proficient in dealing with a wide range of emotional responses and this chapter can help.

Dealing with Negative Reactions

The most important negative reactions you have to manage are your own. Check your thinking, and register your feelings. Does your heart sink at times? Do you feel defensive or irritated with particular people? What aspects about them do you find difficult?

There are no difficult people – just people with difficult ways. Next time you encounter a 'difficult person', ask yourself:

- ✔ **What does this person do?** Perhaps he argues, is demanding, blames others, won't do what you suggest, or doesn't listen.

- ✔ **What does this person want?** Perhaps he wants his own way, to hear the sound of his own voice, or not to be found out.

- ✔ **Do you give him what he wants? If not, why not?** You may think, 'No, I don't like his behaviour, so why should I give him what he wants?'

Sometimes the people you find difficult may in fact want much the same things as you do. They want to be respected, listened to, and praised. When you don't give them any of this because you happen not to like the way they go about things, you often lose some good leverage in coaching. Give people respect, and you have the chance to point out gently the effect their behaviour has on you and probably others.

And, breathe: Keeping calm in a crisis

During coaching, you also come across the negative reactions of others. However well you set up the initial stages of Performance Coaching (establishing rapport, building on the initial relationship, fostering partnership), emotions are likely to intervene at some point. This is inevitable when you deal with human beings!

Take time to think about which negative reactions would give you most trouble – anger, helplessness, superiority. Catch any thoughts that indicate a belief such as:

- ✔ That's an appalling way to behave
- ✔ There's no need to feel/behave that way
- ✔ People shouldn't react like that

These beliefs interfere and limit your professionalism. The following sections in this chapter explain more helpful behaviour.

Fanning the flames or putting out fires?

Table 13-1 shows a range of negative reactions and the constructive – and unconstructive – ways of dealing with them.

Table 13-1		Dealing with Negative Behaviour	
Negative Behaviour	*Your Colleague's Reaction*	*Your Petrol-on-Flames Response*	*Your Performance Coaching Response*
Resentment	Why am I being singled out for this? I have to do everything as it is!	What makes you think you're better than anyone else?	It sounds like this feels like an additional burden on you right now. What would help?
Anger	Who said that about me? I want to know their names. What gives you the right to do this?	Wouldn't you like to know? That's just typical of your management style. You're such a bully!	You seem angry. How do you think your staff might feel? How does this reflect your working relationships?
Helplessness	I know I'm a mess, but what can I do? I've tried getting out of it.	Hmmm, yes, you have made a bit of a mess of things. I'm not sure where to start.	I get the impression that you've made many good attempts. How can we build on that to get success?
Cynicism	Yeah, yeah, so nothing ever really changes but I guess I have to jump through the hoops. I don't suppose this is going to give me any more money?	Good grief, don't you ever get fed up of being so world-weary? It's just not cool any more.	It sounds like you've had a lot of disappointments. It's hard to keep trying when you don't feel you get much back.
Superiority	You can't tell me a thing. I have more experience in my little finger than you will ever have.	I don't think you realise how much coaching work I've done. I've read books and everything!	You're absolutely right. I couldn't possibly match your experience in your area. How do you think we should approach the issue?
Panic	Oh my goodness, I'll never cope. What will they think of me? What if I forget what to say? I'll never get on then.	Stop getting yourself in a twitter – that never helped anyone. You just don't look professional.	Let's think about all the times you've coped, so we can use those techniques again. That will make sure you get on just fine.

Although initially you may feel a bit inept in handling others' strong emotions, keep having a go at turning them into something constructive. Pretending the emotions don't exist is likely to backfire.

Coping with Anger

According to a recent article in the *Sunday Times Magazine*, 45 per cent of people regularly lose their temper at work. Everyone gets angry sometimes and anger comes in many different forms, ranging from mild irritability and frustration to full-blown rage. Even the most mild-mannered of individuals can lose it if circumstances become intolerable to deal with. Some people get angry if their rules about justice and fairness are transgressed. Others are biologically predisposed towards anger. Performance Coaches themselves aren't immune from experiencing anger. However, as the Performance Coach, you need to handle such situations professionally when they occur.

What lights your fuse?

People experience anger for a number of reasons. As the Performance Coach, you need to have an understanding of why people become angry to help you help your colleague understand his situation better before moving on to developing the strategies to manage anger. Such understanding also helps you decide on the most appropriate strategies to defuse the situation.

The reasons why people experience anger are:

- **Biological predisposition or acquired behaviour.** Some evidence suggests that some people may be genetically predisposed towards anger, especially when under stress. However, it's not inevitable that people experience anger and react with aggressive behaviours as a reaction to the pressures of life.

    Anger often runs in families. No one really knows how much this fact is due to genetic influences and how much to picking up angry behaviours from family members. Even if your colleagues were born into families predisposed to expressing anger, this fact doesn't mean that they're doomed to become angry people. Much of human behaviour is picked up in this way and can be put down and new behaviours developed, which is where Performance Coaching comes in.

- **Stressful life events.** Everyone experiences stressful periods from time to time, such as bereavement, job loss, or relationship problems. Even quite positive changes such as marriage, a new job, or a house move can contribute to the stress. However, the events when your colleague feels threatened are likely to be the ones that spark off feelings of anger.

✔ **Thinking style.** People who think in certain ways are more likely to feel angry. Such thinking styles include always putting down or dismissing anything positive or maximising negative events by being overly pessimistic and dramatic. In particular, beliefs about justice and fairness or whether you see people as basically benevolent or out to get you're likely to trigger angry feelings. If your colleague's thinking style is adaptive and healthy, he may still feel worried or frustrated about things, but if he's pessimistic then anger is a more likely outcome.

✔ **Poor coping skills.** Many people have excellent coping skills and can deal efficiently with things. However, people who find coping difficult can experience feelings of anger because they don't have a sense of control over situations.

✔ **Individual personality.** Your colleague's basic personality type is likely to help or hinder his ability to deal with stress and anger. In the late 1960s, cardiologists discovered what have become known as Type A and Type B personalities and, more recently, the Hardy Personality. Type As are ambitious, competitive, hard driving, and more likely to ignore stress symptoms. Type As have a tremendous energy and drive but tend to go down rather spectacularly when they become overloaded, and can become angry. Type Bs are more laid-back and find it easier to keep matters in perspective. The Hardy Personality has all the attributes of a Type A but without the susceptibility to stress.

One of the classic symptoms of a stressed Type A is irritability and anger and even the most charismatic and normally stable Type A character can be prone to angry outbursts over the smallest of issues when he's stressed.

✔ **Lack of social support.** People with good support systems in the form of family, friends, and colleagues are far more likely to ward off the effects of crisis or trauma. The more people an individual has to talk to, the more he protects himself from the full effect of dealing with stress. A lack of a supportive network really shows itself in times of crisis. Often simply letting off a little steam can prevent the build-up of emotion that can later express itself as extreme anger or rage.

✔ **A mask for anxiety.** Anger can often mask feelings of anxiety. When you perceive a threat you respond – by fleeing or fighting. Both mechanisms are based on your sense of fear that something threatening or dangerous is about to happen. Sometimes the best way of dealing with a situation is to use the anger you feel to deal with the perceived threat. At other times the best thing you can do is run away. Angry people are simply showing their fear.

Anger ain't always awful

Anger can be an appropriate response – it gets things done. Consider how many laws have come into being or been changed because people have felt a sense of injustice or unfairness and have taken it upon themselves to bring about a change. Anger can be an appropriate emotion that individuals and society in general can benefit from. Anger is a human emotion and as such is neither good nor bad, it simply is.

Dealing with anger

At some point you, or the colleague you're coaching, is going to have to deal with angry people. Help yourself by having a few behavioural strategies so that you can be as professional and effective as possible.

On rare occasions someone may be totally out of control. If this is the case and you feel that physical violence may occur, you need to remove yourself from the situation and follow your company policy on how to deal with the threat. Your safety comes first.

The following tips are proven ways in which to defuse anger.

- ✔ **Stay calm.** If your colleague is angry, you, as the Performance Coach, need to stay calm. Take deep breaths to calm you down. The calmer you are, the more you model a sense of calmness for the other person.

- ✔ **Listen carefully to your colleague.** Use your active listening skills to hear what your colleague is saying (refer to Chapter 5 for the lowdown on active listening skills). If you can demonstrate that you've heard and understand how bad he feels, this demonstration can provide a safe space for your colleague to let off steam. Use sentences such as:

  - 'I can imagine that was really difficult for you to manage.'

  - 'I can see why you felt so unhappy when . . .'

  - 'It must be very difficult for you, coping with . . .'

- ✔ **Let your colleague finish!** You may be tempted to try to rationalise what your colleague is saying but doing so can actually fan the flames by irritating him further. If you allow him to express his frustration fully, he's likely to run out of energy and become calmer. This method is a bit like letting a train run down a hill and slow down when it's on flat land!

- ✔ **Use your empathy.** You don't have to agree with your colleague's take on the situation. You may think your colleague is wrong or overreacting. However, if you can use your empathy to imagine how he may feel and how the world looks from his perspective, this empathy can help you understand the situation better. Use sentences such as:

- 'I can imagine that many people may have felt upset when . . .'

- 'Yes, from where you're standing it must seem . . .'

- 'Sounds like you felt really put out about that . . .'

Such statements demonstrate your understanding, which is not the same as agreeing. Your aim is to calm your colleague down enough for him to think rationally. He won't listen to reason while his emotions are too strong and you'll waste your time. Wait until his emotions have calmed.

✔ **Use distraction.** When your colleague seems a little calmer, offer him something to drink or ask him to sit down if he's been pacing around. Demonstrate that you want to help and that you won't judge him.

✔ **Show that you're in this together.** Make it clear by what you say that you want to help and that you understand what your colleague is saying, and you're likely to have a productive meeting. Use sentences such as:

- 'Let's see if we can make sense of what has happened and consider how you may deal with the situation in the best way to get the outcome you'd like.'

- 'You sound extremely upset and angry and we need to find a way of you being able to express that in the best way possible.'

Handling Distress

As a Performance Coach you'll come across colleagues who are distressed by work-related matters, personal concerns, or perhaps a mixture of both. Sadness, upset, and distress are the external manifestations of someone who is finding it difficult to cope. As with anger, people may be more prone to expressing distress depending on genetic predisposition, family background, stress levels, range of coping skills, personality type, or lack of supportive relationships. Distress can range from mild upset to full-blown, heart-wrenching misery. Your colleague may come to see you in a highly distressed state or may become distressed as you talk to him about other matters. Handling distress is part of the Performance Coaching process and in this section we explore the skills to cope successfully with distress.

You as the Performance Coach bring your own emotions into every situation. Start by recognising and managing your own emotions before moving on to other peoples'.

The 'do I fetch the tissues?' moment

When someone is distressed, tears may well be part of the process. When your colleague becomes tearful, you may find it comes naturally to offer comfort. Alternatively, you may feel awkward and unsure about how to deal effectively with such emotions. Your own prejudices may also come into the picture. You may find a woman crying more acceptable, due to social norms, than a man. However, men get distressed too, so don't be judgemental. As a Performance Coach, your job is to help normalise the situation, ensure that your colleague doesn't feel embarrassed, and find ways of helping him to cope with his situation. Keep a box of tissues close to hand for those occasions.

On rare occasions, someone may be totally out of control. If this is the case and you have serious concerns for your colleague, contact your Human Resources Department for advice and guidance. You may want to take your colleague to the relevant individual in person.

The following tips are proven ways of dealing with distress.

- ✔ **Stay calm.** When someone becomes distressed you may find yourself wanting to say something comforting to stop that distress. However, if you do say something too quickly, your colleague may interpret it as disapproval. Distress is a human emotion that, like anger, normally runs its course. If you respectfully allow the person to express the emotion fully, the distress is likely to subside.

- ✔ **Normalise the situation.** Often, after your colleague has regained composure, embarrassment sets in. This embarrassment can get in the way of the Performance Coaching process. Normalise the process by expressing to your colleague that upset is a normal human reaction. By doing so, you may ease his sense of embarrassment.

- ✔ **Use your empathy.** Use your empathy and active listening skills to demonstrate to your colleague that you understand his situation. Slow down and check how your colleague is feeling at different points during your discussion.

- ✔ **Monitor body language.** Keep an eye on you colleague's body language to help you monitor how he may be feeling. You rarely need to utter the words 'How do you feel?' if you pay attention to the signals in front of you. If your colleague looks happier, he probably feels happier! (If you want to find out more about body language, check out *Body Language For Dummies* by Elizabeth Kuhnke (Wiley).)

- ✔ **Be caring.** After the coaching session, check whether your colleague feels fit and able to go back to his desk. Offer him the opportunity to take a break. If the need arises, check whether he wants to see someone in your Human Resources department.

Managing Personality Clashes

Clashes in the workplace are a lot like those you have at home. Clashes are often caused by a conflict in roles, responsibilities, and goals – not personalities. You may complain about whose job it is to put the rubbish out, but only when things get really bad do you say that someone's plain lazy.

People in the workplace are quick to point to a 'personality clash'. Sometimes colleagues dislike each other, but most of the time this label is inaccurate. Instead, look at the conflicts caused by work situations and difficult relationships between individuals.

As a Performance Coach your role is to help your colleagues find effective ways of dealing with the conflict situation they finds themselves in. Additionally, you need to understand what may be motivating the conflict and whether other issues, such as bullying, may be at the root of the problem.

Strategies for dealing with personality clashes include:

- **Think about the end result.** Help your colleague keep in mind what he seeks to get out of his interaction with a difficult person. Don't get side-tracked by unrelated issues.

- **Deal with conflicting purposes.** Every story has two sides and both parties have a different take on the situation. Help your colleague to consider both sides of the story and encourage him to explore the possible motivations and feelings that the other person may be experiencing.

- **Monitor communication.** When dealing with a difficult person, it's easy to become defensive or antagonistic. Help your colleague to develop clear communication skills in order to deal more effectively with the situation. If appropriate, suggest additional help such as attending an assertiveness training course.

- **Look for a 'win-win' outcome.** Encourage your colleague to think about what the other person is seeking. Help him devise a strategy where compromise can take place, leading to a better outcome for all concerned.

- **Deal with the real issues.** If it comes to light that your colleague may be the victim of bullying, check your organisation's harassment policy and encourage your colleague to take the appropriate action.

Avoiding 'Scapegoating'

As a Performance Coach you become privy to the information that your colleagues tell you. You may also be in a position where you have demands placed on you by the organisation. If the coaching doesn't go well, you can end up as piggy-in-the-middle; blamed by your colleague for the ills of the organisation and by the organisation for not producing the changes required in your colleague. This section looks at ways to remain professional if you become embroiled in such an unpleasant situation.

It wasn't me: Avoiding the blame

Your colleague may place all the blame for his circumstances on the organisation and see you as an organisational representative. If he thinks in this way, you may be the person who bears the brunt of your colleague's resentment, and become the scapegoat for the individual. Ask yourself:

- ✔ Did you move too fast in the early stages of coaching?
- ✔ Did you ensure that your colleague developed sufficient insight and took responsibility for his own actions and predicaments?
- ✔ Did you present him with any external data you had, such as 360-degree feedback, to support the coaching process? (Refer to Chapter 7 for more on 360-degree feedback.)
- ✔ Did you make clear your objectives in coaching and check that they made sense to your colleague? (Refer to Chapter 4 for more on objectives.)

If you're an internal coach and your manager expects to see certain changes in an individual that don't materialise, you may become the scapegoat that your manager uses for his higher-ups. Again, check the facts:

- ✔ Did you check that your manager's expectations were realistic?
- ✔ How effectively do you feel you've coached your colleague?
- ✔ Could you have taken other approaches?
- ✔ Have there been difficult circumstances of which your boss is unaware?

To avoid being a victim of 'scapegoating', always remain clear about your objectives and ensure a transparency of communication with your colleague and the organisation.

Dealing head-on with organisational issues

To ensure that you're able to stay focused on your task as a Performance Coach, you need a strategy to ensure that you protect yourself, your colleague, and the organisation.

Here are a couple of tips for dealing with organisational issues:

- ✔ **Be clear.** By adhering to the agreed objectives and outcomes of the coaching contract you ensure that everyone is clear about what is wanted and expected. In cases where your colleague or the organisation asks you to undertake any activity outside of this brief, or where their demands may sidetrack the process, you can return to the contract and deal with these requests appropriately. Chapter 4 covers the coaching contract in detail.

- ✔ **Communicate.** Always ensure that you communicate clearly with all parties. When you find yourself in doubt, clarify the situation and, if necessary, ask for time to consider the issue you're faced with so that you can consult relevant individuals (including your coaching supervisor if you have one) about the best way to proceed.

Chapter 14

Overcoming Negativity

· ·

In This Chapter

▶ Motivating people

▶ Taking a reality check

▶ Ensuring trust

▶ Coping with lack of success

· ·

*I*n this chapter we consider trickier times in Performance Coaching. The reality is that at times you won't always get it right, through your own error or because of something outside of your control. At other times, your colleague is going to experience setbacks and failures. This chapter equips you to deal with the stumbling blocks you may encounter.

Overcoming Negative Emotions with Motivation

Motivation is a key to success. As a Performance Coach, your role is to encourage your colleague to increase her level of motivation. Many of your colleagues may be highly motivated when they enter the Performance Coaching process; others won't be. Lack of motivation may be because:

✔ The current situation your colleague faces seems insurmountable.

✔ Your colleague lacks interest in the coaching process.

✔ Your colleague resents the need to make any changes at all.

If your colleague enters the Performance Coaching process with a set of negative emotions about her situation and the coaching process, you need to spend time helping to challenge this thinking. Negative views breed negative outcomes so helping your colleague to create a sense of hope for the future is important.

Performance Coaching is less effective when your colleague:

- ✔ **Does not commit to the process.** If colleagues do not commit to the Performance Coaching process, they're unlikely to gain much benefit. You can increase commitment to the process by using the motivational skills that we outline in Chapters 6 and 8.

- ✔ **Has unrealistic expectations.** If your colleague has unrealistic expectations of what you as the Performance Coach can offer, he's likely to be disappointed. Ensure that you engage in the Behavioural Contracting process (that we describe in Chapter 3) as a way of ensuring that you discuss explicit expectations.

- ✔ **Is defensive.** If your colleague is defensive either through fear or resentment, you need to talk through such feelings and deal with them to achieve a positive end result.

- ✔ **Takes a passive role.** If your colleague thinks that you do all the work and she simply has to turn up, remind her that Performance Coaching is an active process where she needs to take action.

- ✔ **Doesn't take risks.** If your colleague is unwilling to take any risks, nothing is likely to change. Behavioural change means trying to do things differently and your colleague may be fearful of what may happen. As the Performance Coach, encourage your colleague to understand that risk is a part of life and that nothing positive is likely to happen unless she takes a few risks.

Success breeds success – the more positive outcomes your colleague experiences, the more likely she is to take risks and consolidate new behaviours. Encourage people to experiment, to identify what works, and to reinforce the positive impact of such outcomes. Your colleague is likely to retain the new behaviours and, in time, use these behaviours as part of everyday living.

Reaching for the Stars: Raising Aspirations

Ambition is linked with motivation. Life without ambition becomes rather mundane, and your colleague is unlikely to achieve all that she's capable of. As a Performance Coach, your role is crucial in helping your colleague to recognise her full potential and work to achieve it.

People often underplay their abilities and appear to lack ambition even when others can clearly see their potential. As a Performance Coach, your task is to encourage your colleagues to be the best they can be by tapping into their enthusiasm. Table 14-1 shows possible reasons for a lack of ambition and coaching strategies to tackle them with.

Table 14-1	Encouraging Ambition
Reasons for Lack of Ambition	*Coaching Strategies*
Lack of confidence. Your colleague may want to do more but doesn't feel she has the confidence to do so. This lack of confidence may have come about over a lifetime or may be the result of a difficult time at work.	**Identify strengths.** Encourage your colleague to identify her strengths; speak to other people in the company about the way she's perceived. Encourage her to take risks and to try out new behaviours.
Being in the wrong job. Remaining fully engaged is hard for someone who doesn't like her work or the job has changed in such a way that it no longer plays to her strengths.	**Recognise reality.** Sometimes the best thing a Performance Coach can do is to help someone realise that she's in the wrong job. This realisation saves the organisation money, the employee heartache, and the manager the task of managing someone who doesn't want to be there.
Life events. Difficult life events, whether personal or work-related, can lead to a lack of confidence.	**Seek specialist help.** If your colleague's lack of ambition is due to difficult circumstances, you may need to seek appropriate specialist help such as counselling.

Challenging Overconfidence and Lack of Insight

Although most people tend to undervalue what they're able to do and their achievements, some people do exactly the opposite. When you have an over-confident colleague, your challenge is to help the individual gain a more realistic view of her abilities without demoralising her in the process.

Some people put on an act of bravado and appear super-confident when they actually feel very vulnerable inside. This tactic is aimed at throwing people off the scent. Colleagues may see showing their true self as far too threatening an option. Other people believe that the quality of their work and the way they behave is exemplary.

Muhammad Ali said, 'I am the greatest' and got away with it, but most people can't. Muhammad Ali was the greatest world-class boxer in his day so he was only speaking the truth. He had evidence to substantiate his claim of superiority because he'd never been beaten. However, if your colleague is making such statements, they're unlikely to be based on anything other than a subjective reality.

You need to find a way of helping your colleague change her way of thinking to a more realistic one. By enabling someone to gain a true view of her strengths, you give her the chance to gain control of situations she faces and deliver what is expected.

You can help your colleague gather information on how others perceive performance in the form of 360-degree feedback. This information is invaluable in becoming a mirror for how others perceive your colleague's abilities and behaviours. (Refer to Chapter 7 for loads more on using 360-degree feedback.)

Seeing Yourself as Others See You: The Johari Window

Another tool for encouraging colleagues to develop self-awareness and identify their strengths and weaknesses is the Johari Window. Named after the first names of its inventors, Joseph Luft and Harry Ingham, the Johari Window is a useful model of human interaction. A four-paned window, as illustrated in Figure 14-1, divides personal awareness into four different types: open, hidden, blind, and unknown. You can use the Johari Window as a way of encouraging people to consider how they behave, the motivations behind such behaviour, and to consider and what others may think of their behaviour.

	Known to self	Not known to self
Known to others	Open	Blind
Not known to others	Hidden	Unknown

Figure 14-1
The Johari window

In Figure 14-1, each person is represented by her own window.

- ✔ The *open* **public area: 'What I and others know about me.'** The knowledge that the open window represents can include not only factual information, but feelings, motives, behaviours, wants, needs, and desires. For example, a person recognises that she's fair in dealing with others, and other people have noticed this trait too.

✔ The *blind* hidden area: 'Things others know about me, but that I am unaware of.' Everyone has blind spots and this area is where others can see something about the way you are that you don't see. For example, people may see you as creative and fast thinking but you have no idea that you possess those qualities. Or people may perceive you to be aloof and you don't realise that you give off this impression at all.

✔ The *hidden* unknown area: 'Things I know about myself that others do not.' You may have a personality trait that you may not have shown to other people, either because it has never come up or because you choose to keep it hidden. As you get to know people better, you may choose to share this information through what is called *self-disclosure*. People only share personal information when they feel safe with each other. For example, you may be going through a difficult time in your personal life but have chosen not to share this information with your colleagues.

✔ The *unknown* private area: 'Things I and others don't know about me.' You may underestimate the skills you possess. You may not even recognise a natural ability. You may have developed behaviours and attitudes in childhood that you've never thought about but that influence the way you do things now. For example, you may find dealing with conflict hard due to experiencing conflict at home as a child.

Using the Johari Window can help your colleagues gain a realistic view of themselves and expand their understanding of their behaviour.

Careless Whispers: Overcoming Anxiety About Confidentiality

Trust is a key factor in the coaching process and is essential to the successful outcome of your coaching programme. If people have fears about whether the work they undertake with you may become known to others, they're likely to hold back from sharing relevant information with you. Colleagues stop trusting you if they think you're talking about your coaching work with others or are reporting the discussions you have with your manager. Internal coaches who have a role other than their coaching role often find it challenging to ensure that they're seen as unbiased and trustworthy. Imagine how your colleague would feel if she saw you, her Performance Coach, talking to her manager in a hushed manner at lunch. You may be discussing last night's television, but your colleague may feel uneasy.

You can reinforce the confidential nature of the coaching process in a number of ways:

- ✔ **Be clear.** Ensure that you start the coaching process by discussing confidentiality, what it means, and any information you cannot keep confidential, so that your colleague is clear about what confidentiality means and when you would have to break the confidentiality contract. If you have another role, such as being a manager, make a clear distinction between your roles. Chapter 4 has more information about ensuring confidentiality at the beginning of the coaching process.

- ✔ **Never talk about another colleague.** Be very careful about the examples you use when illustrating a point. If you mention another colleague, even if you don't mention that person by name, your colleague may be able to identify her. If so, your colleague may come to the logical conclusion that someone else may be able to identify her in the same way.

- ✔ **Keep your paperwork out of sight.** If you have paperwork on colleagues, ensure that you don't have it on show during your meetings. If your colleague can see paperwork associated with other colleagues, she may raise concerns. Reassure your colleague that you keep any notes or paperwork secure.

- ✔ **Check e-mail correspondence.** Always check with your colleague about whether her e-mail is read by anyone else. By doing so, you demonstrate that you take the issue of confidentiality seriously and can negotiate how to send any coaching information by e-mail.

- ✔ **Seek out concerns.** Ask your colleague if she has any concerns about confidentiality and address these directly.

Overcoming Setbacks

Everyone has setbacks and this is as true for you as for your colleague. Coaching isn't an exact science, and factors outside of your control may get in the way of the coaching programme. Recognise that setbacks are a fact of life, carefully review what happened, and consider what you can gain from the experience for the benefit of future work with colleagues.

Your colleague may experience setbacks, despite working hard, doing everything right, and wholeheartedly engaging in the Performance Coaching process. Such setbacks are demoralising and, as the Performance Coach, your job is to help your colleague view the situation realistically and help her deal with it. The setback may be due to unforeseen circumstances, or brought about by your colleague's mistakes.

When your colleague makes an error, remind her of the saying, 'There's no such thing as failure, only feedback.' Whether something goes well or badly, you can benefit from the situation and apply what you've gained to future experiences.

Strategies for dealing with setbacks

You can apply a number of strategies when someone experiences a setback.

- ✔ **Use your empathy.** Colleagues benefit from being given the space to explore the feelings associated with the setback they've experienced. By showing that you appreciate how difficult the situation is for the person, you're strengthening the rapport you have with her and providing emotional support. Your active listening skills are essential (refer to Chapter 5 for more on active listening).

- ✔ **Analyse what went wrong.** Help your colleague take the situation apart and consider who did what, what was missed, who was involved, and how much responsibility belongs to your colleague and how much to other people and/or circumstances.

- ✔ **Ask what she'd do next time.** Help your colleague to consider what, if in fact there was anything, she'd do differently next time. As the Performance Coach, you can normalise the fact that mistakes happen and that many successful people have made errors of judgement yet have still gone on to become successful. The key to success is knowing how to benefit from experiences for the future.

- ✔ **Look out for negative thinking.** Most people engage in negative thinking during times of stress. You have the opportunity to use the situation your colleague faces to unearth such negative thinking. By identifying negative thoughts such as, 'I failed, so why bother', 'They won't want me', 'I tried once and it didn't work so no point doing it again' and illustrating how such thinking makes matters worse rather than better, you can help your colleague become stress-proof in the future.

- ✔ **Keep things in proportion.** Viewing a setback or failure realistically can be hard sometimes. As a Performance Coach, you can help people to keep their views proportionate to the situation. For example, ask your colleague if she's ever had a setback before and, if so, what feelings she experiences about it now? The passage of time changes the way people feel. Your colleague is unlikely to feel as upset or aggrieved as she did at the time. She may even say that although the situation was difficult at the time, it actually helped her improve in the long run. You can then draw a parallel between the historical situation and how she's likely to view the current situation in a year or so's time.

- ✔ **Take action.** Despite the setback, all may not be lost. You can help your colleague to consider whether she can take steps to correct the situations that have arisen.

Getting back on the horse

Getting back to normal as quickly as possible following a setback is important. The sooner you can return to normal, the sooner you can move on.

When you experience a setback in the Performance Coaching process, you can do a number of things to ensure that you review the situation and discover whether the setback was due to an error in the coaching process, an external situation, or perhaps both.

Collecting all the information you can

Ensure that you gain as much information as possible from all parties about what happened, the circumstances, and any significant aspects of the situation. This information helps you to decide how much of what happened was down to you and problems in the Performance Coaching process and how much may be down to circumstances outside of your control.

Table 14-2 shows an analysis that led to the apportioning of responsibility when a Performance Coaching situation didn't go too well.

Table 14-2	Analysing Setbacks
Situation	I feel bad about the coaching I was doing with Ronnie because it just seems to have fizzled out.
What did you try to do?	I tried to ring but never got a response. I e-mailed as well but he never replied.
What part do you think you played in the situation?	I hadn't really pinned him down to when and how regularly we were going to meet.
What part do you think other people played?	Well, I guess Ronnie didn't get in touch. I know now that his boss sent him away at short notice to work on a project.
What part do you think the circumstances played?	Employees of the company are under a lot of pressure to perform, especially at this time of year.

Coaching hadn't been made an important enough priority in the firm.

Ask yourself the questions in Table 14-1. Now make a pie chart illustrating where the responsibility really lies. A number of factors usually contribute to the situation.

It happens to us all

Yes, really, setbacks happen to everyone and that means *you* as much as it does your colleague. When Performance Coaching goes wrong, you can't do much more than review the situation and take stock from it for the future. Some reasons that account for a setback are out of your control. For example, your colleague may have had a hidden agenda that you couldn't have known about. Circumstances may have changed. Reviewing setbacks isn't about apportioning blame but about acknowledging what contributed to the problem so that you don't repeat mistakes in the future, or affirming confidence in the approaches you've used.

Figure 14-2 shows the responsibility pie of Ronnie's situation. What is clear is that although each of the players has responsibility, the circumstances need addressing first when attempting to remedy the situation.

Figure 14-2: The Responsibility Pie

As well as asking yourself questions about where the responsibility lies, other things you can do include:

✔ **Talking to your colleague.** Review your work with your colleague and try to find out what may have gone wrong during Performance Coaching. Very often talking openly with your colleague can improve the situation because you colleague sees that you're genuinely interested in her situation. In the above example about Ronnie, after you track Ronnie down, you may find that he was feeling too embarrassed to contact you because he felt he'd let you down by disappearing.

✔ **Reviewing your notes.** Go back over your notes, e-mails, and any other documentation you may have and analyse them to see if you spot anything that you might have done differently. For example, did Ronnie give any clues that he may be under too much pressure to commit to coaching?

✔ **Talking to your coaching supervisor, if you have one.** Talk to someone outside the situation who understands the coaching process and the work that you've been doing. A supervisor can help by providing new insights into the situation. For example, she may be able to help you see the situation from Ronnie's, the boss's, and even the business point of view.

✔ **Using your coaching skills on yourself!** In the same way that you help your colleague come to terms with setbacks by using your coaching skills, so you can apply these skills to yourself and the situation you face. If you'd encourage your colleague to accept a situation and gain from it, the same process applies to you. Try brainstorming all the positive steps you can take to investigate or put it right.

Getting back to normal – whatever that may be!

The example of Ronnie may seem quite trivial but many a good Performance Coach beats herself up about similar cases if left to her own devices. You need to be professional in handling setbacks. The steps are the same whether you're facing a trivial or a serious problem.

Think about whether you need any extra support while you recover from the setback. Ensure that your confidence is back in place and that your enjoyment of Performance Coaching isn't irrevocably damaged by the one that got away! The setback may be unfortunate, but isn't the end of the world.

Chapter 15

Managing Organisational Problems

In This Chapter:

▶ Talking sense

▶ Being firm in uncertainty

▶ Keeping the best

▶ Staying out of trouble

*C*ertain issues have a major impact on the effectiveness, productivity, and success of organisations. Companies often say that 'people are our most valued asset'. If so, considering employees' needs and designing and investing in appropriate personal development ought to lead to substantial business advantage. Performance Coaching, while pleasurable and beneficial for the individual undergoing it, must form part of a larger business process. In this chapter we look at several common organisational problems that can benefit from effective Performance Coaching.

Improving Communication

Communication is a major issue in all organisations. Some places can even show you charts of how communication should work. Often, however, reality presents a very different picture. This is usually down to the lack of skill of the people who are meant to be communicating well.

It is jumping the gun a bit to suggest improving communication if you haven't first taken stock of how good it is already. Can you assess communication in your organisation, division, department, or team? If this is the point at which you produce an organisation chart to demonstrate the effective flow of information, be wary. No matter how good the systems are that require people to communicate, they can't compensate if the level of communication skills in the organisation is unsophisticated.

Where a lack of communication or faulty communication exists you usually see a range of behavioural problems at both the individual and the group level. These problems impact on performance, productivity, and staff retention. The organisation becomes dysfunctional. Table 15-1 shows a few examples of the impact of ineffective communication on the organisation.

Table 15-1	Ineffective Communication Styles
Aggressive Communication	**Passive Communication**
People spend time during group discussion on retaliation.	Few people contribute to discussions.
Mistakes are used to punish people.	Group members work in isolation, not as a group.
Unhealthy competition arises between members of staff.	Employees don't share common problems.
People are reduced to playing psychological games and *politicking*. (Putting more effort into manipulating people and circumstances than into getting the work done.)	No progress review or attention is given to how the group is working.
A high level of aggressive behaviour.	A high level of passivity, leaving leader to make decisions.

Auditing communication

If you decide that the company's communication is in pretty dire straits and you resolve to audit communication, some of the questions to consider are:

Who should communicate?   Who does communicate?

What should be communicated?   What is communicated?

How should it be communicated?   How is it communicated?

Look out for any discrepancies between the left- and the right-hand columns. Here are a few areas to consider when checking for communication excellence.

The following questions are useful in Performance Coaching when your goal is to increase excellent communication at work. Check how effective your colleague is in these areas:

✔ **Who should communicate?**

- Colleagues
- Direct reports
- Team members
- Customers
- Shareholders
- Suppliers
- The media
- Consultants
- Government agencies

✔ **What should be communicated?**

- Mission statements
- Vision and values
- New products
- Business goals
- The nature of crises
- Change
- Different roles of individuals and departments
- Good news and bad news
- Terrific performances

✔ **How should it be communicated?**

- Face-to-face
- One-to-one or in groups
- Through coaching
- In writing
- On the intranet
- At the annual conference

Notice how the rumour mill works in your organisation. Are new messages clearly cascaded down from the top in a timely and controlled fashion? Or do you get your insight from the receptionist, who got it from the Director's assistant in the ladies' room? Chatting to the staff at reception is always interesting. Check whether they know what the core business is, and the values or mission statement. Receptionists make first contact with the outside client or customer. Has good communication ensured that they are truly in the loop and are giving the impression or message that your company wants to put across?

Wake up and smell the coffee: A story about communication

We were working for a stylish consultancy. Their offices were gorgeous and their brand showed in everything they did. Visiting them was always a pleasure because there was a fantastic coffee bar in the vestibule. One day when we turned up, the people we were seeing were concerned. When we explored this in a coaching session, we were told: 'Today we came in and the coffee was truly terrible. Cheap catering stuff – just not us at all. So that must mean we're in dire straits – if we can't afford the good coffee, the company must be on its last legs and they're just not telling us. We need to dust off our CVs!'

Following a question from us about other possible explanations, one of the employees made enquiries. It turned out that the wrong order had been delivered, and the caterers thought they'd try the new coffee while they waited for the correct replacement order.

One of the fabulous things about people is their capacity to interpret situations creatively. Don't leave communication to chance or assume you know what other people are thinking. They always surprise you!

Coaching for communication

Communication is a skill that people can develop. This is really good news for you as Performance Coach, because you have a critical role in raising the standard of communication throughout the organisation – both the amount and the level of sophistication of the communication. Armed with information from your audit, you're equipped to focus your Performance Coaching interventions and raise the professionalism of the communication.

Employees feel more highly motivated when they truly understand:

- ✔ The mission of the organisation – the purpose, values, behaviours, and strategies
- ✔ The purpose of the organisation (why it exists)
- ✔ The products and their special features
- ✔ What jobs other colleagues do
- ✔ Their place in the grand scheme of things

Each of these topics contributes to the individual's sense of engagement, commitment, and belonging to the organisation. Performance Coaching makes sure that the individual's own development is in line with the needs, values, and goals of the organisation. This ensures your colleague has the interests of the business at heart.

Critical areas of communication to explore when Performance Coaching include:

- ✔ **Understanding:** How good are your colleagues at listening and understanding the data they receive?

- ✔ **Establishing common ground:** How good are they at building bridges between people?

- ✔ **Perception:** How good are they at assessing and managing the perceptions of other colleagues? Can they see things from another's point of view?

- ✔ **Awareness:** How good are your colleagues at noticing all the nuances of communication going on around them?

- ✔ **Confidence:** How confident are they in their communication skills?

- ✔ **Clarity:** How good are your colleagues at communicating information in a clear and concise form?

- ✔ **Managing conflict:** How good are your colleagues at understanding issues and managing disruptive emotions?

- ✔ **Motivation:** How good are they at stirring enthusiasm and commitment?

- ✔ **Inspiration:** How good are they at convincing and enthusing people, imparting their vision for their product or service, and telling stories?

- ✔ **Equality:** How good are they at handling diversity and difference?

- ✔ **Problem solving:** How good are your colleagues at using a range of creative problem-solving techniques with their people?

Coaching an Uncertain Organisation

Strangely enough, people aren't that bad at coping with difficulty and adversity. What really breaks the human spirit is uncertainty. Uncertainty in a company during times of change can lead to higher levels of anxiety and a range of unproductive behaviours. People find it hard to wholeheartedly support change when they're unsure of what it entails and, more specifically, what their part in it all is meant to be. Uncertainty can be especially rife and pernicious when an overload of new initiatives compound the issues. On the upside, uncertainty can be exciting, giving the hope of new and interesting situations.

Communication plays a vital part in managing uncertainty. Timing is also critical. How do you decide when to communicate that times of change are on the way? Too soon, and people have a long time of uncertainty. Too late, and the rumour mill causes uncertainty anyway. People are creative – given uncertainty, they construct their own version of certainty, however deluded. The pessimists see an Armageddon scenario while the optimists have a vision of a Utopian future. Neither reflects the truth or helps to align people's actions to the needs of the business. It falls upon managers to lead effectively through the uncertain times. The company needs to construct some level of certainty in the midst of complex uncertainty and ambiguity.

Dealing with uncertainty

Coach your colleagues in the following ways to enable them to deal with uncertainty more constructively:

- **Credibility:** People tolerate more uncertainty if they have confidence in you and their leaders and colleagues.

- **Commitment:** If people are committed to and proud of the team, the organisation, and its goals and values, they maintain their trust in the company.

- **Communication:** Regular updates reassure people, even if the information changes dramatically from time to time.

- **Consideration:** People need to know that they are being considered and that you're cognisant of the impact on them of the uncertainty.

- **Clarity:** You need to make clear what specific behaviour is necessary to achieve the overall strategy.

- **Coaching:** You need to coach your colleagues at every stage so that people have certainty, if only for that moment. Help them to see opportunity and excitement rather than threat and fear.

The competencies required here include solid, day-to-day reliable behaviour, giving reassurance in a miasma of uncertainty. Many managers withdraw when they don't have clear, positive news or facts to give. This is not a good method. Instead, you need to engage with people, sharing their emotions, hopes, and anxieties. However, don't overlook yourself. Where does your sense of certainty come from? What makes you feel secure in this uncertain time? Most likely, a deep confidence in your strengths and your value to the organisation, and the resilience and belief necessary to move on in times of change are essential for coping with your own uncertainty, before trying to maintain others' confidence.

Here are some of the behaviours that can help people to weather the difficult uncertain times and feel a certain sense of purpose. This sense of purpose, in turn, is likely to enable you to keep good people. When using Performance Coaching in uncertain times, work on the following:

✔ Construct a desired vision of the future.

✔ Gain support and overcome resistance.

✔ Use the picture of the desired future to keep moving forward.

✔ Make a plan that's not too detailed and specific, because it needs to change as events unfold.

✔ Explore ways of understanding and managing uncertainty.

✔ Be clear about what is fact and what is conjecture.

The optimists aren't always wrong. Sensitively handled, a time of uncertainty can lead to a refreshed and revitalised organisation with the flexibility to do well in these changing times. (Refer to Chapter 9 for loads more about managing change.)

It's good to talk

It's good to talk but it is sometimes even better to listen!

Effective businesses need excellence in communication. High levels of professional communication equate with a sophisticated organisation. Here are some of the applications for improved communication that you can use when you're Performance Coaching:

✔ **Consultation:** This is where you really ask people for their input and act on it – (not where you ask for their input and say, 'Fine, but here's one I prepared earlier'!)

✔ **Education:** Make sure that everyone knows what they need to know to be confident of their role in difficult or changing times. They may not have seen these circumstances before.

✔ **Inspiration:** Knowing the facts about the change is quite different to feeling excited and eager about tackling change. Painting pictures of the future helps people to identify their place in it.

✔ **Confrontation:** Dissent, resistance, or bad behaviour must be dealt with quickly. You need to be ready to have the difficult conversation that can get things back on track fast.

Performance Coaching has a specific role to play in bringing excellence to these areas of communication and ensuring that organisational problems are overcome.

Preventing the Loss of Good People

People tend to know their own worth. If they don't feel valued or if they get the wrong message from the company, they'll leave. You cannot afford to overlook any loss of key personnel. Keeping your key employees has a major impact on your business success. Doing so ensures:

- **Customer satisfaction.** Continuity of service is disrupted by a high turnover of personnel.

- **Settled colleagues.** Familiarity allows people to get on and do the job rather than continually having to adjust to new people.

- **Effective succession planning.** Keeping people gives you the opportunity to spot talent, nurture it, and prepare people to step up to the next role at exactly the right time.

- **Retention of organisational knowledge.** Getting up to speed takes quite a long time. During that time, people accumulate a great deal of information about the organisation – some formal, and much informal (such as how to make that dodgy photocopier work without calling out an engineer). If you lose people, you lose a lot of knowledge.

Here are some of the basic mistakes that can cost you key people:

- Lack of clarity about your expectations of them and their expectations for the future

- No clear discussion about earning potential

- Little feedback about performance

- Failure to hold scheduled meetings such as appraisal, feedback, and development discussions

- No framework within which people see how they can succeed

Saying goodbye to great employees is expensive and disruptive to maintaining the business of the organisation. It costs the company in terms of:

- Loss of productivity

- Expense of external recruitment and training as opposed to home-grown succession

- Lost knowledge and organisational continuity

- Delays in getting up to speed

- Lower morale in the organisation

All for one and one for all?

We had a client who wanted all the directors and senior managers to be coached at the same time. We felt that the CEO and the directors needed to go through some development themselves before we worked with the senior managers, because the directors would then be equipped to mentor and coach their direct reports. The CEO wouldn't have it and so we started them all at once.

What we feared happening, did in fact happen. The senior managers all turned up for their coaching and leapt at the chance of focused development. The directors were travelling the world, missing coaching sessions and falling behind. The directors started to become threatened and defensive just as the senior managers became energised and demanding. A sort of 'whack a mole' game ensued. Every time a newly confident senior manager showed initiative, some of the directors would smack him back into place. At first the managers were irrepressible and kept bouncing back with new ideas but they couldn't sustain this in the face of the repression. Coaching had made the senior managers positive, confident of their abilities, and eager to perform to their best abilities. If this company wouldn't allow them to shine, they'd be out, knowing another company would have them.

The situation came to a head when one of the directors cancelled a senior manager's appraisal for the third time, not realising how well she had prepared for what she thought was an important meeting about her excellent performance and future career in the company. She resigned that day. Others, appalled by her treatment, started to think about leaving too. We had to have some emergency coaching sessions with the directors to get them to see the impact they were having and to prevent the company from disintegrating.

Here are our tried and tested suggestions for reducing or preventing loss:

- ✔ Get the right person in the right job, a job matched to his strengths, to ensure high satisfaction. Review regularly to ensure that job satisfaction remains high.

- ✔ Demonstrate interest in helping people shape the career they really want. Prevent them assuming they're going to have to leave to get something better.

- ✔ Respect colleagues' feedback and ideas about where they aspire to be. Help them to achieve their goals through Performance Coaching. (Have a look at Chapter 7 to find out more about effective goal setting.)

- ✔ Ensure that your colleagues receive regular feedback and recognition for their achievements. (Chapter 6 explains the value of feedback.)

- ✔ Strive to help them to find ways to make work enjoyable.

✔ Consult with people about decisions that are going to change their working lives.

✔ Encourage people to work at the right work-life balance at each stage of their career.

✔ Make sure that people have clear knowledge of what is expected of them.

✔ Celebrate success.

✔ Encourage colleagues to keep looking for opportunities for career progression and coach them so that they're ready for the next move.

✔ Encourage good, supportive relationships within teams and between individuals at work. (Chapter 12 has more on getting the best out of teams.)

If you can be instrumental in providing all this, your only problem is that people may never want to leave!

Coaching used to be seen as remedial and so the worst performers received all the attention. With the recognition of the need to manage talent effectively, this is rarely the case nowadays. Rather than leaving the stars to fend for themselves in an, 'it ain't broke, don't fix it' fashion, the focus is on finding ways of retaining the best talent. You're likely to achieve terrific returns when you Performance Coach these high performers. A small investment of time at carefully judged intervals can ensure that all is well, motivation is high, any issues are dealt with immediately, and the individual's career goes from strength to strength. Resist the temptation to leave high performers to their own devices, assuming they'll maintain results in a vacuum while you concentrate on the more recalcitrant members of staff. (Refer to Chapter 8 for more about talent management.)

Avoiding Litigation

Workplace litigation covers any lawsuit brought against an employer by an employee who claims that his legal rights have been violated. By the time someone is suing, you can guarantee that problems are ingrained and that communication broke down a long time ago. Involving the lawyers is usually a last resort in an incredibly difficult situation.

This section isn't just about keeping out of trouble but rather ensuring professionalism so that the reasons for dissent are dealt with efficiently, professionally, and effectively.

Beating bullying

Bullying involves threatening, offensive, or insulting behaviour – both overt and covert. Discrimination on the grounds of sex, religion, disability, age, or race counts as *harassment*. Issues may be ignorance, lack of awareness, lack of skill, or bad habits. Bullying and harassment must be detected and dealt with fast before harm is done.

Mercer Human Resource Consulting conducted a survey from which they estimated that 1.5 million workers experienced some form of bullying in 2006. We often think of the victims of this sort of behaviour as those with the least power to defend themselves, but senior managers and directors are also affected: six directors in ten admit to experiencing bullying.

The impact of this behaviour is wider than the suffering of the individual victim, affecting the overall performance of the organisation.

No specific legislation currently exists in the UK regarding victims of work-place bullying. However firms who do not protect individuals' rights not to be bullied can face huge claims for compensation at tribunals.

Bullying and harassment are serious workplace issues that affect mental and physical health. Symptoms include:

- Loss of confidence in abilities and judgement
- Withdrawal from friends and colleagues
- Fearfulness, insomnia, and physical symptoms such as inability to concentrate or make decisions, and memory loss
- Severe depression and work-related suicide

The Chartered Management Institute has highlighted poor management as the most significant factor in bullying at work, particularly in the areas of emotion management and communication. Research shows that bullies bully because they see it as fun, fast, and effective. This perception must be changed.

Use Performance Coaching to ensure that all staff, especially managers and supervisors, are aware of the consequences of their behaviour and that development is aimed at implementing and upholding policies that empha-sise respect and professional behaviour at all times.

In bullying or harassment situations, the first steps are:

- ✔ Understand what really happened
- ✔ Check how the incident was perceived
- ✔ Determine what the impact really was
- ✔ Decide on future behaviours and actions

These steps are actually the same whether you're dealing with the victim or the culprit.

Coaching to justice

Here are a few case studies of bullying to contemplate. Performance Coaching can retrieve and resolve each of these situations in which someone may easily sue if they feel they weren't getting justice.

Peter the unconfident bully: Peter had worked his way up through the organisation to become Operations Director in charge of all customer services and sales. The new role was daunting and his confidence took a further nosedive when one of his direct reports accused him of bullying, by making a formal complaint. Peter was appalled. He prided himself on his ability to get along with people, and now he doubted that as well.

During coaching, we realised that Peter had no real understanding of the talents that had contributed to his success. We spent some time drawing up a list of the attributes and actions Peter had taken to get where he was until he admitted to himself that he did have what it took to do a good job, including good people skills. When Peter reviewed the bullying incident, he realised that because he'd been feeling so anxious and tense about his own role, he'd been shorter and more abrupt than he normally would be. He worked on understanding what this had meant to the individual in question and reviewed his

options for making the relationship right. He admitted to his colleague that he'd handled the situation wrongly and looked at developing a positive and mutually supportive future working relationship.

Pauline the unconscious bully: Pauline was the Company Secretary of a large organisation. She was meticulous and exacting in her standards. She worked hard and rarely saw the need to speak directly to her team, e-mailing them instead. It was a shock when one of the younger women reported her to the Human Resources department for her bullying behaviour. As evidence, the young woman had printed off a huge pile of brusque, demanding e-mails. She asserted that Pauline didn't treat her team like human beings, gave them no respect, and didn't even say, 'Good morning'. HR suggested some Performance Coaching.

Coaching commenced with a review of the impact of Pauline's behaviour and an analysis of her values. How had her values developed? How did the values make her behave? What values did other people have? Pauline had no idea that other people didn't automatically share her values. It dawned on her that she thought she had the right to expect high standards of her team but that she had done nothing to inspire them to share her values, hopes, and expectations. Pauline, with the help of Performance Coaching, embarked on communicating with the team and raising performance through a collaborative process rather than resorting to abrupt e-mails.

Phil the easily bored bully: Phil was a bit of a star, but was intellectually arrogant and had no time for people not able to hold their own with him, reducing some people to tears. His performance and results were excellent, so the company had turned a blind eye but now, with alarm, they realised he was beginning to treat clients the same way, so they suggested Performance Coaching.

We realised that Phil enjoyed behaving in this bullying way. He knew that people became distressed but he felt that he was doing them a service. This was no industry for wimps. Instead of appealing to his better nature, we encouraged him to reflect on the trouble he was getting into and the possible negative impact of this on his brilliant career, and to find a better, more fun way of dealing with people. Once he understood that no one was going to try to make him soft and cuddly with people – just smarter and more effective – he was quite happy to review and change his ways.

Your Performance Coaching can then focus on developing more sophisticated skills in:

- ✔ Managing conflict
- ✔ Communication
- ✔ Emotional intelligence
- ✔ Giving difficult feedback
- ✔ Conflict management and negotiation
- ✔ Constructive use of power, politics, and influence
- ✔ Supporting people through change
- ✔ Developing a culture of openness and trust where opportunities for bullying are minimised

Counting the cost of stress

Stress in the workplace is of grave concern and litigation claims are increasing fast. A number of high-profile awards have been paid out recently, which is alarming for employers and can be attractive to unhappy and stressed employees – especially with the increase in 'no win, no fee' legal arrangements.

The Health and Safety at Work Act 1974 sets out the basic obligations for employers to assess and manage risk to employees. Employers have a duty under the Act to ensure, so far as is reasonably practicable, that their workplaces are safe and healthy. Under the Management of Health and Safety Regulations of 1993, employers are obliged to assess the nature and scale of risks to health in their workplace and base their control measures on these risks. Measures such as the Working Time Regulations have been introduced with the aim of reducing the incidence of stress.

Employers have a legal duty to take reasonable care to ensure that employees' health is not placed at risk through excessive and sustained levels of stress arising from the way the workplace is organised, the way people deal with each other at their workplace, or the day-to-day demands placed on them. All employers have a duty to look after the health and safety of their employees.

In the first instance, the role of the Performance Coach is to work with colleagues to ensure that they cope constructively with any pressure they may experience. Areas you can consider are:

- **How much pressure is the person under?** If the pressure is unreasonable, coaching may focus on how he approaches a discussion with his manager. If the pressure doesn't seem unreasonable, coaching might focus on the way he's dealing with the situation.

- **What are his coping strategies?** Most people have a range of coping strategies they've gradually adopted, but not all of them work as well as people like to think. For example, is your colleague avoiding difficult situations, taking time off, drinking loads of coffee, or having one too many drinks of an evening? These are telltale indicators of ineffective ways of coping. You can coach in ways to cope more effectively.

- **What support does he need?** For some people, simply being able to admit to feeling stressed does a lot to reduce the pressure. As Performance Coach, you may have to focus just on supporting a colleague by listening and empathising for a while, rather than helping to find any clear solutions to the problems.

- **What facilities might be useful?** Employers often provide a range of services from a well-equipped gym to a work-sponsored counselling service.

As a result of some of these interventions, Performance Coaches are instrumental in reducing the risk of poor performance or litigation.

Stress is an expense that organisations just cannot afford. The main costs are through:

- Loss of productivity through poor attendance records – one study estimated that 60 per cent of all absences are caused by work-induced stress

- Underperformance

- 12.8 million working days lost in the UK due to work-related stress.

- Bad press, which besmirches the company's reputation

Employers need to bear stress in mind when assessing possible health hazards in their workplace, watching for developing problems, and being prepared to act if harm seems likely. Employers need to know their legal obligations and to take active steps to prevent claims. Stress needs to be treated like any other work-related hazard.

Part V
The Part of Tens

'All right! — Don't listen to me, your performance coach! — Just go ahead with your silly sling and stones instead of a sensible sword and see what happens to you!'

In this part . . .

Here's your chance to digest some simple yet powerful steps leading to excellence. Have a set of resources at your fingertips. Sort out every part of your life through self–coaching. Welcome to the Part of Tens . . .

Chapter 16

Ten Steps to Performance Excellence

In This Chapter

▶ Developing communication strategies

▶ Devising management strategies

▶ Continuing Professional Development

*P*erformance Coaching is about improving and maintaining peak performance. As a Performance Coach, you encourage your colleagues to excel at whatever they do. Excelling is about:

✔ Developing the right mindset

✔ Being prepared to work hard

✔ Knowing where you want to go

✔ Planning how to get there

As a Performance Coach, you have responsibility for offering the help, encouragement, and support your colleague needs to achieve performance excellence. Here's a selection of the very best ways of doing that.

Strive to Achieve Interdependence

Interdependence means the ability to work with others. It's a sign of someone who understands the advantages of working with others, as well as those of working alone.

✔ *Dependence* means relying on others to take care of you. Some people, depend on the organisation, their manager, or superiors to take care of their needs.

✔ *Independence* means making your own decisions and taking care of your-self and working towards developing your own personality and abilities. Some people focus so much on what they're doing that they forget about the bigger picture and that they need to consider other people too.

✔ *Interdependence* means co-operating with others to achieve something that you can't achieve alone. It focuses on achieving the best outcomes by everyone striving to attain a common goal using their individual tal-ents. When you're acting interdependently you not only recognise and use your unique abilities, but also consider the needs of others and the overall aims and objectives.

As a Performance Coach, you can help embed the appropriate skills and strategies required to consolidate the stage of interdependence. People who operate within this model are more likely to prove useful to the organisation and to their colleagues, and to get the job done effectively.

Ensure Good Communication Channels

People often complain that they do not receive enough communication and information about what is happening in the company. Reactive individuals wait for others to pass on the information.

Proactive people seek out the information needed to work at peak perfor-mance. As a Performance Coach, you can encourage your colleague to make the most of formal and informal communication channels:

✔ **Formal Channels**

- **Weekly Meetings.** Encourage your colleague to arrange a weekly meeting with her manager, using this time to ask questions about the department, the business, and any other aspect that may affect her work. Even a regular 10-minute check-in is better than nothing at all.

- **Intranet.** Your organisation's Intranet facilities can keep your col-league up to date on company business.

- **Internal Meetings.** Your colleague can capitalise on the minutes or notes of any regular meetings held even if she's not part of the group.

✔ **Informal Channels**

- **Social Events.** Urge your colleague to find opportunities to unwind with colleagues to make communication flow more easily. Social events provide an avenue for catching up on news and views as well as building relationships.

- **Lunch.** Your colleague can arrange catch-ups with individual colleagues over lunch or a drink after work from time to time.

Good communication channels also require the individual to become skilled at listening to and understanding others. Learning to listen and understand before trying to be understood can enhance communication, limit frustration and confrontation, and create a more effective team working environment.

Work Co-operatively

Working with others ensures success. In any interaction with another person, encourage your colleague to start with a positive attitude and to respond constructively to the other person. If the other person is negative, encourage your colleague to attempt to break the negativity by starting the communication again and by remaining positive, even though the initial response may not have been encouraging. If people continue to act negatively, you may need to encourage your colleague to find ways of dealing with this. However, positive actions tend to lead to positive outcomes. People who engage in co-operative working often find that they are the best networked and most well informed, because others are more willing to share information with them.

You can coach to increase the chances of working co-operatively if:

- Your colleague shows an interest in what others are doing even if this is not directly associated with her own direct area of responsibility.
- Your colleague has something to gain by working with the other person in the future
- Your colleague has something to lose if she does not work together with the other person
- Your organisation encourages a supportive culture

Remind your colleague that you decrease your chances of working co-operatively if you are:

- Envious of other people's achievements
- Protective of your expertise
- Defensive or aggressive

Improve Your Credibility

Encourage your colleague to admit to failure. Doing so is a way of modelling a key component of lifelong learning. Being honest about your own performance gives you an opportunity for development. Many successful people make mistakes – the important thing is how people use these experiences when they occur.

People may feel uncomfortable when they don't know the answer to a question. If this is the case with your colleague, encourage her to admit it. Her peers are more likely to develop a trust in her competency if she's prepared to be open and honest.

One way to model such useful behaviour to your colleague is to demonstrate your ability to deal with situations when *you* don't have the answer. Admit you don't know. Offer to find the answer or information required and provide this at the next coaching session.

Notice Other People's Achievements

People sometimes focus more on impressing others than on acknowledging the achievements of others. Individuals who recognise the achievements of others are far more successful than those who don't, because other people are more likely to seek out the views of someone who's helpful and supportive. This leads to better working relationships and help is more likely to be forthcoming when you colleague needs it.

Encourage your colleague to use every opportunity to acknowledge the achievements of others by:

- Telling the person
- Telling others what you liked about what the person achieved
- Sending an e-mail to the person concerned
- Sending an e-mail to a group that you and the person concerned belong to

When giving praise, remind your colleague to:

- Be clear and precise in what she says
- Say why she thinks her colleague's achievement is worthy of praise

Focus on Outcome

Key performers tend to think in terms of outcomes rather than problems. An outcome is the answer to the questions: *what do we want to happen* and *what do we need to do to make it happen?*

People who think about the problems of taking on a task often become bogged down in what could go wrong. In contrast, people who think about the outcome – what is wanted and how to get it – are more likely to get more of what is wanted, more of the time.

Questions you can get your colleague to ask of herself are:

- What do you want to achieve?
- How will you know you've achieved it? What will you see, hear, and feel to know you've achieved your outcome?
- Imagine you're at some time in the future. What will you have gained by achieving this outcome?
- What resources do you need to achieve this outcome?
- What is the first step you need to take to achieve this outcome?

Refer to Chapter 3 for heaps more about setting goals.

Delegate to Stretch Yourself

Hanging on to the tasks that you can readily complete without too much effort or concern is easy. But people who excel are those who delegate the easy work while taking on work that proves more of a challenge. Delegation provides the opportunity for others to grow but also for people to stretch themselves by taking on more difficult tasks that use their strengths more fully.

In order to delegate really effectively, coach your colleague to have a structure for both handing over the work in the first place and for then monitoring the delegated task without undermining the enthusiasm or ability of the person given the task.

The ten stages to effective delegation are:

1. Identify and define the task – what needs to be done?
2. Select the right person or group of people to delegate to.

3. Check on the individual's ability and provide training if necessary.

4. Explain why the task is being delegated.

5. Be clear about the results you require.

6. Check on the resources required to complete the task(s).

7. Be clear about the delivery and deadline date.

8. Ensure you supply the required support and inform all those who need to know that someone else is undertaking the exercise.

9. Provide feedback on the outcome.

10. Praise the person for her work – a simple 'thank you' goes a long way. However, by taking this a step further and saying what went well and what the person might have done differently, encourages the person when it comes to further work, and provides any relevant information for future skill development.

Let Others Have a Say

As a Performance Coach you come across colleagues who believe that they're only being effective, and will only be seen as effective, when they are the ones doing all the talking. They may perceive other people's opinions as questioning their own ability, which can feel like a threat. However, because people are unlikely to want to listen before they feel they've been heard, your colleague needs to allow others to have their say. This allows the other person to both let off steam and to share concerns.

People who perform to their optimum know that it is worth investing the time and energy in allowing others to express their opinions and to treat these opinions as valid even if they are views that they personally disagree with.

Encourage your colleague to develop the skills of active listening. If your colleague finds holding back difficult, advise her to take a deep breath and count to ten before answering. Doing so ensures that she gives the other person the opportunity to have a say.

Encourage your colleague to:

1. Actively listen to what is being said.

2. Ask questions such as, 'Tell me a little more about what you mean?' and 'I wonder if you could explain your concerns more fully to me'.

3. Develop ways of answering concerns positively by using statements such as, 'I can understand why you might hold those concerns', and 'I can see that this could be confusing'.

4. Provide non-defensive answers such as, 'I can understand why you may have some worries about what I'm proposing. However, while I appreciate these, I believe that if we don't take action now we may be storing up problems for the future.'

Develop Your Influence

Influence is a leadership skill of affecting others through no apparent force or demands – people follow because they believe in you and your abilities. If you have a reputation for getting things done and show that you're consistent, results-driven, and professional, others are influenced by you and, in turn, you influence the world around you.

Influence is also about changing *things*, such as working conditions or deadlines. Coach your colleague to be proactive by focusing her efforts on what she can influence, and has control over, not on what she can't influence.

Proactive people work on changing what they can control and that also means aspects of themselves. By being positive and taking control, colleagues come to recognise how they can influence both other people and their own circumstances.

Get Things Done

Coach your colleague to show people she can perform on the job – not by talking about doing, but by doing. Competency is demonstrated by the outcomes achieved. With a winning attitude, your colleague will strive to improve and invest in herself, others, and the company.

You can help your colleague become more proactive by encouraging her to:

✔ Focus on results and outcome and not on the clock. Deadlines are important and have to be met. However, if you focus on encouraging your colleague to consider the best outcome possible, this is more likely to ensure that the organisation gets the best result and that your colleague can use all of her skills, including her creativity.

✔ Proactive people don't blame others for what goes wrong, they analyse the situation, identify what hasn't worked and why, and then devise another way of dealing with the situation. They discuss errors in a way that encourages understanding and learning, keeps the other person on side, and motivates the individual to do better in the future.

✔ Creating opportunities is one of the hallmarks of a proactive person. Coach your colleague to constantly be on the lookout for new opportunities, ways of developing existing ways of doing things, or new products and systems.

✔ Creativity is one of the attributes of a proactive person. Encourage your colleague to keep notes and perhaps keep a journal to scribble down ideas.

✔ Proactive people know the people they admire and why. They align themselves to these individuals. Coach your colleague to learn from those who have achieved what your colleague wants to achieve. Your colleague can identify people at work whom she admires, read books and articles, and watch documentaries on individuals in the public eye that have the professional qualities that she seeks to develop.

✔ Success means hard work but it also means ensuring that an individual stays healthy emotionally and physically. Help your colleague put into place a work-life balance that allows for hard work but also ensures that she remains happy and well.

Chapter 17

Ten Steps to Coaching Yourself

In This Chapter
▶ Improving your confidence
▶ Becoming more assertive
▶ Getting the most from life

*A*s a Performance Coach, you'll find yourself helping your colleagues with a variety of issues, from the purely professional to the personal. We suggest that you gather around you as many useful resources, books, CDs, information sheets, and self-help materials as possible so that you can use them in your work with your colleagues, or can use them as reminders to yourself whenever you feel you need to do a bit of self-coaching.

Improve Your Confidence

Confidence is an area that you often come across as a Performance Coach, and it's useful to have a range of ideas relating to this to support your work with your colleagues. The following five self-help tips can support the work you're undertaking.

+ Professionalism

- ✔ **Stop discounting yourself!** Recognise your personal qualities and give yourself credit for what you do. Avoid saying things like 'that doesn't count', 'other people could do it better', and 'anyone could have done it'. Instead, congratulate yourself the way you would your best friend.

- ✔ **Appreciate life.** Get yourself a journal and, at the end of each day, write down three things that you're pleased about and why you're pleased. For example, 'I liked the way I spoke to my colleague – I felt so much better about being able to be firm without losing it.' Improving your ability to feel gratitude also increases your confidence.

- ✔ **Look good and feel good.** Changing the way you look can give your confidence a boost. Get a makeover – you don't have to spend a fortune. Find a charity shop in a good residential area and you can find designer clothes and other good-quality items for next to nothing. Find out where your local hairdressing and beauty training schools are, as they need models and charge very little. A personal shopper can make all the difference – other people can see the potential in you that you cannot see in yourself.

✔ **Think about what you need from life.** Think about yourself and your needs – meeting everyone else's needs and forgetting your own is all too easy. Learn to say 'No'. When you find yourself saying, 'I can't', say 'What's the worst that can happen?' instead.

Stand back, take a good look at your life, and make some decisions about those areas that are working and those that are not. Take control and begin to change the things that aren't working for you. Read *Confidence Works: Learn to be Your own Life Coach*, by Gladeana McMahon (Sheldon Press) to find a completely new way of looking at yourself.

✔ **Act 'as if'.** Confident people take risks, so make your risks work for you. If you act *as if* you're confident then you're more likely to become confident. If you're going to a networking event, think of the most confident person you know and ask yourself how he behaves. What does he say, do, and wear? This technique is called modelling and successful people do it without even realising they do. People are attracted to those who smile and are approachable. Try acting *as if you are this type of person*, and you'll be surprised at how many contacts you make, and how much better you feel about yourself.

Create a Positive Lifestyle

If people are to function well in the workplace, they need to consider ways in which to achieve a positive lifestyle at work and at home. The following tips outline ways in which your colleague (and you!) can do this.

✔ **Let go.** How much time and emotional energy do you waste wishing things or people in your life were different? What has happened cannot be undone so why compound it by wasting energy on it? Okay, you would have preferred things to be different, but going over the same ground in your head depletes you and stops you from benefiting from a positive way of being. When you want to challenge your thinking and let go, take a deep breath and say, 'I would have liked things to be different but if I keep on thinking this way I'll make things worse and not better'. This type of thinking style is more likely to help you move on.

✔ **Put things right.** When something goes wrong, think about why it went wrong (so you can avoid the same situation in the future) and then do something about it. If you said something better left unsaid or forgot to do something you should have done, acknowledge the situation and act in a positive way. Say sorry – it won't kill you. Explain what happened and put it right if you can. People who develop a positive lifestyle know that making a mistake is not a problem – what makes the difference is knowing how to deal with it and move on.

✔ **Stop putting yourself down.** When you put yourself down you decrease your ability to live in a positive way. Look people in the eye, smile, hold your body upright and say 'thank you' when someone compliments you. If you catch yourself putting yourself down – stop. Instead of saying, 'I'm useless', 'I can't', or 'typical of me to get it wrong' say, 'I found that hard' or 'I guess it will take a bit more practice'.

✔ **Just because you think something, doesn't mean it's true.** Thoughts are funny things that can play tricks on your unsuspecting mind, making you act in ways that do you no good whatsoever. Imagine you see someone you know in reception. You smile and wave but get no response. What is your immediate thought – 'Oh, he didn't see me' or 'what have I done wrong?' You have a choice. You can tell yourself something negative and make yourself feel bad or you can change the way you think into something that makes you feel better about yourself, other people, and the world. What evidence do you have to suggest you did something wrong? Where's the sense in thinking the worst?

Manage Your Money

You and your colleagues are likely to experience financial difficulties at times. Financial difficulties may require specialist financial help. However, sometimes such financial difficulties are short-term and only require some minor adjustments. The following tips deal with just this type of situation.

✔ **Track your spending.** Track your spending habits for one month. Make a note of every single penny you spend. This will provide you with typical information about where your money is being spent. Many people are surprised at just how much money they spend on all sorts of non-essential items, such as drinks or takeaways. Tracking your spending allows you to make decisions about whether you wish to continue spending at the same rate on the same things.

✔ **Set yourself a proper budget.** Having tracked your spending you need to set yourself a realistic budget. A budget helps to give you precise control over what you have to pay, how much you can save, and how much you can spend. Budgets can set you free. The key to successful budgeting is to be realistic – otherwise you won't stick to your budget. For example, if you try to save too much and don't leave yourself enough weekly spending money for fun activities, you're likely to take money out of your savings, which is self-defeating. To help you with your budgeting you can download a useful budget planner from the National Debtline at www.nationaldebtline.co.uk.

✔ **Set up a series of savings accounts.** Rather than set yourself up one savings account, set up a series of accounts to cover all the items you want to save for, such as a holiday, clothes, or Christmas. Set up a standing order to each so that the money is taken directly from your account on a monthly basis. This way you not only get interest on the money you save but also know how much money you have for each item you're saving for.

✔ **Beware of impulse spending.** Before you spend anything, ask yourself, 'Do I really *need* this item, or do I just *want* it?' You may find that many of the items you purchased were bought on impulse. Window shopping costs nothing and if you don't trust yourself to keep to this plan, then only take a small amount of money with you and leave your purse or wallet in a safe place. If you do see a real bargain you can always go back for your money.

✔ **Lower credit card balances.** Use your credit cards sensibly – use only one and choose the one that gives you the best deal in terms of monthly interest payments. Pay off your credit card at the end of each month so that you don't incur interest payments. The savings that you can make on major items such as fridges and cookers when sales are on can be too good to miss and a credit card purchase can be an excellent way to benefit from just such a deal. Work out the saving you can make on the item and set this against the interest payment on the card – that way you know how much you've really saved. If you cannot trust yourself to use your credit card wisely, allow a family member or trusted friend to look after it.

Get Creative

People often produce their best results when they feel creative, because creativity increases enthusiasm. These tips provide ways of rekindling creativity.

✔ **Take time to reflect.** Creativity is unlikely to happen if you're rushing around preoccupied with the usual daily activities. Block out time on both a daily and weekly basis simply to reflect on life. Use your existing 'dead' time (such as when travelling by train – not by car!) to develop the art of daydreaming and allow the thoughts that are out of conscious awareness to surface.

✔ **Listen to music.** Various types of music, especially classical music and in particular Mozart, have an effect on increasing creativity and thinking ability. Listen to music during your reflective time. MP3 players now make it possible to listen to music while travelling and you can be exposed to the benefits of music throughout the day.

✔ **Generate ideas.** The more ideas you can generate, the more likely your chances of finding something that works. Carry a journal around with you to note down ideas and thoughts.

Float into Relaxation

Switching off can be a challenge for many people and if you or your colleague is experiencing a stressful time at work, making time for relaxation is very helpful.

You can use relaxation any time, anywhere, and in any situation in order to restore a sense of self-control, even if only momentary. Relaxation helps by releasing and relieving tension, promoting sleep, enhancing your natural coping skills, and promoting clear and logical thinking.

Here are a few exercises – be careful if you suffer from breathing difficulties or have high blood pressure.

Breathing:

1. Breathe in deeply through your nose for the count of four.
2. Breathe out through your mouth for the count of five. As you breathe out, consciously relax your shoulders and stomach muscles.
3. Repeat the steps three or four times.

Five-Minute Tension-Release:

1. Sitting in a chair, breathe in and press your feet hard into the floor. As you breathe out, relax.
2. Breathe in and lift your feet up until only your heels are on the floor. Feel the tension in your calves. Breathe out and lower your feet to the floor.
3. As you breathe in, squeeze your knees and thighs together. As you breathe out, relax your knees and thighs.
4. Breathe in, squeeze your buttocks together, and pull your stomach in. As you breathe out, allow your buttocks and stomach to relax.
5. As you breathe in, clench your hands into fists and press your arms into your sides. As you breathe out, release your fingers and turn your palms up, resting them on your legs.
6. Breathe in and turn your head to your left. Breathe out and return your head to the centre. Repeat the exercise, this time turning your head to the right.
7. Breathe in, clench your teeth, and screw your eyes up tightly. As you breathe out, relax your face. You're now all relaxed!

Using Imagery:

1. Make yourself comfortable and close your eyes.

2. Imagine yourself in a beautiful walled garden at the time of the year you like the most. Walk around and enjoy being there.

3. Notice a wooden door in one of the walls and make your way over to it. Open the door to find yourself in your own very safe, personal place, where you feel at peace with yourself.

4. Enjoy being there either on your own or with anyone you choose to be with.

5. When you're ready, make your way back to the door, knowing this place is always there for you anytime you need it.

6. Close the door firmly and make your way back into the garden.

7. When you're ready, open your eyes.

Deal with Criticism Assertively

As a Performance Coach, you often face situations where you or your colleague may find dealing with receiving criticism difficult. The following tips provide strategies for dealing with criticism.

- ✔ **Be clear.** Be clear about what the criticism is about. This may mean asking for examples of the behaviour being commented on: 'You say I am unreliable. It would be helpful if you could give me some examples of those situations where you believe I acted that way?'

- ✔ **Take your time.** Ask for more time to consider what has been said. After all, it can be difficult to identify what you may think or feel immediately. For example, 'I can appreciate you feel strongly about what you see as my unreliability. However, although you've given me some examples, I need to think about what you've said and I suggest we talk tomorrow.'

- ✔ **Agree if appropriate.** Agree with what has been said if the criticism is valid and discuss future changes. For example, 'I've thought about what you said and I can see that I haven't always kept you in the picture and have changed my plans on occasion without telling you.'

- ✔ **Disagree confidently.** If you don't agree with what is being said then disagree confidently. For example, 'I've thought about what you said and I don't agree. Many of the instances you talked about involved other people rather than being directly attributable to me.'

Give Criticism Assertively

Giving criticism can be as hard as receiving it. People can learn from the thoughts and views of others and if handled in the right way you can get the point across without insulting the other person or being unkind. As a Performance Coach you may well find situations where your colleague is required to give criticism but doesn't feel he has the skills to do so. The following tips can help with this process.

- **Always discuss in private.** Find a private place to give criticism. Many people react instantly without thinking about the consequences of doing so. If you want someone to think about what you're saying you need to respect the other person's feelings.

- **Balance is the key.** Acknowledge the person's good as well as bad points, and make sure what you say is genuine. Some people try to make up something as a way of placating the other person. This type of false behaviour will be picked up immediately and the person will lose respect for anything you say.

- **Keep it professional.** Avoid becoming too personal. Keep comments to the facts of the situation. Avoid exaggerating the faults of the person concerned – the other person may feel hurt or unfairly treated and you lose your credibility.

- **Focus on the behaviour not the person.** Criticise the person's behaviour rather than his character. Behaviour is something a person has control over. Criticism is best given in ways the person can understand and can change. For example, 'It would be helpful if you told me when I do something to upset you rather than holding on to your feelings and then losing your temper with me over something minor.'

- **Describe your feelings, listen, and be specific.** Describe your feelings. For example, 'I find it very difficult to concentrate on my work when you talk to me all the time.' Listen to what the other person has to say because effective communication requires active participation and active listening. Be specific about what you want to happen. For example, 'I would really like it if we could agree a way of talking that ensures that you feel listened to but allows me to have time to work quietly.'

Increase Your Chances of Success

Most people want to be more successful at work. The following tips provide a framework for improving success.

✔ **Take a look from the outside.** De-personalise your experiences so you keep perspective – and keep your blood pressure down. When you find yourself feeling under attack, stand back and imagine a force field around you. Remind yourself that staying calm is in your best interests.

✔ **Check that the rules are working for you.** Everyone has 'life rules' that help in making choices. Make sure you're not operating on any rules that have reached their sell-by date. For example, 'If I take every opportunity, I'll be successful' may have been a great rule to get your career started but may now spread you too thinly if you're established at work.

✔ **Ask your way to success.** If you don't ask, you don't get! Be assertive. Good communication skills mean easier relationships, fewer misunderstandings and emotional upheavals, and this means more energy to use developing the life you want. Ask for what you want and you'll be surprised at how much you get.

✔ **Use your time well.** There are 168 hours in a week. If you sleep for 8 hours a night you're left with 112 hours to do everything else. Don't waste your time – you need to split your time into work, rest, and play if you want to be a rounded person. Successful people know that time is at the heart of success and use the time they have to best effect. Make plans and use your time wisely. Remember to make time to laugh (it relaxes you and so enables you to make better decisions), and to call friends (which helps you to develop a useful personal and professional network).

✔ **What goes around comes around.** You get what you focus on. If you think negative thoughts, you end up with negative outcomes. Focus on positive people and learn from them, read positive books, and listen to positive radio programmes. Use your car journey to listen to inspirational tapes and turn 'dead' time into development time.

Successfully Manage Your Time

Most people wish for more hours in the day, but be realistic and focus on time management instead, to use your precious time effectively. The following strategies can help:

✔ **Clear the clutter!** Whether at home or at work, organisation is the key to freeing up time. If you can't bear to throw anything out, get someone to help you or ask an organised friend or colleague to share his organisational system with you. Throw out your junk mail as soon as it arrives and file paperwork on a regular basis so you can find it when you need it. Remember to repeat the de-cluttering exercise on a quarterly basis.

✔ **Manage telephone calls.** When you're bombarded with telephone calls, you need to be as efficient as possible in dealing with them. Try the following:

- Keep a clock nearby and allocate an amount of time to deal with the call. Many people waste time talking about nothing at all and then wonder where the time has gone. If you find you tend to get side-tracked by conversations, allocate three minutes for general chit-chat before moving on to the business in hand.

- Summarise the conversation with the action points to be taken and by whom. Doing so ensures you've both understood.

✔ **Control interruptions.** Very often you may find yourself being diverted from a task and interruptions can steal time if you allow them to. To avoid this happening:

- Visit other people so you can control the amount of time you spend with them.

- Learn to say 'No' – if you don't, you end up using your time to do things that you don't need to, or that aren't your problem.

- Where possible, allow your voicemail to take calls for you or have calls diverted to enable you to deal with the project in hand.

✔ **Make to-do lists.** Record the tasks you need to do by using a simple A, B, C system that helps you decide how urgent the item is. Without such a system you're likely to end up wasting time on non-essential items and leaving more urgent ones.

- **A:** Urgent items for immediate attention.

- **B:** Important items that require attention in the near future.

- **C:** Non-essential or non-urgent items.

Place sticky notes in full view to remind you to carry out urgent tasks.

✔ **Strive for home/work balance.** Achieving a home/work time balance isn't easy. However, you can help yourself by:

- Using 'dead' time such as travelling time to tidy your bag and check your organiser so you can start to think about what you need to do.

- Deciding on your personal priorities and entering them in your diary. The busier your work life, the more you need to plan ahead.

- Making sure you take short breaks during the day so that your brain and body have a chance to relax.

Keep Stress Under Control

Stress can be very destructive, both psychologically and physically. Some basic stress management tips can be useful for you and to supplement your coaching programme:

- ✔ **Accept reality.** Many people allow themselves to become excessively stressed and overtired before they admit that something's wrong. Don't wait until you're exhausted to do something. You don't get a reward for knocking yourself out. When you realise that the demands you face are greater than your resources, take action.

- ✔ **Ask for help.** If you have too much to do, speak to your manager and explain the situation. Ask for guidance – that's what your manager is there for. Make a list of all the tasks you have to manage, which ones are taking most time, what's holding you up, and what help you need.

- ✔ **Look after yourself.** Eating, relaxing, and sleeping well are the key factors in managing stress. Keep a supply of fruit, nuts, and water close by so you don't snack on unhealthy choices. If you find sleeping a problem, engage in some relaxation before you go to bed, avoid caffeine at night, and perhaps do some gentle exercise.

- ✔ **Take regular breaks.** Don't stay stuck to your desk all day. Make sure you move around, even if to walk to the water machine or kitchen. Take all your available holiday too.

- ✔ **Talk to people.** Socialising is another way of switching off. Have a few minutes chat about non-work activities with your colleagues. You may also feel reassured when you realise they feel stressed too.

- ✔ **Get your support systems in place.** Ensure that your partner and family share the chores. Work can be demanding but if you're also expected to undertake more than your fair share of domestic tasks, you feel overloaded.

- ✔ **Take control.** No one else but you can take control of your life and this means making a commitment to yourself. No one ever got to his deathbed and said he wished he'd spent more time at the office!

Chapter 18

Ten Useful Resources

In This Chapter

▶ Reading for coaching inspiration

▶ Surfing Web sites for useful information

▶ Finding out about professional bodies

*I*n this chapter we provide information on the best resources to help you in your work as a Performance Coach. So much information is out there that you may feel a bit swamped, but we've picked the cream of the crop.

You'll probably discover many more sources of information, but you won't go wrong starting with these!

Finding Wise Words in Books

Naturally, this is the finest book on Performance Coaching you'll ever find, but delve into the following books for additional inspiration.

✔ *Essential Business Coaching* **by Averil Leimon, Francois Moscovici, and Gladeana McMahon (Brunner Routledge, 2005).** This book covers a whole range of business-related coaching subjects and provides useful additional information about developing your coaching skills in the workplace.

✔ *Coaching for Performance* **by Sir John Whitmore (Cambridge University Press, 2007).** Sir John Whitmore developed the widely used GROW Model, for enhancing performance at work. The book provides a practical model commonly used by managers for its accessible framework.

✔ *Behavioral Coaching* **by S. Skiffington and P. Zeus (McGraw-Hill, 2005)** This book focuses on how to achieve behavioural change in the workplace. Its practical style means ease of use as it provides the reader with the relevant information required.

✔ *Excellence in Coaching,* **edited by Jonathan Passmore (Kogan Page, 2006).** An industry guide for anyone working in the coaching arena, this book provides information on a range of approaches and issues related to coaching.

Entangling Yourself in Web Sites

The Internet is a marvellous tool for finding information, but the sheer number of Web sites can be overwhelming. Here's the pick of the pops when it comes to sites providing Performance Coaching information.

✔ **Coaching and Mentoring Network, www.coachingnetwork.org.uk.** This site provides independent advice, information, and guidance on a range of coaching-related issues and has a range of useful articles and an active forum.

✔ **Positive Psychology, www.authentichappiness.com.** This is a useful resource if you're interested in fostering and promoting a positive attitude in the workplace. You can find on-line questionnaires and a number of articles on the site.

✔ **Coaching at Work, www.cipd.co.uk/coachingatwork.** *Coaching at Work,* a magazine from the Chartered Institute of Personnel and Development, provides an up-to-date reference archive, practical tips, and a place for you to exchange news and views.

Getting Advice from Professional Bodies

Here's the low-down on the most helpful and well-respected professional bodies in Britain and beyond.

✔ **Association for Coaching (AC), www.associationforcoaching.com.** Established in 2002, the AC is an independent, non-profit professional body for coaches, coach trainers and providers, academic institutions, and organisations. The AC has a professional code of conduct, a vetting procedure, a course recognition and accreditation scheme, industry research, frequent coaching and professional development events and professional forums, together with an International Conference and other member-focused services. With worldwide membership, the AC is run by coaching professionals committed to raising the standards and awareness of coaching throughout Europe and beyond.

✔ **European Mentoring and Coaching Council (EMCC),** `www.emccouncil.org/`. EMCC promotes good practice and the expectation of good practice in mentoring and coaching across Europe.

✔ **International Coach Federation (ICF),** `www.coachfederation.org`. The International Coach Federation is *the* professional association for personal and business coaches worldwide with over 12,000 members in 80 countries, and over 650 members in the UK.

Appendix

Forms

· ·

*T*his Appendix is jam-packed with forms for you to photocopy and fill in during Performance Coaching.

Performance Coaching Checklist

This form is useful for structuring, assessing, and recording your coaching sessions.

Process Stage	Questions Asked	Techniques Used	Points for Feedback
Agreeing aims			
Awareness			
Analysis			
Action			
Assessment			

Coach Them!

Start to make plans for when you're going to apply the coaching skills you're developing.

Who You'll Coach	Your Aims	Timescale

Setting Goals

Think of a goal of your own from your personal or professional life. You might want to lost weight, learn French, or get promoted within the year. State your ultimate goal at the top of the ladder, and starting at the bottom, break down all the steps to achieve it. Your ladder may end up with a hundred steps. What matters is that you're now in a position to take the first step, making your ultimate goal more of a possibility.

Delegating Tasks

Many managers are too busy carrying out tasks to have the time to develop their staff. Coaching requires a considerable investment of time and energy in the short term to reap long-term gains.

An excellent coaching opportunity arises when you can delegate a task or project, which someone else would regard as a career development.

In the following table, list everything your job entails. For each task decide:

- Who could do it now, if necessary? Highlight in green.
- Who could do it, if he or she received some coaching? Highlight in yellow.

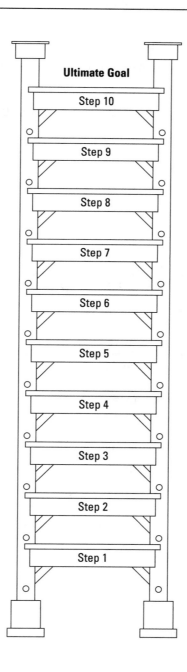

Ultimate Goal

Step 10

Step 9

Step 8

Step 7

Step 6

Step 5

Step 4

Step 3

Step 2

Step 1

- ✔ What is left (tasks that only you can do)? Highlight in pink.
- ✔ How would you like to develop your job when these other tasks are taken care of?

Task	Who Could Do it?	What Coaching Would He or She Need?

Performance Coaching Evaluation

Here's an evaluation form for your colleague to answer after Performance Coaching:

Answer the following questions (with 1 meaning that you don't agree and 5 meaning that you very much agree).

Coaching Fundamentals

Did your Performance Coach:

- ✔ Keep agreed appointments?
- ✔ Allow you to set the agenda for your sessions?
- ✔ Keep a check on the points agreed during your sessions and feed these back to you including reviewing points from previous sessions?
- ✔ Share experiences and ideas as options for you to consider?

Coaching Process

Did your Performance Coach:

- ✔ Establish rapport with you – listening to what you said and displaying empathy with your thoughts and ideas, giving clear responses and summaries, and communicating openly with you?
- ✔ Explain clearly any necessary concepts, information, and techniques, giving concise and constructive feedback?
- ✔ Ensure that you retained responsibility to solve your own problems and change your own behaviour, committing to a Coaching Agenda.
- ✔ Assert him/herself without being aggressive or passive?

✔ Show that he/she was knowledgeable, skilful, and willing to liaise with other appropriate experts?

✔ Demonstrate good time-management practices?

✔ Communicate a genuine belief in the potential for people to improve their performance?

✔ Manage any relevant emotional issues that occurred during the coaching (if appropriate)?

✔ Act as a good role model?

Coaching Outcomes

Answer the following questions as best you can:

✔ Are you now able to assess your current levels of competence effectively (if appropriate)?

✔ Has your work performance improved?

✔ Are you able to maximise opportunities to progress?

✔ Are you able to set yourself development targets and prioritise your development needs?

✔ Are you able to set yourself new goals?

✔ Do you feel positive about your development?

✔ Did Performance Coaching raise your morale?

Organisational Benefits

Rate the following statements between 1 and 5 (with 1 meaning 'I don't agree' and 5 meaning 'I very much agree').

✔ Providing Performance Coaching demonstrates to me that this company cares about my development.

✔ My motivation has increased as a result of coaching.

✔ I'm more likely to stay with the company as a result of receiving coaching.

✔ I'm able to demonstrate how coaching has improved my personal performance at work.

✔ My coaching has *directly* resulted in business benefits.

✔ My coaching has *indirectly* resulted in business benefits.

Coaching Objectives

Write down your original objectives and rate each one 1 to 5, with 1 being 'I haven't met this objective' and 5 being 'I have definitely met this objective'.

Sample Coaching Contract

Administrative Details

Organisation Name:	
Corporate Sponsor Name:	
Corporate Sponsor Position:	
Coaching Client Name:	
Coaching Client Position:	
Date of Initial Scoping Meeting:	

Coaching Objectives/Required Outcomes

Outcome Measurements

Number of sessions agreed:

Feedback Procedures

Confidentiality

Recognising the need for discretion and confidentiality, all parties agree to take into account all aspects relating to the law and duty of care.

Additional agreements/details (if any):

I agree to abide by the terms and conditions supplied to me.

Corporate Sponsor Name:		Date:
Coaching Client Name:		Date:
Coach Name		Date:

Talking Feelings

This exercise helps you become more emotionally literate.

Picture yourself in situations in which you've experienced the emotions listed in the following table. Write down what you see, feel, and experience in your imagination. You don't have to tackle all the emotions. Try the ones you have most difficulty with.

Accepted	Disappointed	Lonely
Affectionate	Free	Loving
Afraid	Frustrated	Rejected
Angry	Guilty	Repulsed
Anxious	Happy	Respectful
Attracted	Hopeful	Sad
Belonging (in community)	Hurt	Satisfied
Bored	Inferior	Shy
Competitive	Intimate	Superior
Confused	Jealous	Suspicious
Defensive	Joyful	Trusting

Your Positive Introduction

Write a 300-word Positive Introduction of yourself at your very best. Make sure it has a beginning, middle, and end, and is about one concrete moment in time.

Read through your Positive Introduction and ask yourself:

✔ What strength does the Introduction illustrate?

✔ Is it a signature strength?

✔ Do you use the strength often? Where?

✔ What is the effect of that strength on you?

✔ What is the effect on others?

✔ Does the strength get you into trouble? If so, why do you still use it?

The Seven-Stage Problem Solving Model

Steps	Questions/Actions
1. Problem identification	What's the problem/challenge I'm facing?
2. Goal selection	What do I want to achieve?
3. Generation of alternative ways of proceeding	What can I do to achieve my goal?
4. Consideration of consequences	What are the pros and cons of the course of action I propose?
5. Decision-making	What am I going to do?
6. Implementation	Doing it!
7. Evaluation	What worked and why? Do I need to amend my action plan?

Using Psychogeometrics

Choose the shape which best describes you.

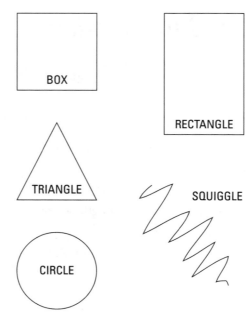

BOX

RECTANGLE

TRIANGLE

SQUIGGLE

CIRCLE

What is your mix?

Box	Triangle	Rectangle	Circle	Squiggle
Traits				
Organised	Leading	In transition	Friendly	Creative
Detailed	Focused	Exciting	Nurturing	Conceptual
Knowledgeable	Decisive	Searching	Persuasive	Futuristic
Analytical	Ambitious	Inquisitive	Empathic	Intuitive
Determined	Competitive	Growing	Generous	Expressive
Common words used				
Logistics	Interface	Unsure	Lovely	Experiment
Deadlines	Escalate	Consider	Gut level	Challenge
Allocate	Jargon	Maybe	Comfort	Create
Policy	Thrust	Delegate	Team	Develop
Efficiency	Return on Investment	Options	Co-operate	Conceive
I did it!	You do it!	Why?	No problem!	What if?
Male appearance				
Conservative	Stylish	Erratic	Casual	Sloppy
Short hair	Appropriate	Changeable	No tie	Dramatic
No facial hair	Expensive	Facial hair	Youthful	Dirty
Female appearance				
Understated	Tailored	Erratic	Overweight	Varied
Navy, grey, or brown clothes	Manicured	Extreme	Feminine	Artistic
Thin	Briefcase	Unusual	Faddish	Fat/Thin
Office style				
Every pencil in place	Status symbols and awards	Disorganised mishmash	Homelike and comfortable	Messy, bleak, or dramatic

Box	*Triangle*	*Rectangle*	*Circle*	*Squiggle*
Body Language				
Stiff	Composed	Clumsy	Relaxed	Animated
Controlled	Jaunty	Nervous	Smiling	Theatrical
Nervous laugh	Pursed mouth	Giggle	Full laugh	Sexual cues
Precise gestures	Large gestures	Flushed face	Excessive touching	No touching
Personal Habits				
Loves routine	Interrupts	Forgetful	Easy-going	Spontaneous
Always prompt	Early arriver	Nervous	Joiner	Interrupts
Planner	Joke teller	Late or early	Sloppy	Disorganised
Precise	Fidgety	Outbursts	Socialiser	Daydreams

FENO-menal Feedback

When you need to give constructive criticism, consider facts, effect, need, and outcome (FENO). Keep your feedback brief but clear. Complete this form before tackling your colleague face to face.

FENO	*What you need to say*
Facts	
Effect	
Needs	
Outcome	

Four Windows on Reality

When coaching, put yourself in different shoes to get different perspectives.

Team   *Boss*

Customers   *Self*

Team Performance Checklist

Use this checklist to evaluate team performance.

Team Performance	1 Poor	2	3	4	5 Excellent
Clear objectives					
Good decision-making process					
Agreed guidelines about team behaviour					
Trust, cooperation, and support					
Constructive conflict (people have the confidence to dissent)					
Clear roles, responsibilities, and leadership					
Sound relationships with other groups					
Analysis of team's performance					

The Responsibility Pie

Make a Pie Chart, illustrating where responsibility really lies for any problems you or your colleagues experience.

Label each section according to the amount of responsibility.

Use the pie to determine who you need to speak to and what actions you need to take to sort things out.

Index

• *Numerics* •

360-degree feedback exercise, 115–116

• *A* •

AC (Association for Coaching), 250
acceptance
  as aspect of respect, 58
  non-judgemental attitude promoting, 60
  of person versus behaviours, 58
  stage of change, 131
ACE coaching structure, 25–27
acting 'as if', 240
action category (MBTI), 110, 111–112
action stage
  in ACE model (Coach), 26–27
  coaching question examples, 19
  overview, 17
  in six-session model, 45, 46–47
  telling people what to do, avoiding, 34
action-oriented team roles, 181
active listening, 70–71, 236
advancement. *See also* career
    management; improvement
  as coaching aim, 23
  frustrations for coached individuals, 36
  impact of recession on, 148, 149
  raising aspirations, 204–205
  talent management for, 120, 123
advising from one's experience, avoiding, 10
advocacy versus inquiry, 185
affiliation, 94, 162
age demographics for workforce, 120
aggressive communication, 214
agreeing aims stage
  Behavioural Contract, 42, 45
  Coaching Agenda, 46
  coaching for recovery versus excellence,
    40–41
  coaching question examples, 18

continual development, 44
  overview, 16
  in six-session model, 45, 46
aims or goals. *See also* agreeing aims stage
  of analysis stage, 17
  breaking down into steps, 28–30, 44
  for career, 158
  for change, 98–99
  clear and measurable, establishing,
    32–33, 41
  Coaching Agenda, 46
  in coaching contract, 64, 259
  coaching contract purpose, 63
  Coaching Objectives, 42
  of coaching questions, 18–19
  conflicting purposes, 199
  excellence, 40–41
  first 100 days in new career, 162
  getting ahead, 23
  getting better, 23
  improvement as primary aim, 10–11, 16
  for initiating Performance Coaching, 25
  ladder to success, 28–30, 254, 255
  linked to pay or bonuses, 33
  misconceptions about, 9–10
  need for, 22
  for performance, current versus future, 23
  performance recovery, 40
  setting objectives in new job, 165
  in seven-stage problem-solving model,
    108, 260
  taking the long view, 25
  team objectives, rating clarity of, 177
  for teams, 172
  understanding in new job, 164
Ali, Muhammad (boxer), 205
all or nothing thinking, 132
ambition, encouraging, 204–205. *See also*
    advancement
Analyse, as 'A' in ACE model, 26–27
analysing setbacks, 209, 210–211

analysis stage
  in ACE model (Analyse), 26–27
  coaching question examples, 19
  ensuring your colleague is ready to
      change, 41–43
  knowing your colleagues, 35
  overview, 17
  taking stock, 16
anger
  appropriate, 196
  forms of, 194
  Performance Coaching response to, 193
  prevalence at work, 194
  reasons for, 194–195
  stage of change, 131
  tips for defusing, 196–197
Angry One (difficult team member), 184
anxiety
  anger masking, 195
  about confidentiality, 15, 63, 207–208
  due to bullying, 223
appearance, improving yours, 239–240
assertiveness, 244–245, 246
assessment stage. *See also* evaluation;
      outcomes
  clear and measurable goals, 32–33
  coaching fundamentals questions, 49
  coaching not the answer, 51
  Coaching Objectives questions, 51
  coaching outcomes questions, 50
  coaching process questions, 49
  coaching question examples, 19
  colleague unable to change, 52
  considering outcomes from the start, 27
  cost-benefit analysis, 27
  feedback useful for, 33
  final meeting (session 6), 47–48
  importance of, 31
  measuring outcomes, 31–33, 50
  mini-reviews in coaching sessions, 48
  organisational benefits questions, 50–51
  overview, 17–18
  return on investment (ROI), 27
  reviews, 48
  self-report questionnaire for, 31–32
  in six-session model, 45, 47–51
  when no progress has been made, 31, 52
assets, people as most valued, 13, 34, 146

Association for Coaching (AC), 250
attitudes, changing by changing
      behaviours, 129
auditing communication, 214–215
authoritarian feedback, avoiding, 99
autonomy, 94, 162
awareness, as critical communication
      area, 217
awareness stage
  chemistry meeting, 44, 45
  coaching question examples, 18
  importance of, 17
  knowing your colleagues, 35
  overview, 16–17

• *B* •

balancing life and work, 166–169, 247
balancing old and new talent, 143
'before' and 'after' self-report, 31–32
Behavioural Coaching (Skiffington and
      Zeus), 249
Behavioural Contract, 42, 45
behaviours. *See also specific kinds*
  changing attitudes by changing, 129
  comparing people, care in, 99
  difficult team members, 182–185
  giving positive feedback about, 100
  for managing uncertainty, 218–219
  persons versus, 58, 99, 184, 191, 245
  signs of stress, 137
Belbin Team Roles
  action-oriented roles, 181
  assessing roles suited to members,
      180–181
  cerebral roles, 181, 182
  handling members not suited to the role,
      181–182
  overview, 178–179
  people-oriented roles, 181
bias, avoiding in team coaching, 188
Big Bully (difficult team member), 183
biological predisposition to anger, 194
blame
  for performance downturn, avoiding, 150
  scapegoating, 199–201
  of self for failure, 146

blind hidden area of Johari Window, 207
body language
  defined, 67
  of distressed colleague, 198
  examples, 68, 69
  eye contact, 68
  facial expressions, 68
  gestures, 69
  non-verbal cues, 68–69
  percent of communication through, 68
  posture, 69
  with probing questions, 76
  reading emotions in, 87–88
  SOLER acronym for, 70
boldfaced text in this book, 1
book resources, 249–250
boundaries
  confidentiality concerns, 15, 62–63,
    207–208
  establishing ground rules, 61–65
  making clear, 57
box shape in psychogeometrics, 113–115,
  260–262
breathing for relaxation, 242
budgeting, 241
bullying, 223–225
burnout, avoiding, 40–41

• *C* •

CA Magazine report, 15
calmness, 192, 196, 198
career drivers, 93–95. *See also* motivation
career management
  attention required for, 157
  balancing life and work, 166–169
  career plan development, 160–161
  first 100 days in new career, 162–166
  identifying personal values, 161–162
  planning ahead, 157–159
  short-, medium-, and long-term goals, 158
  understanding strengths
    and limitations, 159
  win/win scenario with, 158
career progression during recession, 148
caring for distressed colleague, 198
catastrophising, 133

CBI (Confederation of British Industry), 168
cerebral team roles, 181, 182
challenging
  Colombo approach, 82
  contradictions, 83
  dangers of, 80
  defined, 80
  failure to honour commitment, 83–84
  faulty assumptions, 82–83
  holding back personal concerns, 81
  illogical thinking, 84
  ineffective versus effective, 84–85
  key skills of, 82
  lack of insight, 205–206
  for managing uncertainty, 219
  overconfidence, 205–206
  prerequisites for, 81
  timing for, 82–84
change
  adapting coaching to pace of, 43
  aiming for, 98–99
  clarifying requirements at the outset,
    42–43
  coaching through, 130–134
  coaching to cut costs of, 129–130
  continuum of, 128
  controlling negative thoughts, 132–134
  drop in confidence and competence due
    to, 129
  failure of initiatives, 128
  helping colleagues use support systems,
    135, 137
  importance of responsiveness to, 127–128
  in management style, overcoming
    concerns about, 15
  non-judgemental attitude as aid to, 60
  prevalence in modern times, 127
  professional handling of, 128–129
  questions to ask when coaching for, 134
  respect as aid to, 60
  route to embracing effectively, 129
  stages of, 130–131
  in team role preferences, 180
  understanding stress from, 135–138
  understanding the impact of, 131
Character Strengths and Virtues (Peterson
  and Seligman), 97

Chartered Institute of Personal Development (CIPD), 128
Chartered Management Institute, 223
checklists
  Performance Coaching, 253
  Team Performance, 263
chemistry meeting, 44, 45
circle shape in psychogeometrics, 113–115, 260–262
clarity
  about changes required, 42–43
  clear and measurable goals, 32–33, 41
  as critical communication area, 217
  about criticism, 244
  about new career responsibilities, 165
  setting boundaries, 57
  uncertainty more manageable with, 218
clear goals, establishing, 32–33
Cleese, John (actor), 10
closed questions, 72, 73
clutter, clearing, 246
Coach, as 'C' in ACE model, 26–27
Coach Them! form, 254
Coaching Agenda, 46, 47
Coaching and Mentoring Network Web site, 250
Coaching Assignment, 46, 47
Coaching at Work Web site, 250
coaching contract, 63–65, 258
Coaching for Excellence, 40–41
Coaching for Performance (Whitmore), 249
Coaching Objectives, 42, 51
coaching questions
  ACE model, 26–27
  analysing setbacks, 210
  assessing what went wrong, 150–151
  career planning, 160–161
  challenging, 84–85
  clarifying changes for Behavioural Contract, 42–43
  closed, 72, 73
  coaching agenda, 21–22
  Coaching Objectives questions, 51
  about communication, 214–215
  counteracting negativity, 103
  delegating tasks, 36, 256
  for difficult team members, 184–185
  FENO technique for criticism, 101
  formal review, 48

fundamentals questions, 49
hypothetical, uses for, 72
identifying limitations, 159
identifying motivators, 95
identifying strengths, 98, 159
knowing your colleagues, 35
leading, avoiding, 72
mapping organisational needs, 125
motivational, 74–75
multiple, avoiding, 72
negative reactions, 193
about negative thoughts, 132, 133–134
open, 72–73, 75
organisational benefits questions, 50–51
organisational culture, 124
outcomes questions, 50
for performance recovery, 152–155
PIE problem-solving model, 108
probing, 75–77
process questions, 49
prompting self-feedback, 100
retaining talent, 123
seven-stage problem-solving model, 108
stage 1: agreeing aims, 18
stage 2: awareness, 18
stage 3: analysis, 19
stage 4: action, 19
stage 5: assessment, 19
stages of change, 131
tailoring coaching to organisational life cycle, 141
talent management philosophy, 121
team attributes for success, 174–176
team members difficult to deal with, 180
team strengths and weaknesses, 180
trying out tests, 112
when coaching for change, 134
coaching yourself
  controlling stress, 248
  creating a positive lifestyle, 240–241
  giving criticism assertively, 245
  improving confidence, 239–240
  increasing chances of success, 245–246
  managing money, 241–242
  receiving criticism assertively, 244
  rekindling creativity, 242–243
  relaxing, 243–244
  time management, 246–247

'command and tell' management style, 10
commitment
  challenging failure to honour, 83–84
  coaching contract agreements, 64, 259
  gaining colleagues', 24
  by individual being coached, 63
  Performance Coaching less effective
      without, 204
  of personnel, day-to-day attention
      required for, 129
  retaining talent, 122–123
  taking the long view, 25
  uncertainty more manageable with, 218
common ground, 217
communication. *See also* feelings
  active listening, 70–71
  aggressive, 214
  assessing, 213
  auditing, 214–215
  on benefits of coaching, 24–25
  blind spots, identifying, 186
  body language, 67–69, 87–88
  challenging, 80–85
  chemistry meeting, 44, 45
  coaching for, 216–217
  on coaching for recovery versus
      excellence, 44
  coaching questions, 214–215
  confidentiality concerns, 15, 62–63
  critical areas, 217
  emotional intelligence in, 85–90
  ensuring good channels, 232–233
  establishing ground rules, 61–65
  formal channels, 232
  improving in organisations, 213–217
  ineffective styles of, 214
  informal channels, 232–233
  to limit time-consuming
      misunderstanding, 168
  for managing uncertainty, 217–218, 219
  meeting outside the coaching context, 57
  misinterpretation due to lack of, 216
  monitoring for difficult colleague, 199
  motivation aided by, 216
  motivational questions for, 74–75
  non-verbal cues, 68–69
  about note taking, 47
  open questions for, 72–73

  about organisational issues, 201
  paraphrasing, 77–79
  passive, 214
  premature closure, avoiding, 77
  probing questions for, 75–77
  question types for, 72–75
  reading emotions, 87–89
  reflecting feelings, 79–80, 89–90
  reflective listening, 74
  as root of team problems, 173
  about setbacks, 211
  setting boundaries, 57
  setting out a space for, 71
  showing respect, 58–61
  SOLER acronym for attending, 70
  in teams, ensuring effectiveness of,
      185–186
  telling people what to do, avoiding, 34
  timing challenging, 82–84
  timing probing questions, 76
  voice tone, pitch, and pacing, 68, 69–70,
      76, 88
  about who is being coached and why, 37
companies. *See* organisations
comparing people, care in, 99
competence level
  change and drop in, 129
  colleague unable to change, 52
  of colleague versus coach, 18
  demonstrated by outcomes, 237
  as intrinsic work value, 161
  situations outside yours, 11, 12
competition, as root of team problems, 173
completer finisher (Belbin Team Role),
      179, 181
Confederation of British Industry
      (CBI), 168
confidence
  bullying's impact on, 223
  challenging overconfidence, 205–206
  change and drop in, 129
  as critical communication area, 217
  dealing with colleague's lack of, 205
  improving yours, 239–240
  issues for bullies, 224
  low, as root of team problems, 173
  rating team performance regarding, 177

confidentiality
  in coaching contract, 64, 259
  legal issues, 62
  overcoming concerns about, 15, 63,
    207–208
  resolving conflicts, 62
  tips for reinforcing, 208
conflict management, 217
confronting. *See* challenging
continual development, 44
contracts
  Behavioural Contract, 42, 45
  coaching, 63–65, 258
contradictions, challenging, 83
conventions in this book, 1
co-operation
  performance aided by, 233
  rating team performance regarding, 177
co-ordinator (Belbin Team Role), 179, 181
coping skills, anger from poor, 195
corporate client, 64
corporate culture. *See* culture of
    organisation
corporations. *See* organisations
cost-benefit analysis, 27
courage, as signature strength, 97
creation stage of organisational life cycle,
    140
creativity
  as attribute of proactivity, 238
  as career driver, 94
  impact of growth on, 142
  as intrinsic work value, 162
  rekindling yours, 242–243
credibility
  performance aided by, 234
  uncertainty more manageable with, 218
credit card balances, lowering, 242
crisis, keeping calm in, 192
criticism. *See also* feedback
  for behaviour, not person, 99, 245
  FENO technique, 100–101, 262
  giving assertively, 245
  giving constructively, 100–101
  Performance Coaching versus, 9
  receiving assertively, 244
  softening with light touch and
    humour, 187

in team coaching, 187
tips for giving, 99
of yourself, stopping, 241
culture of organisation
  defined, 124
  impact on talent, 124–125
  sustaining during recession, 147
  understanding in new job, 163, 164–165
customer satisfaction, retaining talent
    for, 220
cynicism in colleagues, 193

• *D* •

Darwin, Charles (evolution theorist), 127
deadlines versus outcomes, 237
decision-making
  rating team performance in, 177
  in seven-stage problem-solving model,
    108, 260
defensiveness in colleagues, 204
defusing anger, 196–197
delaying gratification, 104–105
delegating tasks, 35–36, 235–236, 254, 256
denial stage of change, 131
dependence, 231
depression, 131, 168, 223
designated client, 64
destabilising effects, 36–37
Devil's Advocate (difficult team
    member), 183
difficult colleagues or situations. *See also*
    criticism; feedback; negativity,
    counteracting
  anger, 194–197
  coaching questions for teams, 180
  dealing with negative behaviour, 192–194
  distress, 197–198
  finding the best in, 59, 60–61
  keeping calm in crisis, 192
  negative reactions in colleagues, 192–194
  negative reactions in oneself, 191–192
  non-judgemental attitude in, 58–60
  Performance Coaching not useful for, 11
  personality clashes, 199
  persons versus behaviours, 58, 99, 184,
    191, 245
  reducing team challenges, 173

scapegoating, 199–201
in teams, dealing with behaviours,
182–185
Dillinger, Susan (psychogeometrics
developer), 113
directness, as key to team success, 175
disciplinary action, 11
distraction for defusing anger, 197
distress
handling, 197–198
seeking specialist help for colleague's,
205
doubts about effectiveness, overcoming,
14–15
downturn. *See* recession

education, for managing uncertainty, 219
Effect, in FENO technique for criticism,
100–101, 262
e-mail, confidentiality issues for, 208
EMCC (European Mentoring and Coaching
Council), 251
emotional conflicts, 11
emotional intelligence, 85–90
emotions. *See* feelings
empathy
for dealing with distress, 198
for dealing with setbacks, 209
for defusing anger, 196–197
developing, 58
using for understanding, 60
energy category (MBTI), 109, 110
engagement
dealing with colleague in wrong job, 205
of employees, survey on, 13
as key to team success, 174
low, as cost of stress, 227
EQ (emotional intelligence quotient), 86
equality, as critical communication area,
217
Essential Business Coaching (Leimon,
Moscovici, and McMahon), 249
European Mentoring and Coaching Council
(EMCC), 251
Evaluate, as 'E' in ACE model, 26–27
evaluation. *See also* assessment stage
in ACE model (Evaluate), 26–27

of communication in organisation, 213
considering outcomes from the start, 27
Performance Coaching Evaluation form,
256–257
before performance recovery, 150–151
in PIE problem-solving model, 108
in seven-stage problem-solving model,
108, 260
of team strengths, 177–178
excellence, coaching for, 40–41
Excellence in Coaching (Passmore, ed.), 250
expansion, 148–149. *See also* growth stage
of organisational life cycle
expectations
consequences of overworking on, 167
unrealistic, 204
expertise, 94, 161
external coaches, 13
extraversion type (MBTI), 110
extrinsic work values, 161, 162
eye contact, 68, 70

facial expressions, 68
Facts, in FENO technique for criticism,
100–101, 262
failure
of change initiatives, 128
clarifying negative outcomes
at the start, 42
coaching example for, 146
helping colleague deal with, 208–209
to honour commitment, challenging,
83–84
negative thoughts from, 132
family, impact of overworking on, 167
fatigue from overworking, 167
faulty assumptions, challenging, 82–83
feedback
acknowledging others' achievements, 234
asking colleague to self-critique, 103
for behaviour, not person, 99
in coaching contract, 64, 259
comparing people, care in, 99
confidentiality concerns, 62
counteracting negative self-critique, 103

feedback *(continued)*
  criticism, constructive, 100–101
  criticism, giving assertively, 245
  criticism, receiving assertively, 244
  encouraging from others, 99
  examples, 102
  FENO technique for criticism,
    100–101, 262
  after first formal meeting, 46
  immediacy in giving, 101
  issues interfering with effectiveness, 103
  motivating people with, 101–103
  positive, as prerequisite for challenging, 81
  positive, giving effectively, 99–100
  positive, questions prompting self-
    feedback, 100
  during recession, 149
  360-degree feedback exercise, 115–116
  timing for giving, 101–102, 103
  tips for giving, 99
  using to assess changes, 33
feeling type (MBTI), 111
feelings. *See also specific kinds*
  body language portraying, 87–88
  embarrassment about, 87
  emotional conflicts, coaching not useful
    with, 11
  emotional intelligence, 85–90
  importance of, 85
  managing emotions, 86
  as minefield, 85
  naming, 88–89
  negative, from negative thoughts, 132
  reading emotions, 87–89
  during recession, 149
  recognising others', 86, 87
  recognising your own, 86–87
  reflecting, 79–80, 89–90, 197
  self-control, 86
  signs of stress, 137
  Talking Feelings exercise, 259
  tone of voice portraying, 88
  vocabulary portraying, 88
FENO technique for criticism, 100–101, 262
'fight or flight' response, 136. *See also*
    stress
firing, 11, 149

first 100 days in new career
  aims, 162
  clarifying responsibilities, 165
  considering training needs, 166
  focus for, 163
  learning how things work, 164
  making the right impression, 163
  setting objectives, 165
  settling in easily, 163–164
  understanding the organisation, 164–165
Five-Minute Tension-Release exercise, 243
flexibility, 109, 176
flow, being in, 96
focus
  for first 100 days in new career, 163
  as key to team success, 175
  negative versus positive, 246
  on outcome, 235, 237
  task-focus versus 'me'-focus, 146
formal communication channels, 232
forms and tools
  Coach Them!, 254
  coaching contract, 65, 258
  delegating tasks, 254, 256
  FENO technique, 100–101, 262
  Four Windows on Reality, 263
  ladder to success, 28–30, 254, 255
  Myers-Briggs Type Indicator (MBTI),
    109–112
  Performance Coaching Checklist, 253
  Performance Coaching Evaluation,
    256–257
  PIE problem-solving model, 108–109
  Positive Introduction, 259
  psychogeometrics, 113–115, 260–262
  questionnaire information, 115
  responsibility pie chart, 210–211, 263–264
  seven-stage problem-solving model,
    107–108, 110, 260
  Talking Feelings exercise, 259
  Team Performance Checklist, 263
  360-degree feedback exercise, 115–116
Four Windows on Reality form, 263
friends, impact of overworking on, 167

• *G* •

Galwey, Tim (*Inner Game* book series), 8
gestures, 69
goals. *See* aims or goals
gratification, delaying, 104–105
growth stage of organisational life cycle
  handling expansion, 148–149
  overview and challenges, 140
  tailoring coaching to, 141–142
  talent management during, 148–149
guilt, fighting, 168

• *H* •

harassment, 223
Hardy Personalities, 195
Health and Safety Work Act, 226
health, ensuring, 238, 248
helplessness in colleagues, 193
hidden unknown area of Johari Window,
  207
Human Resource colleagues,
  working with, 12
humanity, as signature strength, 97
hypothetical questions, 72

• *I* •

ICF (International Coach Federation), 251
icons in margins of this book, 4
ideas, generating, 243
illogical thinking, challenging, 84
imagery for relaxation, 243
immobilisation stage of change, 130
implementation in problem-solving
  models, 108, 260
implementer (Belbin Team Role), 179, 181
improvement. *See also* advancement
  continual development, 44
  getting ahead, 23
  getting better, 23
  as primary coaching aim, 10–11, 16
  road blocks, 51–52
impulse spending, avoiding, 242
independence, 232
inertia stage of change, 131

influence
  as career driver, 94
  developing yours, 237
  as intrinsic work value, 161
informal communication channels, 232–233
Ingham, Harry (Johari Window co-
  inventor), 206
in-house coaches, 13, 14
Inner Game book series (Galwey), 8
inquiry versus advocacy, 185
insight, challenging lack of, 205–206
inspiration
  as critical communication area, 217
  for managing uncertainty, 219
interdependence, 232
interest in others versus self-interest, 185
internal coaches, 13, 14
International Coach Federation (ICF), 251
Internet resources
  for Performance Coaching information,
    250
  professional bodies, 250–251
  questionnaire information, 115
  survey on impact of overwork, 168
interruptions, controlling, 247
intrinsic work values, 161–162
introducing coaching to workplace
  chemistry meeting, 44, 45
  delegating tasks, 35–36, 235–236, 254, 256
  emphasising benefits, 24–25
  finding the time, 35–36
  keeping people happy, 36–37
  knowing your colleagues, 35
  procrastination, avoiding, 36
  tailoring coaching to individuals, 35
  telling people what to do, avoiding, 34
  WIIFY and WIIFT factors, 24
introversion type (MBTI), 110
intuition type (MBTI), 111
italic text in this book, 1

• *J* •

job satisfaction, strengths related to, 96
Johari Window, 206–207
journaling, 239
judgement category (MBTI), 110, 111

judging
  avoiding, 58–59, 89, 99
  as barrier to respect, 59
  developing a non-judgemental attitude, 59–60
  in feedback, avoiding, 99
  MBTI type, 111
  when reflecting feelings, 89
justice, as signature strength, 97

• K •

knowing your colleagues
  being open to understanding, 60
  building foundations of relationship, 55–57
  chemistry meeting, 44, 45
  impact of growth on, 148
  questions to ask, 35
  during recession, 149
knowledge. *See also* self-awareness or self-knowledge
  retaining talent for, 220
  as signature strength, 97

• L •

ladder to success
  creating from goal statements, 33
  illustrated, 29–30, 255
  for setting goals, 28, 254
leadership
  developing, as preparation for recession, 147
  developing your influence, 237
  rating team performance regarding, 177
leading questions, avoiding, 72
Leaning, in SOLER acronym, 70
Learning and Development colleagues, working with, 12
legal issues
  avoiding litigation, 222–227
  bullying, 223–225
  for confidentiality, 62
  due to workplace stress, 225–227
  harassment, 223
  litigation as sign of ingrained problems, 222

Leimon, Averil (*Essential Business Coaching*), 249
lifestyle, positive, 240–241
limitations. *See* weaknesses or limitations
listening skills
  active listening, 70–71, 236
  allowing completion by the other, 71
  attending, 70–71
  for defusing anger, 196
  encouraging, 236–237
  for managing uncertainty, 219
  paraphrasing, 77–79
  performance aided by, 236–237
  reflective listening, 74
  using silence, 71
  when challenging, 82
logging work and non-work activities, 168
long view of coaching, taking, 25
long-term career goals, 158
looking good, 239–240
loss stage of change, 130
love, as signature strength, 97
Luft, Joseph (Johari Window co-inventor), 206

• M •

makeover, 239–240
managing careers. *See* career management
managing money, 241–242
managing organisational problems
  avoiding litigation, 222–227
  coaching uncertain organisations, 217–219
  improving communication, 213–217
  preventing loss of good people, 220–222
managing talent. *See* talent management
Manchester Consulting (US) review, 15
mapping organisation's needs, 125
MBTI (Myers-Briggs Type Indicator), 109–112
McMahon, Gladeana (*Essential Business Coaching*), 249
meaning
  as career driver, 94
  search for, as intrinsic work value, 161
  search for, as stage of change, 131
measurable goals, establishing, 32–33

measuring outcomes. *See also* assessment
    stage
  determining measurable outcomes, 50
  establishing measurable outcomes, 32–33
  micro versus macro level, 50
  motivating using achievements, 104
  overview, 31–33
  questions to ask, 50
medium-term career goals, 158
meetings. *See also* communication
  arranging room for, 71
  chemistry meeting, 44, 45
  final (session 6), 47–48
  first, formal (session 1), 46
  ongoing sessions, 46–47
  outside the coaching context, 57
  six-session model, 45–51
Mega-neg (difficult team member), 183
Mercer Human Resource Consulting, 223
Metrix Global ROI study, 14
mind-reading, 133–134
minimising team weaknesses, 182–185
misconceptions of Performance Coaching,
    9–10
mistakes
  costing key people, 220
  helping people deal with, 132
  setbacks after, 208–209
monetary rewards
  as career driver, 94
  insufficient for retaining talent, 123, 148
money management, 241–242
monitor evaluator (Belbin Team Role),
    179, 181
monofont text in this book, 1
Moscovici, Francois (*Essential Business
    Coaching*), 249
motivation
  aiming for change, 98–99
  career drivers, 93–95
  communications aiding, 216
  considering your best performance,
    97–98
  considering your motivators, 92–93
  as critical communication area, 217
  deeper motivators, 95
  delaying gratification, 104–105

  feedback for, 99–103
  justificatory motivators, 93
  as key to success, 203
  list of signature strengths, 97
  measuring achievements for, 104
  motivational questions, 74–75
  not assuming all people are like you, 92
  overcoming negative emotions with,
      203–204
  raising aspirations, 204–205
  during recession, 149
  role in Performance Coaching process, 203
  shallow versus deep motivators, 93
  talent management for, 123
  using key strengths, 96
  when progress is slow, 104–105
motivational questions, 74–75
multiple questions, avoiding, 72
music, creativity increased by, 242
Myers-Briggs Type Indicator (MBTI),
    109–112

naming feelings, 88–89
Needs, in FENO technique for criticism,
    100–101, 262
negative communication in teams, 185
negative outcomes, clarifying, 42
negative reactions. *See also specific kinds*
  dealing with behaviours, 192–194
  keeping calm in crisis, 192
  overcoming with motivation, 203–204
  respect for difficult colleagues, 192
  in yourself, 191–192
negative thoughts
  all or nothing thinking, 132
  catastrophising, 133
  during failure, 146
  focus on positive versus, 246
  impact of, 132
  mind-reading, 133–134
  questions to ask about, 132, 133–134
  as reason for anger, 195
  after setbacks, handling, 209

negativity, counteracting. *See also* difficult
  colleagues or situations
  anxiety about confidentiality, 207–208
  in colleague's self-critique, 103
  Johari Window as tool for, 206–207
  with motivation, 203–204
  motivational questions for, 75
  raising aspirations, 204–205
  setbacks, 208–212
non-judgemental attitude
  change aided by, 60
  developing, 59–60
  importance of, 58–59
non-verbal cues
  body language, 67–69, 87–88
  examples, 68, 69
  eye contact, 68
  facial expressions, 68
  gestures, 69
  percent of communication through, 68
  posture, 69
  with probing questions, 76
  SOLER acronym for, 70
  voice tone, pitch, and pacing, 68,
    69–70, 76
normalising situation with distressed
  colleague, 198
note taking, 47
nurturing oneself, 168

• O •

Occupational Health colleagues, working
  with, 12
old-school management style, 10
online resources. *See* Internet resources
Open, in SOLER acronym, 70
open public area of Johari Window, 206
open questions, 72–73, 75
organisational life cycle
  averting the end, 144
  balancing old and new talent, 143
  creation stage, 140
  cross-fertilisation between divisions, 144
  as curve rather than cycle, 144
  expansion in, 148–149
  growth stage, 140, 141–142, 148–149
  needs and challenges, 140–141

performance recovery, 150–155
preservation stage, 141, 144
prime stage, 139, 140–141
recession in, 144–148, 149
re-energising, 144
simplified version, 139–140
tailoring coaching to stage of, 141–142
varying among divisions and
  departments, 144
organisations. *See also* introducing
  coaching to workplace
  avoiding litigation, 222–227
  continuum of change in, 128
  dealing with organisational issues,
    200–201
  evaluating benefits for, 50–51
  gaining commitment to Performance
    Coaching, 24–25
  importance of responsiveness to change,
    127–128
  improving communication, 213–217
  linking coaching results to success, 37
  mapping the needs of, 125
  measuring culture impact on talent,
    124–125
  performance recovery, 150–155
  preventing loss of good people, 220–222
  talent management benefits for, 119
  uncertain, coaching, 217–219
  understanding in new job, 163, 164–165
outcomes. *See also* assessment stage
  in coaching contract, 64, 259
  considering from the start, 27
  deadlines versus, 237
  evaluating, 50
  in FENO technique for criticism, 100–101,
    262
  focus on, 235, 237
  measuring, 31–33, 50, 104
  negative, clarifying at the outset, 42
  in PIE problem-solving model, 108
  positive, clarifying at the outset, 43
  separating content of discussions from, 62
  in seven-stage problem-solving model,
    108, 260
overconfidence, challenging, 205–206
overworking, consequences of, 166–168
ownership, as key to team success, 176

• P •

pace of coaching, 43
pacing of speech, 70
panic
  attacks from overworking, 168
  avoiding during recession, 145
  dealing with colleague's, 193
paraphrasing, 77–79
partnership, working in, 66
passivity, 204, 214
Passmore, Jonathan, ed. (*Excellence in Coaching*), 250
past history, as barrier to respect, 59
people-oriented team roles, 181
perceiving type (MBTI), 112
perception, as critical communication area, 217
perception category (MBTI), 109, 110–111
performance
  acknowledging others' achievements, 234
  becoming proactive, 237–238
  considering your best, 97–98
  credibility improvement for, 234
  current versus future, 23
  defined, 8, 21
  developing your influence for, 237
  ensuring communication channels for, 232–233
  focus on outcome for, 235, 237
  getting ahead, 23
  getting better, 23
  improvement as primary coaching aim, 10–11, 16
  interdependence aiding, 231–232
  listening as aid to, 236–237
  managing during recession, 147
  recovery in individuals, 40
  recovery in organisations, 150–155
  road blocks, 51–52
  talent versus, 121
  Team Performance Checklist, 263
  team, rating, 176–177
  types of, 23
  working co-operatively for, 233
Performance Coaching Checklist, 253
Performance Coaching Evaluation form, 256–257
Performance Coaching (Whitmore), 7
Performance Recovery Coaching, 40
performance recovery in corporations
  assessing what went wrong, 150–151
  becoming resilient, 152–153
  moving on as a priority, 151–152
  planning for, 153
  questions to ask, 153–155
  reasons problems aren't solved, 150
performance recovery in individuals, 40
personal values, identifying, 161–162
personality clashes, 199
personality types and anger, 195
Peterson, Christopher (*Character Strengths and Virtues*), 97
physical signs of stress, 136
pie chart for setback responsibilities, 210–211, 263–264
pitch of voice, 69
plant (Belbin Team Role), 179, 181, 182
Pleaser (difficult team member), 184
positive communication in teams, 185, 187
positive feedback. *See also* feedback
  acknowledging others' achievements, 234
  for behaviour, not person, 99
  giving effectively, 99–100
  motivating people with, 101–103
  as prerequisite for challenging, 81
  questions prompting self-feedback, 100
  in team coaching, 187
  tips for giving, 99
Positive Introduction from, 259
positive lifestyle, 240–241
positive outcomes, clarifying, 43
Positive Psychology Web site, 250
posture, 69
power, 94, 161
prejudices, as barriers to respect, 59
premature closure, avoiding, 77
preservation stage of organisational life cycle, 141, 144
pressure
  assessing, 226
  turning stress into, 138
Price Waterhouse Coopers ROI, 15
prime stage of organisational life cycle, 139, 140–141
proactivity, 237–238

probing questions, 75–77
problem solving
  as critical communication area, 217
  flexible approach with, 109
  PIE model for, 108–109
  reasons problems aren't solved, 150
  recognising problems early, 148
  seven-stage model for, 107–108, 109, 260
process of coaching
  evaluating, 49
  managing, 24–27
  overview, 10
  six-session model, 45–51
  stages of, 15–19
procrastination, 36
professional bodies, 250–251
psychiatry, Performance Coaching versus, 9
psychogeometrics, 113–115, 260–262
purposes. *See* aims or goals

• *Q* •

question types. *See also* coaching
    questions
  closed, 72, 73
  hypothetical, 72
  leading, 72
  motivational, 74–75
  multiple, 72
  open, 72–73, 75
  probing, 75–77

• *R* •

reading emotions, 87–89
realism
  challenging overconfidence or lack of
    insight, 205–206
  for colleague in wrong job, 205
  Four Windows on Reality, 263
  letting go wishing things were different,
    240
  after setbacks, 209
  thoughts versus truth, 241
  toward stress, 248
  unrealistic expectations, 204

recession
  business advice affecting Performance
    Coaching, 145–146
  coaching example, 149
  ignoring, avoiding, 145
  inevitability of, 144–145
  panic during, avoiding, 145
  people as most valued assets, 146
  performance recovery after, 150–155
  planning for, 147–148
recognising feelings
  naming emotions, 88–89
  others', 86, 87
  reading emotions, 87–89
  yours, 86–87
rectangle shape in psychogeometrics,
    113–115, 260–262
redeploying people during recession, 147
re-entry after coaching, impact of, 37
reflecting feelings, 79–80, 89–90, 197
reflective listening, 74
relationships. *See also* communication;
    team coaching; teams
  building foundations of, 55–57
  outside the coaching context, 57
  rating team performance, 177
  time needed for developing, 55
  types of, pros and cons, 56–57
relaxation exercises, 243–244
Relaxed, in SOLER acronym, 70
relief stage of change, 130
remediation, Performance Coaching
    versus, 9
reputation, as barrier to respect, 59
resentment in colleagues, 193
resistance to coaching, overcoming
  change in management style, 15
  confidentiality concerns, 15, 63, 207–208
  doubts about effectiveness, 14–15
  time requirements, 14
resource investigator (Belbin Team Role),
    179, 181, 182
resources
  books, 249–250
  professional bodies, 250–251
  Web sites, 250

respect
avoiding judging, 58–59
barriers to, 59
during coaching, 58
defined, 58
developing, 59–60
for difficult colleagues, 192
finding the best in people, 59, 60–61
importance of, 55
of person versus behaviours, 58, 192
as prerequisite for challenging, 81
showing, 58–61
silence as sign of, 71
for team members, 173
responsibilities
clarifying in new job, 165
rating team performance regarding, 177
for setbacks, pie chart for, 210–211,
263–264
retaining talent. *See also* talent
management
basic mistakes costing key people, 220
benefits of, 220
coaching for, 222
costs of losing good employees, 220
monetary rewards insufficient for, 123,
148
overview, 122–123
during times of change, 123
tips for, 221–222
return on investment (ROI), 14–15, 27
reviews, 48. *See also* assessment stage
risks
acting 'as if' confident, 240
encouraging willingness to take, 204

● *S* ●

scanning for recession, 147
scapegoating, 199–201
searching stage of change, 131
security, 95, 162
self-assessments
asking colleague to self-critique, 103
questions prompting self-feedback, 100
self-report questionnaire, 31–32
in 360-degree feedback exercise, 115–116

self-awareness or self-knowledge. *See also*
testing
challenging overconfidence or lack of
insight, 205–206
exercise for discovering strengths, 98
issues for bullies, 224–225
Johari Window for, 206–207
lacking in people, 101
as prerequisite for challenging, 81
questions prompting self-feedback, 100
recognising your feelings, 86–87
search for, as stage of change, 131
360-degree feedback exercise, 115–116
self-blame for failure, 146
self-disclosure, 207
self-doubt stage of change, 131
self-interest versus interest in others, 185
self-report questionnaire, 31–32
Seligman, Martin (*Character Strengths and
Virtues*), 97
sensation type (MBTI), 110
setbacks
analysing, 209, 210–211
getting back to normal after, 210–212
inevitability of, 208, 211
pie chart for responsibilities, 210–211,
263–264
strategies for dealing with, 209
yours, 209, 211, 212
seven-stage problem-solving model,
107–108, 109, 260
shaper (Belbin Team Role), 179, 181
shock stage of change, 130
short-term career goals, 158
signature strengths, 97
silence, using, 71
Silent One (difficult team member), 183
six-session model
evaluation, 49–51
final meeting (session 6), 47–48
first formal meeting (session 1), 46
ongoing sessions, 46–47
overview, 45
reviews, 48
Skiffington, S. (*Behavioural Coaching*), 249
sleep, getting enough, 169
SOLER acronym, 70

Solera System for sherry, 143
specialist (Belbin Team Role), 179, 181, 182
speech. *See* communication; voice
spending, managing, 241, 242
Square, in SOLER acronym, 70
squiggle shape in psychogeometrics,
    113–115, 260–262
stages
  of change, 130–131
  of organisational life cycle, 139–141
  of Performance Coaching, 16–19, 26–27
  of problem-solving, model for, 107–108
  of task delegation, 235–236
status, as career driver, 95
strengths
  considering your best performance,
      97–98
  identifying, 159, 205
  job satisfaction related to, 96
  Johari Window for identifying, 206–207
  playing to people's, 96
  playing to yours, 160
  self-knowledge exercise, 98
  signature, list of, 97
  talent management for, 123
  in teams, charting team roles, 180
  in teams, identifying, 177–178
  in teams, respect for, 172
  360-degree feedback exercise, 115–116
  understanding for career management, 159
  understanding to aid change, 130
  understanding yours, 98
  unequal in different areas, 96
stress
  areas to consider, 226
  behavioural signs of, 137
  from change, 135–136
  controlling, 248
  costs of, 226–227
  emotional signs of, 137
  'fight or flight' response, 136
  Health and Safety Work Act, 226
  helping colleagues use support
      systems, 137
  legal issues, 225–227
  overworking, 166–168
  physical signs of, 136
  as reason for anger, 194

turning into healthy pressure, 138
  in Type A personalities, 195
Stress Carrier (difficult team member), 183
structuring the process. *See also specific*
    stages
  ACE model for, 25–27
  need for, 15
  question examples for stages, 18–19
  six-session model, 45–51
  stage 1: agreeing aims, 16, 18
  stage 2: awareness, 16–17, 18, 26–27
  stage 3: analysis, 17, 19, 26–27
  stage 4: action, 17, 19, 26–27
  stage 5: assessment, 17–18, 19
success. *See also* assessment stage;
    outcomes
  bred by success, 204
  clarifying at the outset, 43
  coaches' qualities promoting, 55
  emotional and physical health needed
      for, 238
  increasing your chances, 245–246
  ladder to, 28–30, 33, 254, 255
  linking coaching results to, 37
  measuring outcomes, 31–33, 50
  motivation as key to, 203
  team attributes for, 174–176
succession planning, 148, 220
suicide, 168, 223
superiority, 193, 225
support
  for balancing life and work, 169
  for dealing with stress, 226
  helping colleagues use resources,
      135, 137
  lack as reason for anger, 195
  need for providing, 28
  rating team performance regarding, 177
  for yourself, 248

taking notes, 47
taking the long view, 25
talent
  challenges of attracting, 120–121
  measuring company culture impact on,
      124–125

mobility of population, 121
performance versus, 121
supply and demand issues for, 120
talent management
for advancement, 120, 123
attracting talent, 122
balancing old and new talent, 143
challenges of attracting talent, 120–121
coaching directors and senior managers at once, avoiding, 221
coaching leaders of tomorrow, 123
defined, 119
during expansion, 148–149
identifying talent, 122
importance for organisations, 119, 122
investment bank example, 120
monetary rewards insufficient for, 94, 148
for motivation, 123
perspectives exercise, 121
planning for recession, 147
retaining talent, 122–123, 220–222
for strengths, 123
talent versus performance, 121
Talker (difficult team member), 183
Talking Feelings exercise, 259
targets. *See* aims or goals
task-focus versus 'me'-focus, 146
team coaching
for adjusting to change, 130
assessing roles suited to members, 180–181
avoiding pitfalls, 188
Belbin Team Roles method, 178–182
building a code of conduct, 187
case study, 186–188
for difficult members, 182–185
ensuring effective communication, 185–186
identifying strengths and weaknesses, 177–178
for individual members, 173, 187
key attributes of success, 174–176
for members not suited to the role, 181–182
minimising weaknesses, 182–185
Team Performance Checklist, 263
team worker (Belbin Team Role), 179, 181

teams
basics needed for, 172
dysfunctional, coaching individual members of, 173
flourishing, attributes of, 178
identifying strengths and weaknesses, 177–178
rating performance of, 176–177
roots of below-par functioning, 173
situations not useful for, 171–172
size issues for, 171–172
Team Building Anyway days, 171
Team Performance Checklist, 263
tears, handling, 198
telephone calls, managing, 247
telling people what to do, avoiding, 34
temperance, as signature strength, 97
termination, 11, 149
testing
Myers-Briggs Type Indicator (MBTI), 109–112
psychogeometrics, 113–115, 260–262
360-degree feedback exercise, 115–116
trying out tests, 112
uses for, 109
thinking, negative. *See* negative thoughts
thinking style, as reason for anger, 195
thinking type (MBTI), 111
360-degree feedback exercise, 115–116
time
deadlines versus outcomes, 237
demands preventing Performance Coaching, 11
finding for coaching, 35–36
making by delegating tasks, 35–36, 235–236, 254, 256
managing, 246–247
overcoming concerns about coaching requirements, 14
pace of coaching, 43
procrastination, 36
for reflection, 242
taking breaks, 248
timing
for challenging, 82–84
for giving feedback, 101–102, 103
for probing questions, 76

to-do lists, 247
tone of voice
  overview, 69
  percent of communication through, 68
  with probing questions, 76
  reading emotions in, 88
tools. *See* forms and tools
Towers Perrin survey, 13
training needs in new job, 166
transcendence, as signature strength, 97
triangle shape in psychogeometrics,
    113–115, 260–262
tripartite agreement, 66
trust
  developing in teams, 173
  as prerequisite for challenging, 81
  rating team performance regarding, 177
  setting clear boundaries, 57
Type A personalities, 195
Type B personalities, 195

 • *U* •

uncertainty
  behaviours for managing, 218–219
  challenges of, 217–218
  communication vital to managing,
    217–218, 219
  enabling people to deal with, 218–219
understanding, as critical communication
    area, 217
unknown private area of Johari Window,
    207
unrealistic expectations, 204

• *V* •

values, identifying personal, 161–162
visualisation for relaxation, 243

vocabulary, feelings portrayed by, 88
voice. *See also* non-verbal cues
  pacing, 70
  percent of communication by tone of, 68
  pitch, 69
  with probing questions, 76
  tone, 68, 69, 76, 88

• *W* •

water cooler coaching, 10
weaknesses or limitations. *See also*
    criticism
  identifying, 159
  Johari Window for identifying, 206–207
  in teams, charting team roles, 180
  in teams, identifying, 177–178
  in teams, minimising, 182–185
  360-degree feedback exercise, 115–116
  understanding to aid change, 130
Web resources. *See* Internet resources
'what's in it for them' (WIIFT) factors, 24
'what's in it for you' (WIIFY) factors, 24
Whitmore, John
  Coaching for Performance, 249
  Performance Coaching, 7
wisdom, as signature strength, 97
working in partnership, 66

• *Z* •

Zeus, P. (*Behavioural Coaching*), 249

FOR DUMMIES®

Do Anything. Just Add Dummies

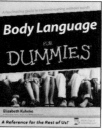

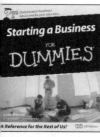

FOR DUMMIES®

Do Anything. Just Add Dummies

HOBBIES

978-0-7645-5232-8

978-0-7645-5395-0

978-0-7645-5476-6

Also available:

Art For Dummies
(978-0-7645-5104-8)

Aromatherapy For Dummies
(978-0-7645-5171-0)

Bridge For Dummies
(978-0-471-92426-5)

Card Games For Dummies
(978-0-7645-9910-1)

Chess For Dummies
(978-0-7645-8404-6)

Improving Your Memory
For Dummies
(978-0-7645-5435-3)

Massage For Dummies
(978-0-7645-5172-7)

Meditation For Dummies
(978-0-471-77774-8)

Photography For Dummie
(978-0-7645-4116-2)

Quilting For Dummies
(978-0-7645-9799-2)

EDUCATION

978-0-7645-5434-6

978-0-7645-5581-7

978-0-7645-5422-3

Also available:

Algebra For Dummies
(978-0-7645-5325-7)

Astronomy For Dummies
(978-0-7645-8465-7)

Buddhism For Dummies
(978-0-7645-5359-2)

Calculus For Dummies
(978-0-7645-2498-1)

Cooking Basics For Dummies
(978-0-7645-7206-7)

Forensics For Dummies
(978-0-7645-5580-0)

Islam For Dummies
(978-0-7645-5503-9)

Philosophy For Dummies
(978-0-7645-5153-6)

Religion For Dummies
(978-0-7645-5264-9)

Trigonometry For Dummie
(978-0-7645-6903-6)

PETS

978-0-470-03717-1

978-0-7645-8418-3

978-0-7645-5275-5

Also available:

Labrador Retrievers
For Dummies
(978-0-7645-5281-6)

Aquariums For Dummies
(978-0-7645-5156-7)

Birds For Dummies
(978-0-7645-5139-0)

Dogs For Dummies
(978-0-7645-5274-8)

Ferrets For Dummies
(978-0-7645-5259-5)

Golden Retrievers
For Dummies
(978-0-7645-5267-0)

Horses For Dummies
(978-0-7645-9797-8)

Jack Russell Terriers
For Dummies
(978-0-7645-5268-7)

Puppies Raising & Training
Diary For Dummies
(978-0-7645-0876-9)

FOR DUMMIES®

The easy way to get more done and have more fun

LANGUAGES

978-0-7645-5193-2

978-0-7645-5193-2

978-0-7645-5196-3

Also available:

Chinese For Dummies
(978-0-471-78897-3)

Chinese Phrases
For Dummies
(978-0-7645-8477-0)

French Phrases For Dummies
(978-0-7645-7202-9)

German For Dummies
(978-0-7645-5195-6)

Italian Phrases For Dummies
(978-0-7645-7203-6)

Japanese For Dummies
(978-0-7645-5429-2)

Latin For Dummies
(978-0-7645-5431-5)

Spanish Phrases
For Dummies
(978-0-7645-7204-3)

Spanish Verbs For Dummies
(978-0-471-76872-2)

Hebrew For Dummies
(978-0-7645-5489-6)

MUSIC AND FILM

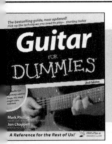

978-0-7645-9904-0

978-0-7645-2476-9

978-0-7645-5105-5

Also available:

Bass Guitar For Dummies
(978-0-7645-2487-5)

Blues For Dummies
(978-0-7645-5080-5)

Classical Music For Dummies
(978-0-7645-5009-6)

Drums For Dummies
(978-0-471-79411-0)

Jazz For Dummies
(978-0-471-76844-9)

Opera For Dummies
(978-0-7645-5010-2)

Rock Guitar For Dummies
(978-0-7645-5356-1)

Screenwriting For Dummies
(978-0-7645-5486-5)

Songwriting For Dummies
(978-0-7645-5404-9)

Singing For Dummies
(978-0-7645-2475-2)

HEALTH, SPORTS & FITNESS

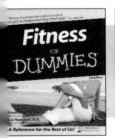

978-0-7645-7851-9

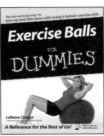

978-0-7645-5623-4

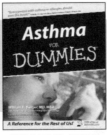

978-0-7645-4233-6

Also available:

Controlling Cholesterol
For Dummies
(978-0-7645-5440-7)

Diabetes For Dummies
(978-0-470-05810-7)

High Blood Pressure
For Dummies
(978-0-7645-5424-7)

Martial Arts For Dummies
(978-0-7645-5358-5)

Menopause FD
(978-0-470-061008)

Pilates For Dummies
(978-0-7645-5397-4)

Weight Training
For Dummies
(978-0-471-76845-6)

Yoga For Dummies
(978-0-7645-5117-8)

FOR DUMMIES®

Helping you expand your horizons and achieve your potential

INTERNET

978-0-470-12174-0

978-0-471-97998-2

978-0-470-08030-6

Also available:

Blogging For Dummies, 2nd Edition
(978-0-470-23017-6)

Building a Web Site For Dummies, 3rd Edition
(978-0-470-14928-7)

Creating Web Pages All-in-One Desk Reference For Dummies, 3rd Edition
(978-0-470-09629-1)

eBay.co.uk For Dummies
(978-0-7645-7059-9)

Video Blogging FD
(978-0-471-97177-1)

Web Analysis For Dummies
(978-0-470-09824-0)

Web Design For Dummies, 2nd Edition
(978-0-471-78117-2)

DIGITAL MEDIA

978-0-7645-9802-9

978-0-470-17474-6

978-0-470-14927-0

Also available:

BlackBerry For Dummies, 2nd Edition
(978-0-470-18079-2)

Digital Photography All-In-One Desk Reference For Dummies
(978-0-470-03743-0)

Digital Photo Projects For Dummies
(978-0-470-12101-6)

iPhone For Dummies
(978-0-470-17469-2)

Photoshop CS3 For Dumm
(978-0-470-11193-2)

Podcasting For Dummies
(978-0-471-74898-4)

COMPUTER BASICS

978-0-470-13728-4

978-0-470-05432-1

978-0-471-74941-7

Also available:

Macs For Dummies, 9th Edition
(978-0-470-04849-8)

Office 2007 All-in-One Desk Reference For Dummies
(978-0-471-78279-7)

PCs All-in-One Desk Reference For Dummies, 4th Edition
(978-0-470-22338-3)

Upgrading & Fixing PCs For Dummies, 7th Edition
(978-0-470-12102-3)

Windows XP For Dummies 2nd Edition
(978-0-7645-7326-2)